Approaching post–World War II poetry from a postmodern critical perspective, this study challenges the prevailing assumption that experimental forms signify political opposition while traditional forms are politically conservative. Such essentialist alignments of forms with extraformal values, and the oppositional framework of innovation versus conservation that they yield, reflect modernist biases inappropriate for reading postwar poetry. Blasing defines postmodern poetry as a break with modernism's valorization of technique and its implicit collusion with technological progress. She shows that four major postwar poets — Frank O'Hara, Elizabeth Bishop, John Ashbery, and James Merrill (two traditional and two experimental) — cannot be read as politically conservative because formally traditional or as culturally oppositional because formally experimental. All of these poets acknowledge that no one form is more natural than another, and no given form grants them a superior position for judging cultural and political arrangements. Their work plays an important cultural role precisely by revealing that meanings and values do not inhere in forms but are always and irreducibly rhetorical.

CAMBRIDGE STUDIES IN AMERICAN LITERATURE AND CULTURE

Politics and Form in Postmodern Poetry

Books in the Series

Continued on page following the index.

Politics and Form in Postmodern Poetry

O'Hara, Bishop, Ashbery, and Merrill

MUTLU KONUK BLASING

Brown University

CAMBRIDGE
UNIVERSITY PRESS

Published by the Press Syndicate of the University of Cambridge
The Pitt Building, Trumpington Street, Cambridge CB2 1RP
40 West 20th Street, New York, NY 10011-4211, USA
10 Stamford Road, Oakleigh, Melbourne 3166, Australia

First published 1995

Printed in the United States of America

Library of Congress Cataloging-in-Publication Data
Blasing, Mutlu Konuk, 1944–

Politics and form in postmodern poetry : O'Hara, Bishop, Ashbery,
and Merrill / Mutlu Konuk Blasing.

p.   cm. – (Cambridge studies in American literature and
culture)

Includes bibliographical references (p.   ).

ISBN 0-521-49607-1 (hardcover)

1. American poetry – 20th century – History and criticism.
2. Politics and literature – United States – History – 20th century.
3. Bishop, Elizabeth, 1911–1979 – Political and social views.
4. Merrill, James Ingram – Political and social views.   5. O'Hara,
Frank – Political and social views.   6. Ashbery, John – Political and
social views.   7. Political poetry, American – History and criticism.
8. Postmodernism (Literature) – United States.   9. Literary form.
I. Title.   II. Series.
PS310.P6B58   1996
811'.5409358 – dc20   94-4113
                                                               CIP

A catalog record for this book is available from the British Library.

ISBN 0-521-49607-1 Hardback

For Randy and John

Contents

Acknowledgments

Parts of the second, third, and fourth chapters originally appeared, in somewhat different form, in the following: "From Gender to Genre and Back: Elizabeth Bishop and 'The Moose,' " *American Literary History* 6(2): 265–86 (1994). Reprinted by permission of Oxford University Press. "The American Sublime, c. 1992: What Clothes Does One Wear?" *Michigan Quarterly Review* 31(3): 425–31 (1992). Reprinted by permission. "Rethinking Models of Literary Change: The Case of James Merrill," *American Literary History* 2(2): 299–317 (1990). Reprinted by permission of Oxford University Press.

Introduction
Poetry after Modernism

The history of twentieth-century poetry has been read largely with a bias for the aesthetic values that gained currency with modernism. Privileging technical experimentation and novelty has precluded approaching post–World War II poetry in ways that take into account the different rhetorical and formal options available to poets after the early decades of the twentieth century. I want to begin by addressing this pervasive bias, its historical background, and its values as they have shaped discussions of postwar American poetry.

The consensus is that the history of American poetry since World War II represents a contest between a formalist academic consolidation of early modernism's experimental impulse and an antiformalist revolt that reaffirms presence and process in open forms. This heroic drama of a central agon between the forces of reaction and progress – with its farcical repetition in the current competition between the New Formalists and the Language poets – assumes that postwar experimental poetry is continuous with modernist experimentalism; that the technical continuity of open forms bespeaks a continuity of moral, metaphysical, and political agendas; and that early modernist and postmodern poetry alike pose avant-garde oppositional challenges to the cultural establishment. In one way or another, experimental techniques are taken to be the most significant marker of twentieth-century poetry, with the attendant implication that modernism's technical break with nineteenth-century poetry was, in fact, a substantive break

1

as well and ushered in a new aesthetic informing poetry to this day, despite some setbacks.

Such a figuration of contemporary poetry's history subscribes to a progressive model of literary change as a continuing liberation from, or a repeated series of breaks with, the forces of tradition.[1] And the plot of this politicized scenario of liberation turns on technique: poetic techniques are seen to carry ideological freight, and specific sociopolitical, ethical, and metaphysical values are thought to inhere in particular forms. Thus a sonnet can become a "fascist" form, in William Carlos Williams's term, and disruptive compositions can make for substantive cultural criticism. Whether presented from conservative or liberal perspectives, critical evaluations of modernist and postmodern poetry alike privilege experimental technique as the test of its modernity and link radical techniques to oppositional politics. In other words, whether one deplores or applauds modernism's experimental tendencies, aligning forms – open or closed – with political values – radical or conservative – remains constant.[2]

I would argue that this essentialist, ahistorical alignment of given technical strategies with moral, metaphysical, or political values is a historically specific confusion. Before we can even begin to conceive of a history of postwar poetry, we need to identify such a conflation of different discourses as itself representing a modernist aesthetic ideology, a reification of what can only be metaphoric links, and therefore not very useful in tracing the difference between modern and postmodern poetry. Indeed, in order to plot a history of this period, we need to address the rhetoric – the unstable, historically changing rhetorical function – of given techniques after the initial period of modernist experimentation. Of course, a pervasive repression of rhetoric – by poets and critics both – may in fact constitute experimental modernism's rhetoric, which promotes technological and scientific values. Modern and late-modern experimental writers repeatedly suggest that technically disruptive work is scientific, objective, and presentational – the very opposite of rhetorical and representational writing.[3] And posing technique as the antithesis of rhetoric precludes engaging the rhetoric of experimental techniques themselves.

I will use the term "postmodern" to designate poetry that breaks with the modernist faith in the truth-value of poetic techniques and registers the intervention of rhetoric in any such connection between forms and values. My use of the term differs from its prevailing use to refer exclusively to experimental work, as in Donald Allen's retitling his *New American Poetry* (1960) with the "newer" term *The Postmoderns* (1982). Likewise, Paul Hoover's Norton anthology, *Postmodern American Poetry* (1994), reserves the term for experimental verse, updating Allen by adding Language poets. Hoover's easy reduction of a historical period to technical experimentation and oppositional politics typifies the bias shaping discussions of postwar poetry: "As used here, 'postmodern' means the historical period following World War II. It also suggests an experimental approach to composition, as well as a worldview that sets itself apart from mainstream culture" (xxv). In my definition, "postmodern" marks a historical *and* a poetic difference: it describes any poetic practice that questions modernist assumptions. Thus not only experimental poets like Frank O'Hara and John Ashbery but formal poets like Elizabeth Bishop and James Merrill are postmodern, for whatever their technical differences, they do not buy into the modernist reification of poetic techniques and its underlying humanist belief in the values of progress, modernity, science, and natural truth. By contrast, what used to be called "contemporary" poetry – open-form poetry that evades the rhetoric of its forms and sets out to reclaim the avant-garde energies of early modernism – might be termed more properly "late modern."

A poet like Charles Olson exemplifies a contemporary or late-modern spokesman for modernity, who is more modern than the moderns. Poets loosely associated with Olson – including Robert Duncan, Denise Levertov, Allen Ginsberg, Robert Creeley, Gary Snyder, and on down to the Language poets – are late modern in this sense, for their work continues to repress the rhetoric of their forms. Olson argues that we live in " 'the post-modern, the post-humanist, the post-historic, the going live present' " (in Perkins 1987: 500). "The harmony of the universe" is "post-logical" or "kinetic" – "the order of any created thing" – and poems must accordingly be "kinetic" (Olson 1966: 55, 61). This given base of an organic order authorizes open forms, which access inherent orders without imposing our puny, human orders on process. Olson's valuing presence and process or *kinesis* over discourse leads him to isolate technique as what holds out against discourse and keeps the poem open and "kinetic," as Burton Hatlen demonstrates in his essay on "The Kingfishers" (1989). In Olson's terms, a processual poem does not destroy but transmits energy and makes sure that the spent energy returns to complete the "circuit" (61–62). "Keep moving," Olson advises, "USE the process" (17); in the words of "The Kingfishers," we get "not accumulation but change, the feed-back proves, / the feed-back is / the law" (170). Olson's source for feedback seems to be Norbert Wiener's *Cybernetics.* There, however, feedback is a way of controlling process: "When we desire a motion to follow a given pattern the difference between this pattern and the actually performed motion is used as a new input to cause the part regulated to move in such a way as to bring its motion closer to that given by the pattern" (in Hatlen 1989: 563). The "law" of feedback assumes purposive motion; the end is already given, and the issue becomes how to use process to get there.

It is difficult to see how such a teleological model of composition that is technically open but conceptually closed is "postmodern" or "posthumanist"; in fact, this engineering concept epitomizes the collusion of technology and humanism, instrumental reason and progress – the very Enlightenment values Olson rails against. Since he already knows that his ends are organic, good, and right beyond question, he need only find the most efficient means to achieve them. Meanwhile, mystifying his technique and repressing his rhetoric ensure that his work is *kinesis,* not discourse. His kind of rhetoric is not rhetoric but natural truth; rhetoric is for other people, as Eliot said of Pound's hell.

Indeed, Pound's poetic may well serve as the modernist paradigm, which continues to inform contemporary or late-modern poetry. Those who read modernism as a substantive break with Romanticism regard Pound as the representative modernist, who articulates an "era." Hugh Kenner's view of Pound as central is expanded by Marjorie Perloff's reading of postwar poetry: "The pivotal figure in the transformation of the Romantic (and Modernistic) lyric into what we now think of as postmodern poetry is surely Ezra Pound" (1985: 181). Postmodern poetry, which she defines as an avant-garde writing best exemplified now by the Language poets, is thus continuous with Pound's work and, at the same time, represents a reaction against or advance beyond modernism. Pound, then, emerges as a special case – a "true" or avant-garde modernist distinct from "false" modernists like Eliot and Yeats. In this reading, Pound first breaks with Romantic and Symbolist poetics; the second time around, a recovery of his processual and presentational values enables the postmodern break with the symbolist aesthetics of the academically sanctioned modernism of Yeats and Eliot. David Perkins also regards Pound as the pivotal figure on this basis: his imagism is taken up, with some modifications, by the Deep-Image poets and others who work the nature versus civilization vein (1987: 557), and his *Cantos* lead to Olson, Black Mountain poetics, and beyond.

Those who read Pound as both the paradigmatic modernist and the source of a postmodern poetic reaction to modernism aim to establish historical continuity between poetic practices and ideologies that may well be discontinuous. Pound comes to serve as a type, whose discontinuous compositions project – as their antitype – all the varieties of experimental poetry that come after him.[4] Yet such a teleological assumption of the literary-historical continuity of twentieth-century poetry begs the historical question, answering it before we can ask it.

If we must look to Pound for a modernist aesthetic that established a tradition, we would have to begin with his concept of the image and his commitment to free verse to see the rhetoric of modernist poetics. His idea of the image has not only influenced a variety of twentieth-century poets but constitutes the revolutionary and informing core of his career as a whole, since the image–vortex–ideogram evolution leads directly from his early work to the *Cantos*.[5] What is indeed new about his image is precisely its repression of rhetoric. The impulse to purge rhetoric from poetry appears to be a general modernist impulse;[6] for example, Yeats's indictment of rhetoric as "the will trying to do the work of the imagination" (1961: 215) insists on separating imagination from will, so as to keep figuration (imagination) uncontaminated by persuasion (will) – to sever the link between rhetoric as figuration and as persuasion. And Pound praises Yeats for stripping "English poetry of its perdamnable rhetoric. He has boiled away all that is not poetic" and prepared the way for "Twentieth century poetry," which, Pound predicts, will "move against poppy-cock" and will be "harder and saner . . . 'nearer the bone.' It will be as much like granite as it can be, its force will lie in its truth, its interpretive power," rather than in the attempt to "seem forcible by rhetorical din, and luxurious riot" (1968a: 11–12). The new poetry will be "austere, direct, free from emotional slither" (12) – scientific, hygienic (21), masculine (1975: 41), and modern.

Pound's imagism represents this tendency to oppose rhetoric and poetry by aligning "interpretive power" with "truth" rather than with rhetoric. For Pound, rhetoric – associated with the "kolossal," the "monumental," the "pretentious," the "decorated" (1968a: 443, 216) in verse – is the antithesis of the "image": "The 'image' is the furthest possible remove from rhetoric. Rhetoric is the art of dressing up some unimportant matter so as to fool the audience for the time being. . . . Even Aristotle distinguishes between rhetoric, 'which is persuasion,' and the analytical examination of truth" (1970a: 83). An image is "absolute metaphor"; it is "real because we know it directly" – we "perceive" or "conceive" it without the mediation of rhetoric or profane metaphor. It is "thought" itself, not "argument and gibe and opinion," mere "shells of thought" (85–87). The image presents "truth" – "universal, existing in perfection, in freedom from space and time" – and is scientific and analytic in its method; "the statements of 'analytics' are 'lords' over fact. They are the thrones and dominations that rule over form and recurrence" (91). By contrast, rhetoric misrepresents "truth" and is decorative or "ornamental" (1975: 374) in method.

And Pound characteristically associates rhetoric with certain poetic forms: imagist verse frees itself of rhetoric by freeing itself of meter. Aspiring to an "absolute rhythm," which "corresponds exactly to the emotion," the poet can jettison meters in favor of a rhythm "more real, more a part of the emotion of the 'thing,' more germane, intimate, interpretive than the measure of regular accentual verse" (1968a: 9, 12). Free verse is a technique that, Pound believes, will combat "rhetoric," meaning insincere and discursive language alike. It will safeguard the poet from worn-out diction and hackneyed subjects;[7] more, it will free language from discourse. Grammar, which enables logical discourse and representation, also serves meter by supplying all those unaccented words, including the copula; these "systems" reinforce one another, and Pound attacks on all fronts.

Pound's presentational image suppresses and naturalizes the rhetoric of figuration by representing figuration as spontaneous and immediate perception. Nonmetrical verse and verbal economy – literally, deleting grammatical connections, which also stylizes language and performs the function of meter – are deployed to represent unmediated perception. Eventually, even the grandly persuasive and highly didactic thrust of the *Cantos* can be naturalized, and rhetorically motivated arguments can be presented as self-evident, absolute truths revealed by the "adequacy" of Pound's technique.

Pound's "image," constituted of two superimposed images, is in effect a metaphor, a perception not of a " 'thing' whether subjective or objective" but of a relation between subjective and objective "things." But the image represses the sequential nature of this relation in "trying to record the precise instant when a thing outward and objective transforms itself, or darts into a thing inward and subjective" (1970a: 89). Pound's complex, two-part image figures itself as immediate perception by defining perception itself as dialogical at base. If Pound thereby complicates perception, he also naturalizes metaphor, moving it from the sphere of linguistic operations to the realm of psychological processes.[8] Now "original" perception, which is itself dialogical, is best embodied in a "simultaneous" juxtaposition of images, not represented by the sequential and hierarchical structure of metaphor (where tenor precedes vehicle in time and import). The image absorbs the spatial displacement and temporal difference of figuration into an instantaneous experience, which occurs in the literal aporia that tropes bridge, in leaping from one half of the image to the other. Hence the image offers "freedom from time limits and space limits" (1968a: 4).

Since the sequential structure of metaphoric substitution implies motivation, will, and persuasion, to repress the sequentiality of figuration is to repress rhetoric as willful persuasion. The relation between the two parts of the figure thus becomes "necessary" and "natural"; it could not be otherwise, for it is not rhetorical or motivated. The figure is not a substitution but the right name for the process, and inherent in right naming is the moral dimension of "rectitude" or will. After his encounter with Fenollosa's work, Pound's thinking expands to cover larger processes, but his vorticism continues to repress rhetoric. Appealing to psychological process (simultaneous perception) or natural process (metamorphic change), Pound's "image" or "vortex" presents natural transformations of force, not merely grammatical or figural changes; his figures, like the "primitive metaphors" Fenollosa describes, "do not spring from arbitrary *subjective* processes" but, indeed, "follow objective lines of relations" and duplicate "the operations of nature" (1936: 26). If temporal, successive change is a natural fact, there may not be different figurations of succession; it is not a subject for rhetoric. Similarly, the basis for Pound's attraction to Chinese compounds is that they "write" relations (1960: 21); they provide a model of writing that can present the operations of nature itself, without the time lag of metaphor.

Such techniques as embody subjective and objective processes become the means of accessing natural truth – not rhetorical models of nature and of our relationship to it. If language is used properly and scientifically – if it is purified of the contamination of rhetoric and historical corruption – its operations will coincide with those of natural process. Thus the "test" of "a man's sincerity" – whether he gives us rhetoric or truth, whether he obscures or interprets nature – is his "technique" (1968a: 9). Reifying technique and repressing rhetoric by appealing to universal, natural truths are the hallmarks of Pound's modernism. Such a mystification or sacralization of technique, authorized by nature, marks a late phase of organicism, which continues to inform the Olsonian strand of contemporary verse.

In the *Cantos,* Pound's ideogrammic method extends the logic of the image. The text trades in historical data: Pound chooses his "luminous details," which may not appear significant at first glance but, when rescued from their historical contexts and superimposed on other such details, illuminate transhistorical truths. The reader must supply the links between the instances the poet provides, but this is not difficult, since relations are really self-evident in the mere citation of facts. Pound represses both his "persuasive" motives for selecting his "typifying" facts and his figuration of the relations between them by omitting relational terms, whether tropological, logical, or narrative. Thus purifying his language technically enables him to present motivated choices as self-evident facts, historical differences as reducible to universals, and political or moral values as absolute natural truths. The text superimposes "facts" rescued from their changing historical contexts, so that we can see natural and transcendent truths through them and perceive repeated patterns as well as unchanging truths. In this way, Pound's modernist aesthetic bridges historical, natural, and transcendent levels of experience.

Although his poetic may have been influenced by T. E. Hulme's ideas, the function of Pound's techniques is continuous with Romantic humanism, which Hulme denounces precisely for confusing these levels.[9] Indeed, in critiquing this humanist and Romantic confusion of categories and insisting on separating ethics and aesthetics, Hulme anticipates Paul de Man's critique of Romantic "aesthetic ideology," which offers another way of approaching Poundian poetics. "What we call ideology is precisely the confusion of linguistic with natural reality, of reference with phenomenalism," de Man writes (1986: 11). Romantic and modernist organicism alike figure poetic language as incarnational, an aesthetic synthesis embodying in concrete terms the union of linguistic meaning and phenomenal reality. In Christopher Norris's version of aesthetic ideology, the pernicious political implications of the "aesthetic" lie in its claims to "reconcile" such irreconcilable oppositions as "time and eternity, subject and object, mind and nature, or the phenomenal and noumenal realms." Thus the aesthetic can serve as a model of some ideal "of socio-political life where conflicting interests would at last be perfectly reconciled, to the point of transcending all mere contingencies of time and place" (1990: 264). The "unity in multiplicity" model of the "organic" work projects an aesthetic model of social organization, whether Confucianism ("The Confucian is totalitarian" [Pound 1975: 85]), fascism, or communism. Pound's politics and poetics are thus of a piece, culminating tendencies that are inherent in organicist poetics. His novelty consists in his deploying discontinuous techniques to authorize and authenticate totalitarian unities, and vice versa.

From this perspective, Poundian organicism is more reformist than avant-garde; it questions existing social, cultural, and aesthetic structures and values only from the viewpoint of universal, natural truths, and it justifies technical aberrations by appealing to such self-evident truths and their *necessary* link to values. When natural, universal truths come into question, both philosophically and politically, the grounds for an effective experimentalism erode, for technical experiments can no longer be justified as enabling a privileged access to truth by cutting through conventions, historical occlusions, or rhetorical falsifications. A belief in universal values and progressive techniques informs modernist aesthetics and reflects the larger collusion of humanism and technology that, as Gianni Vattimo (1988), Andreas Huyssen (1986), and others have argued, characterizes the modern era.

If naturalizing rhetoric is a modernist practice, the postmodern tendency of poets like O'Hara, Bishop, Ashbery, and Merrill is to regard any link between empirical, historical, or natural experience and transcendent truth, which alone can yield value, as only rhetorical and therefore political. No "truth" can lead to an ethical, political, or aesthetic imperative without a rhetorical translation, a motivated figuration of a link. Postmodern poetry highlights this moment of rhetorical intervention and, focusing on representation and the persuasive goals of figuration, breaks with Romantic and modernist organicisms alike, which have ceased to be convincing.

Accordingly, postmodern poets regard all poetic techniques – whether canonical or experimental – as conventional and instrumental, without any inherent authority; techniques serve rhetorical rather than revelatory functions. And the modernist legacy is an inheritance that can be used for any number of rhetorical purposes. While postmodernism may look like a kind of neoclassicism, its authority is less historical than rhetorical, for historical coherence and cultural consensus are very much in doubt – which is itself one of the legacies of modernism. If neither universal truths nor a unified history or a dominant cultural practice that could substitute for metaphysical authority is available, by the same token a greater wealth of conventions becomes available. After modernism, different formal options open up, enabling poets to use a wider range of historical resources – if in a necessarily

dehistoricized way. When the history of poetry in English is not figured progressively, and the historically unprecedented nature of the
present may be effectively gauged by traditional measures, a poet like
Merrill can address a postmetaphysical condition in meters and rhymes.
When novelty becomes an old value, then, the past offers novel options. If this situation represents a change, it is not exactly progress,
and it does not require scrapping the past. Merrill and Ashbery alike
can distance themselves not only from the various pasts they invoke
but from "progress"; failure to do so would be to repeat the progressive
past.

Thus even technical continuities with modernist experiments represent functional discontinuities. For example, while Ashbery's pas-
tiches jumbling together perspectives, periods, and styles owe
something to modernist collages, he has little faith that his techniques
have greater epistemological value or can more effectively and more
inclusively present the complexity of a noncontingent reality or truth.
In Fredric Jameson's terms, pastiche has a different function than its
technical precursor, collage: pastiche is "blank parody," which lacks
"any conviction that alongside the abnormal tongue you have momentarily borrowed, some healthy linguistic normality still exists"
(1991: 17). Technically, pastiche and collage are both impure mixtures,
but while a modernist collage represents a stable referent via polyvocal
signifiers, a postmodern pastiche is deviation without norm, polyvocality without reference. And Ashbery's experimentalism, invoking a
variety of past representational models stripped of their proper functions, ironically amounts to a kind of rote traditionalism, a historical
bind he often thematizes.

Similarly, while O'Hara's open forms technically belong in the
modern and contemporary experimental tradition, he acknowledges
the rhetorical nature of the link between free forms and the "freedoms" authorizing them or supposedly effected by them. His insight
demystifies technique and helps expose the repression of rhetoric that
runs from Pound through most of contemporary poetry, for to con-
fuse discourses and conflate poetic, political, ethical, and metaphysical
thinking and values is indeed the persuasive thrust of organicism from
the Romantics on. For postmodern poets, there is no escape from

representation; all is figuration, and all figuration exercises power over what it represents. Emphasizing the mediation of representation and the rhetoric of their techniques, they question "innocent" organicism, experimentalism, and traditionalism alike.

Postmodern poetry, then, destabilizes the modernist polarities of old versus new, canonical versus avant-garde, and exercises options that become historically available only after modernism, when the ideology of making it new has become part of the past. When the connection between the values of aesthetic novelty and technological progress becomes increasingly clear, achieving a critical distance from a technology-driven culture requires a critical distance from modernist aesthetic values as well. Poetry that registers such distance includes work by traditional poets like Bishop and Merrill, who cannot be reduced to formalists, for they challenge the canonical authority and metaphysical closures encoded in their forms. But such poetry also includes work by poets who use open forms but decline to mystify them; Ashbery and O'Hara, for instance, base their authority on neither an organicist natural truth nor a scientific model of technical progress. Indeed, both are known to write in traditional forms, whether for exploratory purposes (Ashbery) or for parodic effects (O'Hara), just as Bishop and Merrill sometimes experiment with free verse. In my reading, then, a poet's engagement with the motivation for his or her formal and technical choices is more important than the specific technical choices made; for instance, James Breslin's examples of technically antithetical poetry – Merrill's "textbook" formalism (1984: xiv) and O'Hara's "disruptive" antiformalism (xv) – have more in common than not. Similarly, formalism can exist in open as well as traditional forms, whenever forms – whether free or conventional – are thought to carry inherent rather than rhetorical value and invoke nature or tradition as their authority.

Focusing on the break between a given style or set of techniques (whether experimental or traditional) and the discourses they can only represent – the moral, political, and metaphysical positions they can only signify – puts rhetoric at the center of discussions of form. This approach would allow us to distinguish strategies continuous with modernist formalism from those that are essentially discontinuous with modernist assumptions and constitute a distinct literary practice. When we read technical procedures not as icons of the discourses they have been associated with but as representations, we see that their rhetorical functions, motives, and import may vary from poet to poet and from time to time. A model of literary history that registers functional discontinuities within formal continuities, and formal discontinuities within functional continuities, can supply both the rigor and resiliency necessary for a reading of the much-noted diversity of postwar poetry.

We need to understand literary change as a network of continuities and discontinuities, wherein forms and their functions, techniques and their rhetorical and metaphysical implications, follow different histories, trace different lines, and do not always and invariably mesh. A figuration of poetic history that dissociates forms from functions and admits the instability of technical markers would enable us to accommodate the most significant poetry after modernism, by poets who published their first books in the years immediately following World War II. Any convincing figuration of postwar poetry, I should think, would have to include Merrill as well as Ashbery, Bishop as well as O'Hara. Poundian readings of twentieth-century poetry make no distinctions among formal poets and necessarily dismiss them all as accomplished but somehow beside the point. A credible account of postmodern poetry cannot write off such major poets as Bishop and Merrill as isolated aberrations.

Organicist and functionalist models of composition reduce form to content or function; whether poems are Whitman's "leaves of grass" or Williams's "small (or large) machine[s] made of words" (1954: 256), they go to show, as "it got phrased by one, R. Creeley," that "FORM IS NEVER MORE THAN AN EXTENSION OF CONTENT" (Olson 1966: 16). The heresy for this creed would be the idea that form may not be organically or functionally inevitable but may, in fact, be only rhetorically engaged. In critical terms, however, only when the relation between content and form is figured as figuration can we conceive of a *poetic* history, as opposed to either a history of poetic production that subsumes poetic changes to social, intellectual, or political developments or one that models poetic history as a progressive narrative of overcoming. A poetic history may not necessarily be best figured as a narrative, which is itself only one of many modes of poetic organization. And recognizing a distinctly poetic history – a history not simply of poetic forms but of their deployment for various purposes – with its separate politics is the first step in mapping the history of American poetry, which begins by interrupting the narrative of English poetic history and by politicizing and historicizing formal choices themselves.

An American poetic historiography must allow for both a synchronic variety of formal options and a diachronic variety of the political purposes they may serve at different times. Neither a synchronic typology of forms nor a diachronic development alone but a grid would make for a convincing model of American poetic history, for it could register both the political pressures that modify formal typologies and the formal negotiations of political imperatives. Such a history could plot differences between poets in a given chronological period as well as between periods. And unless we differentiate how formal techniques may function in different ways – because the same forms may appeal to different rhetorical figures for their authority and because their rhetorical functions may change through time – we cannot make any substantive historical or political distinctions.[10]

Certainly the politics of free forms is complicated and unstable throughout American poetic history, and that may be one reason open forms and oppositional political values have been so easily confused. The issue of the continuities and discontinuities between English and American poetry is obviously too complex for me to deal with here, but it is safe to say that technical options – whether rejecting or subscribing to English forms – have been politicized by American poets at least since the nineteenth century. One way to resist the political authority of traditional norms and conventions is to devise new techniques that appeal to nature or science and technology, thought to be suprapolitical through the modern period. Because someone like Whitman politicizes literary-historical authority, his technical departures from the norm signify as democratic and politically anti-institutional revisions at the same time that they are authorized on the grounds of self-evident truths. When this organicism boomerangs with Pound at a different historical juncture, natural truths and the totalitarian orders they authorize come with different politics. Pound's rejection of a single, historically authoritative tradition in fact frees him to repossess an absolute – historically noncontingent, scientifically objective – universal authority for poetry. In this way, we get an elitist art divorced from any institutional power base and a technically experimental art that deploys antihierarchical compositional methods to recuperate metaphysics and hierarchical aesthetic, ethical, and political values.

Yet despite his totalitarianism, Pound's work still reminds us of the unstable relation between poetic forms and politics. By dissociating literary authority and tradition from "the conventional taste of four or five centuries and one continent" (1970a: 90), he also dissociates traditional forms from their institutional bases and can in fact use them when they serve his purposes. Although Pound would repress his rhetorical intervention, his poetry illustrates that, in practice, any given form may serve a variety of rhetorical purposes. Once the link between forms and their canonical authority is broken, the political potential of any given form cannot be contained within any one poet's explicit political agenda, and poets with very different politics have learned from Pound. Further, history keeps revising the politics of forms. When politically and culturally conservative poets like the Fugitives turned to conventional forms, for example, Pound appeared as a potentially radical force, and his poetics became useful for politically leftist agendas. The politics of a given form is unstable and changes through poetic history.

The discontinuity between poetic techniques and political or metaphysical values became even more glaring in the postwar period. After the United States emerged as an imperial power itself, liberational and oppositional techniques – from free verse to subversive syntax – began to display their own power politics. The technical revolt against New Critical formalism in the fifties by poets like Olson, Ginsberg, Levertov, Duncan, Snyder, and Creeley was part of a sociopolitical revolt against the U.S. empire and its institutions, and this historical coincidence has contributed to the slippage between poetic techniques and political values that informs histories of contemporary poetry. In the sixties, liberational poetic techniques – used now to protest the Vietnam War – moved from the margins to the center, with no little irony, when poets like Galway Kinnell, James Wright, Robert Bly, Philip Levine, Adrienne Rich, W. S. Merwin, and Donald Hall, who began writing formal poetry, converted to free verse. After this point, free verse was poetically mainstreamed and politically neutralized. Historically, then, free verse has signified anti-British, antihierarchical, and democratic political values (Whitman); totalitarian and hierarchical sociopolitical values marching to nature's way (Pound); radical or Marxist politics (Louis Zukofsky, Charles Reznikoff, George Oppen, Langston Hughes, Muriel Rukeyser, Amiri Baraka); and liberal politics (Williams, Levertov, Ginsberg). Free verse can be antiformalist (Whitman, O'Hara) or formalist (Pound, Olson, Zukofsky); it can appeal for its authority to nature (Snyder, Mary Oliver, Charles Wright), to the unconscious (Deep Imagists), or to the mechanics of language (Language poets).

Once free forms are established and cannot be read as even technically – let alone politically – radical, generalizing about their cultural position and politics becomes impossible. The issue is further complicated when the norm of free verse is questioned and traditional forms begin to offer attractive alternatives. Compared with naturalized free verse, metrical verse that flaunts its artifice commands greater political distance from any number of naturalized conventions governing cultural discourses and thus has greater political potential – and not only as satire, either. After 1960, forms "strait-jacketed by the 'closed' forms of rhyme and meter" – in Frank and Sayre's disparaging oversimplification (1988: x) – no longer necessarily signified political conservatism or metaphysical closure, and poets could write formal verse without being formalists. Thus any essentialist alignment of certain techniques with specific sociopolitical, ethical, and metaphysical values is ahistorical and inadequate for reading poetry after modernism.

Postmodernism, Andreas Huyssen writes, "operates in a field of tension between tradition and innovation, conservation and renewal, mass culture and high art, in which the second terms are no longer automatically privileged over the first; a field of tension which can no longer be grasped in categories such as progress vs. reaction, left vs. right, present vs. past, modernism vs. realism, abstraction vs. representation, avantgarde vs. Kitsch. . . . Such heroic visions of modernity and of art as a force of social change (or, for that matter, resistance to undesired change) are a thing of the past" (1986: 216–17). What this means for poetry is that open forms are not automatically "free" and closed forms are not automatically "reactionary." Even to argue – as Thomas Byers does, for example (1992) – for a strong historical, if not essential, connection in the United States between metrical verse and conservative politics and between disruptive compositional strategies and radical politics does not help, at this historical juncture, the work of criticism, which is to judge how forms are troped and what rhetorical and political functions they perform in any given instance at a particular time. History does not stay put, and it should not be used to recuperate metaphysics; the historical link, for example, belongs to the nineteenth century and dissolves the minute we get a Pound. Once again, when someone like Pound deploys avant-garde techniques for politically reactionary and culturally elitist ends, the nineteenth-century model of aligning experimental writing with opposition or even revolution no longer applies. And to maintain a historical connection between free forms and radical politics in the 1990s is to ignore the history of modernism itself.

Given the political neutrality of technical options, the more recently articulated conservative position of the New Formalists is equally problematic, whether they argue that "free verse" is "totalitarian" ("nicely adapted to the needs of the bureaucratic and even the totalitarian state," in Frederick Turner and Ernst Pöppel's words [1983: 307]) or suggest that metrical verse is indeed more "natural" ("Given the demands and restrictions of the human body, it may well turn out that free verse is inherently barred from the very grandest heights of poetry," in Brad Leithauser's terms [1987: 12]). For the New Formalists also identify techniques with content and maintain an essentialist opposition. Thus, although they set out to challenge modernist values, they end up reinscribing them, for techniques still carry political values – only now it is metrical verse that is politically freer and closer to nature. An organicist naturalization of open forms, as in Olson's use of "breath" as a unit of measure, and a formalist naturalization of conventions, as in Turner and Pöppel's defense of meter by similarly invoking the breath/heartbeat ratio, both ignore the intervention of rhetoric in formal choices. By contrast, poets who call attention to the persuasive function of their formal choices grant us a critical perspective on what we are reading, and poems that resist naturalizing their conventions – whether experimental or traditional – open up a political perspective, whether or not they are explicitly political and whatever the specific or partisan politics of their authors.

I would like to reapproach the political issue via de Man's idea of the "aporia" between the materiality of language and its meaning. De Man traces an irreducible divide between grammar and meaning, between tropes as such and their meanings, between words or sentences and the statements they make, between letters and the words they spell, down to the distinction between the letter as a material, blank mark and the letter as a sign, a mark recognizable as a function in a sign system. This gap in language – this permanent "errancy of language which never reaches the mark" – is what Walter Benjamin calls "history," de Man writes (1986: 92). History in this sense may be understood as the political linkage between structure and meaning, between an "inhuman" materiality of events and the "human" history of "meaningful" events. Thus, in de Man's words, "the nonmessianic, nonsacred, that is the *political* aspect of history is the result of the *poetical* structure of language" (93).

If we appropriate this scheme for poetry, the divide between form and content becomes the condition for the functioning of poetic language. The prevailing dogma that the specialness of poetic language lies in the inseparability of its form and content then appears to be a historically specific ideology, a particular convention of getting from the conventionality of the signifier to intentional meanings. This is the generic convention or ideology of Romantic and modern organicist models of poetic language, and it has shaped readings of all kinds of poetry, at the expense of repressing historical differences.

Only by insisting on the separateness of form and content can we make historical distinctions between varieties of poetry. That is, if we locate the gap between form and meaning inside poetic structure, we can address the rhetorical – that is, political and historical – bridgings of this aporia. Rhetoric, the motivated troping of the literal material into the figurative superstructure, leaves this negotiation between form and meaning open to view – to *further* negotiation. Any scheme that would repress this intentional negotiation and argue the inseparability of a poem's material base and its meaningful superstructure would be a species of aesthetic ideology.

Rhetoric as a political, persuasive figuration of the material code into meaning bears witness that meanings are not inherent in the material. If poetry has a generic and general political function, it may be to show us *how* it constructs itself as a discourse that in turn constructs a meaningful world, nature, and self. Thus poetry always has a sociopolitical valence, because it foregrounds the distance between its structure – the generic, linguistic, and representational codes that govern its substitutions – and its meaning. Poetry is no more reducible to any given set of formal practices than to meanings; it names the distance between the two. It is the text of the historically and metaphysically unstable rhetoric that persuades the trope, letter, or form to mean. Any naturalization of the code as inherently meaningful fits the material fact into an already meaningful whole of some purposive, progressive history.

From this perspective, any claims for the inherent value of any given form must be viewed with suspicion. For example, it is not necessarily true that free verse will make us free or that "we shall never again be a free people until we have poets who sing to us in unfree verse" (T. Fleming in Byers 1992: 397). If both open and closed forms are neutral conventions, poetry's underlining its constructedness – the implicit, generic persuasions of its forms and conventions, including the criteria that distinguish poetic discourse from others at a given instance and mark it *as* a separate discourse – may well constitute its usefulness. That is, the more nonutilitarian and special poetic language sounds, the more it represents itself as convention-bound and emphasizes its own figuration, the more it fulfills its unique and generic, inherently critical political function. And poetry that either represses the conventions that go into its construction, or claims to be nonrhetorical and natural and to reveal truths of any stripe, is implicitly totalitarian, for it leaves the reader no room to evaluate its rhetoric, since to perceive its rhetoric would be to cancel it out as poetry, on its own terms.

Once the rhetoric of poetic techniques is recognized and motivation comes into play, poetic choices enter a larger economy and become implicated in cultural and political rhetorics. W. H. Auden saw modern poets living in a society "governed by the values appropriate to Labor," where "the so-called fine arts have lost the social utility they once had" (1989: 74). For him, nostalgia for a past when poets had a public role leads to two heresies – *l'art engagé,* or "art as propaganda," and an art that endows "the gratuitous with a magic utility of its own" (76). But poets who acknowledge the politicization of aesthetic choices exercise a third option, which exceeds Auden's terms. When poets self-consciously attend to the larger persuasions embedded in their forms and figuration, they acknowledge that their medium itself is tainted; it cannot offer either an aestheticist or a political refuge.

The challenge that faces postmodern poets is not "what to make of a diminished thing," not how to subsist marginally, but what to make of a suddenly centralized and increased thing. Poetic discourse understood as rhetorical is inescapably political; by the same token, it makes taking any overt political position suspect. And if the luxury of legislating for "mankind" is no longer available, neither is the luxury of an aestheticist formalism that would offer, in Ashbery's words, an "exotic / Refuge within an exhausted world" (1975: 82). Since his "exhausted world" is not only "too late" or worn out but choked with exhaust fumes – that is, a historically, politically, and economically specific landscape – to claim distance from it is to take a position in and on it after all. In other words, even aestheticism is not what it used to be; it is politically tainted, because the "exhaustion" is not just metaphysical but historically specific. If, in this blurring, the aesthetic can also be political, the political can also be decorative.

Allowing for such "contamination" does not mean dissolving the categories of "aesthetic" and "political"; indeed, they must be kept distinct if we are to see their interplay in the domain of rhetoric, which, again, is both figuration (including formal as well as tropological figuration) and persuasion (including formal as well as discursive suasion). Collapsing aesthetics and politics – whether by reducing aesthetics to politics or by reducing politics to aesthetics – erases either the figuration or the persuasion of poetic rhetoric. Any passage between politics and aesthetics crosses categories and figures the relation between them as metonymy, analogy, synechdoche, or irony. Aestheticism and polemics (under the signs of metonymy and synechdoche) are equally political or rhetorical, equally lacking any inherent or essential authorization. And neither canonical nor disruptive aesthetic forms can have greater truth-value unless we invest a transcendent value in "tradition" or "change," just as neither conservative nor radical politics can claim greater truth without investing an inherent value in hierarchical or egalitarian sociopolitical orders, in free or planned economies. Any conflation of aesthetics and politics – whether by saying modernist forms are inherently liberational or elitist; whether by arguing traditional forms inherently serve the system or enable more socially accessible and therefore effective writing – remains within the framework of modernism and invokes some version of aesthetic ideology.

The relation of aesthetics and politics has to be refigured after modernism, and one way to begin is to separate the two categories; acknowledging their interplay or "contamination," however, might temper political or aestheticist self-righteousness. Neither an aestheticism that represses politics, nor a politicization that erases aesthetics, presents a viable option, because the category of the poetic is, in fact, special. Poetic rhetoric is figuration and persuasion *at once,* and each function of poetic language keeps exceeding the other, which excess sets in motion uncontrollable side effects. Poetic language is both formal and discursive; repressing the discourse under the sign of formal-aesthetic value and elevating discourse over the aesthetic equally lose the poetic. Unless we want to do away with the category of the poetic, we have to give up ambitions of either completely aestheticizing or politicizing it.

For if politics always intrudes on the aesthetic, the aesthetic always manages to muddle the politics. For example, Cary Nelson's politically motivated attempt to retrieve work suppressed by canonized modernism itself excludes, on the one hand, "genteel" poetry – Edna St. Vincent Millay and Mina Loy warrant resurrection but Elinor Wylie and Sara Teasdale do not, even though they, too, were marginalized – and, on the other, overly polemical poetry – John Reed, for one, does not make the cut. Nelson judges the excluded poets "relatively unable to do vital cultural work for current audiences" (1989: 55); "vital cultural work," as distinct from mere political correctness, is the function now assigned to the "aesthetic." Nelson insists that literary history and canonization should be kept distinct, but I would argue that literary history is as rhetorically motivated as canon making. Since value – and, therefore, politics – is implicit in all such rhetorical projects, we need to resist illusions of objectivity, whether engendered by "universal aesthetic standards" or by the mere fact of the material existence of texts marketing themselves as poetry.

If the politics of poetry after modernism is complicated, if no singular tradition or norm – against which historical and political contingencies may be measured – exists, if neither experimental nor canonical forms can be seen as transparent signifiers of determinate political values, how can a poet achieve any critical distance to speak of personal and cultural experience? I would suggest that only a desacralized, demystified poetic language that declines morally, politically, or aesthetically superior positions can still resist being totally appropriated, for taking superior positions only inscribes poetry all the more firmly in the prevailing discourses of domination. Implicating poetic language and rhetoric in larger cultural discourses, while acknowledging the difference of poetic discourse, its history and its conventions (again, whether of free or canonical forms), would enable a critical distance from within and protect against the "heresies" of both an aestheticist formalism and propaganda. Only such a "complicitous critique," in Linda Hutcheon's apt phrase (1988), can avoid the political self-righteousness of a pure critique, which can only reduce to pure complicity.

The idea that poetry has no public function at all unless it plays an instrumental role in improving our lives or altering social arrangements is itself a modern notion. For the attempt to make poetry a utilitarian discourse is a historically specific response to its increasing cultural marginalization since the eighteenth century; perhaps predictably, however, reinforcing the dominant value of utility has only confirmed poetry's "uselessness." I am proposing that poetry's public function is to grant a perspective on how all meanings are rhetorical and therefore political. Writing is no more "natural" than the world, and if poets are to show how they construct their world, they need more, rather than less, rhetorical sophistication.

We can approach the question of poetry's public function from the other extreme, which would deny poetry any political role at all. For example, Auden remarks that "verse in its formal nature protests against protesting; it demands that to some degree we accept things as they are, not for any rational or moral reason, but simply because they happen to be that way; it implies an element of frivolity in the creation" (1989: 364). While it is true that poetry in its formal nature – in precisely what distinguishes it as poetry – "protests against protesting," it need not follow that "we accept things as they are," because poetry is more than form. And if form tempers the discursive content, the discursive content also tempers form. This transaction hinges on rhetoric, the persuasive troping of form into meaning, which makes for a politically and historically specific representation of "things as they are." Foregrounding this representational mediation also calls "things" into question, for "things as they are" is not a given. Poetry may imply "an element of frivolity in the creation" of "the way things are" if "we" are in a frivolous mood; if we are in a critical mood, however, we could say that poetry implies an element of arbitrariness in "the way things are," for "things" could be otherwise. Since no given arrangement can claim any necessity, we could conclude that we must "accept things as they are," but we could as easily draw the different conclusion that "things" must be changed. Poetry is not quite "outside" the way things are, but it is not quite "inside," either; representing "things," or duplicating them with a difference, it only shows that they could be different – better, worse, or just different. This, I should think, would be a valuable contribution to any citizen's political education.

Postmodern poets achieve a critical distance from their culture also by turning to the past, which is neither Pound's "live" past nor Eliot's simultaneous tradition. And they do not invoke the past in order to affect the future; faith in a future-affecting memory informs progressive models – whether evolutionary or revolutionary, Romantic or modernist. A progressive history, the medium where truth unfolds, is a

humanist history, to which modernism subscribes. Postmodern memory, which does not recall the past as an authority and is not motivated
toward the future, has a different rhetorical function: it opens up a
historical perspective, from which the construction of the present and
the self becomes apparent. Such memory allows for a critical distance
on the present, without investing any given tradition with metaphysical or historical authority and without rejecting the past, which
would only recuperate progressive, humanist models of history.

I take "postmodern" to indicate a different figuration of history
than modernism's progressive model, which inevitably ascribes political and epistemological value to experimental techniques. Again, the
term is commonly used for a variety of movements that are continuous
with modernism and confined by its values and options, from Olson's
"projective verse" to Language poetry. For example, Charles Bernstein
in *A Poetics* reaffirms the greater epistemological and political value of
"new" forms: "*Poetry is aversion of conformity* in the pursuit of new
forms," and "I care most for poetry as dissent, including formal dissent." Poets have serious cultural work to do: they must "throw a
wedge into [the] engineered process of social derealization," which
"means we can't rely only on the tools and forms of the past, even the
recent past, but must invent new tools and forms that begin to meet
the challenges of the ever-changing present" (1992: 1–3). To my
mind, the "challenges" of the present call for interpretive intervention
rather than "new tools" or "wedges," for different figurations of the
poet's function rather than retooling legislators of humankind. But a
program centered on technical progress evades such rhetorical issues.
Since Bernstein aligns "artifice" with novel "programmatic" structures
(69) rather than with rhetorical deployment, he has little use for
something as "tediously / repetitive & witlessly contrived" (39) as
"metrical versification," although meter surely became artificial
enough once modernism denaturalized it.

Perloff, a committed defender of Language poetry, also maintains
that programmatically antireferential and asyntactic language or "radical artifice" – a term resonant with the modernist confusion of aesthetic technique and political value – can alone resist duplicating "the
discourse of the media" (1991: 78). Since the media have appropriated

the poet's traditional domain of feelings, sensitivity, authenticity, and the self, poets like Levine, Bly, and James Wright, with their image-based poetry in "transparent" language, may as well be on *Donahue;* any line we cannot imagine hearing on *Donahue* is, for Perloff, poetry (51, 52, 48). What she labels "procedural verse," for example, combats "reference" and therefore "commodity fetishism" (186) by moving "from the impasse of 'free speech' rhythms to the 'rhythm of cognition'" (170) based on "mathematics." Self-imposed mathematical constraints, better than meter or grammar, reveal "hidden resources" of language (140); offer "a form of *discipline,* forcing the artist to break with ego, with habit, with self-indulgence" (150); and make for "a more profound poetic grammar" (170). Thus, although such procedures aim to combat now-exhausted "free verse," they perform the same function, and appeal to the same arguments for their authority, as Pound's free verse. They have greater epistemological value, are more "scientific" and less rhetorical, and give us a profounder and purer – culturally, politically, and ideologically un-contaminated – use of words than traditional meters, which now include free verse.

A poetic that appeals to the "discipline" of "mathematics" is blind to the issue of rhetoric and duplicates Pound's "discipline," for it does not ask: Who chooses the arbitrary mathematical constraint that will maximally motivate each sign if not the "ego"? What carries out such tiresome plans to the bitter end but "habit"? What purpose to such work but "self-indulgence"? If the alternative is communication and the attendant commodification of subjectivity, so be it, and poets had better find a way to get on with it. For poetry enjoys no special dis-pensation; neither meter nor mathematics can save it from commo-dification. Indeed, a procedural nonreference seems to me to be an extreme case of formalism, which can only play into the commodity fetishism it sets out to combat.

Similarly, their repression of rhetoric redounds on the political pro-gram of the Language poets, which is to critique "bourgeois subjec-tivity," and their ambition to be purely critical ends up absolutely indistinguishable from pure complicity. Ironically, a Marxist like Ja-meson finds such poets, who are leftists politically, "apolitical" and "ahistorical." A lesson is to be learned here: how *do* we distinguish the attempt to be purely critical of bourgeois subjectivity from pure complicity? Representing the self as thoroughly "written" by a network of culturally dominant sociopolitical and economic discourses and aiming to "eliminate subjectivity" (Perloff 1991: 115) also eliminate any critical distance, because the technical apparatus deployed in this representation is not rhetorically engaged. If we are all overdetermined social constructs, Language poetry is indeed what we would write; how, then, can we judge any particular construction or even see it as such? And why would a poetry that sets out to challenge the specialness of poetic language market itself as *poetry?* While Language poetry sets out to demystify poetry that appeals to bourgeois subjectivity, in the end it mystifies its own techniques as iconic by failing to engage rhetorically its own representational means and techniques and remains within a progressive reification of technology that marks its culture. In fact, to read Language poetry as critical, the reader has to bring in a superior vantage point, helpfully provided by ample prose "explanations" and "defenses"; such purgations of polemical rhetoric in prose keep the poetry "pure."

Language poetry, then, is more properly a late-modern poetic, minus Olson's organicism; Language poets claim to have progressed beyond Black Mountaineers "to undermine the univocal, the presumptions about speaker and subject still carried out in a breath-projected model, with the bodily origins of that metaphor" (Palmer 1989: 9). Adopting Wittgenstein's view of language enables them to "advance" beyond organicism while maintaining the organicist equation of language and perception: "Language is not something that *explains* or *translates* experience, but is the source of experience. Language is perception, thought itself" (Messerli 1987: 2). Such a coincidence of language and perception – whether on organicist or Wittgensteinian grounds, whether nature or language is figured as the ground – is perfectly consistent with Poundian aesthetics and rules out acknowledging the intervention of rhetoric. "Meaning" in this poetry is not "self-contained" like a "jelly-bean, but is inseparable from the language in process – the transformation of phoneme into word, the association of one word to the next, the slip of phrase against phrase, the forward movement and reversal of the sentence – the way one experiences life itself" (3).

Up until the last phrase, this description would apply to any poetry, but the last phrase claims for Language poetry a greater verisimilitude to the way "one" (a metonymy for "all") "experiences life." And what if I don't experience it that way? What if I want a poetry that shows me that its "way" is *not* the way "one experiences life itself"? If I resist this naturalization of someone's rhetoric, then I am outside the community of the saved: "Language work resembles a creation of a community and of a world-view by a once divided-but-now-fused Reader and Writer" (B. Andrews in Messerli 1987: 4). This "community" by fusion, with its unified worldview, is totalitarian. Apart from my aesthetic values, my political value here is that, at this point, I cherish the poets who do not have such designs on me – who are not out to "fuse" with me – and who admit their rhetoric, which always bespeaks a democratic respect for difference. Then, if I choose to "fuse," I do so with open eyes.

From my perspective, New Formalism is as inadequate as Language poetry in offering alternatives to the melodrama of canonical forms versus experimental forms, reaction versus progress. Indeed, New Formalism mirrors Language poetics: it is equally academic in believing in the inherent virtue of one form or another, and equally inclined to marshall an array of particular techniques for a specific cultural and political program. Both movements oppose the mainstream – writing-program-programmed lyric poetry in naturalized free verse – and I fully share their discontent. But, I would argue, there are alternatives outside the oppositional framework of Language poetry versus "lyric" poetry, of free versus formal verse. In any case, both Language poetry and New Formalism are best situated within the context of certain sociological changes that have affected the production and consumption of poetry since the seventies, and their considerable sociological and historical interest does not quite translate to literary interest.

My comments on Language poetry and New Formalism are meant primarily to show the persistence into the nineties of an early-modern figuration of the relationship between form and content.[11] But I will concentrate on four poets of the generation immediately following modernism. Since one of my purposes is to question the way the history of postwar poetry has been plotted, I have chosen poets with established, more or less canonized bodies of work. For they foreground the critical issue: if we want to be able to read and appreciate all of these poets, each of whom is considered major by one faction or another, we would have to retell the history of the period after modernism and work outside its paradigmatic analogies between technical practices and political agendas, which have fostered an ideological partisanship that is becoming more and more irrelevant poetically.

Although some of these poets admired one another's work, they do not share a poetic program or a political agenda, but they all challenge, in different ways, any easy alignment of poetics and politics. Any framework relying on a substantive or political opposition between traditional and experimental forms is irrelevant for approaching their work. All of these poets acknowledge the rhetoric of their forms by challenging the larger political and cultural assumptions associated with the forms they employ, thus frustrating expectations shaped by modernist values.

Since "the gender of modernism"[12] has become a critical issue, not only the historical position but the shared sexual orientation of these four poets may be of significance in their questioning of modernists' universalism and organicism, with its implicitly heterosexist values. The poets I have chosen define their values without invoking universals, offer alternatives to organicism, and are homosexual; I am not convinced, however, that sexuality can be factored into poetic history in any general, systematic way without invoking some metaphysical given. To generalize about sexuality – or any other nonliterary determinant, whether biological, biographical, or social – in poetry is to politicize it in a deterministic way. I am arguing that we have to keep politics and poetics distinct if we want to think about poetic history. Thus I would be just as cautious about translating nonliterary contingencies into poetic significance as about translating poetic effects into political power.

In the end, I have chosen to read these poets because they offer more aesthetic pleasure and a more complex engagement with the politics of poetry than I find elsewhere. They seem to me the indispensable poets after modernism – both for the quality of their work, which is their contribution to poetic history, and for their vision of "different" visions outside oppositional models, which is their gift to cultural history.

Frank O'Hara
"How Am I to Become a Legend?"

"I don't think of fame or posterity (as Keats so grandly and genuinely did), nor do I care about clarifying experiences for anyone or bettering (other than accidentally) anyone's state or social relation, nor am I for any particular technical development in the American language simply because I find it necessary," writes Frank O'Hara (1971: 500) in a statement for the *New American Poetry* in 1959. In 1965, when asked, "You think it's important to be new?" he responds, "No, I think it's very important not to be bored though" (1975b: 9). These two comments could serve as the coordinates for plotting O'Hara's experimentalism. In his writings on painting and poetry he insists on the value of innovative, unconventional, "living and interesting" work (13), not out of any reformist zeal but to forestall boredom. The fear of boredom, a repeated concern throughout his writing, places him in a specific cultural economy, itself geared to the continuous production and consumption of novelty to ward off boredom. O'Hara does not mystify avant-garde art as oppositional but locates its impulse to technical innovation within the cultural and economic mainstream. Experimental art is exciting, he suggests, precisely because it does not oppose but shares the cultural dynamic and responds to the stresses and strains of a specific historical moment.

By 1950, experimental arts belong in the complex of the late-capitalist economy, and such art cannot in good faith claim a morally superior vantage point from which to judge the culture. Discussing

Andy Warhol's films, O'Hara objects to the traditional notion of the avant-garde as an "embattled vanguard":

> There is no underground and there is certainly no embattlement. Andy Warhol gets more publicity than any other single living American artist right this minute. . . . I don't mean that I'm saying that it isn't a good thing; I think it's terrific. But it is not being underground; that's a lot of romantic nonsense . . . it is part of your culture. . . . It is not attacking us really in a certain way, and there's no reason to attack a culture that will allow it to happen, and even foster the impulse – and create it. Which is a *change*, you see, from the general idea of, that all avant-garde art has to be attacking the bourgeoisie, and the bourgeoisie has now been so completely absorbed by the rest of society that it can't even have its prejudices any more. (1975b: 8–9)

The changed status and function of experimental art link to sociopolitical and economic changes in the culture as a whole, which render an oppositional or "attack" position irrelevant: "Now, you do not have to have the Russian Revolution or the French Revolution or the Civil Rights Movement in order to get irritated by other people's ideas. All you have to do is be one individual who is tired of looking at something that looks like something else" (9).

I have quoted O'Hara at some length to show that his commitment to the value of experimental work does not rest on the notion that avant-garde aesthetics signify oppositional politics. What is true of art applies to experimental poetry as well, although poetry is a less valuable commodity than, say, painting. "As for measure and other technical apparatus," in the words of his famous 1959 essay "Personism," "that's just common sense: if you're going to buy a pair of pants you want them to be tight enough so everyone will want to go to bed with you. There's nothing metaphysical about it" (1971: 498). And if you're going to write a poem, you don't want it to bore; you want it to be "sexy" enough so everyone will want to read it. There's nothing metaphysical about it: it makes economic sense – as a marketing strategy. O'Hara's stance is distinct from the academicism of the Right *and* the Left. The pants have to fit your body, so laboring in received forms is beside the point. But so is adhering to Olson's metaphysical precepts and striving for a puritanical "tightness": "With the influence of Levertov and Creeley you have another element which is making *control* practically the subject matter of the poem. That is your *control* of the language, your *control* of the experiences and your *control* of your thought," so that it is the "experience of their paring it down that comes through more strongly and not the experience that is the subject" (1975b: 23).

Such formalism of the experimental stripe contrasts with O'Hara's processual values that are resolutely nonreformist – that is, neither radical nor puritanical. O'Hara's erotic metaphor of the "tight pants" for his kind of form–function alliance suggests a "lyric" ideal, and his economic metaphor situates this ideal in the postmetaphysical arena of the marketplace, where value is exchange value. In his impure figuration, eros and economics play into poetic discourse, whose exchanges and substitutions are not governable or repressible by technological efficiency. He rejects the modernist reification of technique: poetry is not "as useful as a machine" (1971: 18); it is not a set of "instruments" (309); and it should not be given over to a "cult of mechanics, of know-how" (1975b: 43). Poetry involves a certain amount of waste or excess and uncontrollable side effects; it is prodigal, like its culture.

And it must entertain: "In a capitalist country fun is everything. Fun is the only justification for the acquisitive impulse, if one is to be honest" (1975a: 5). O'Hara's aesthetic belongs in the larger historical context of the commodification of the avant-garde in the 1950s. When Edward Lucie-Smith, interviewing O'Hara, brings up the European judgment of the New York art world – "because the dynamic is a financial dynamic" – O'Hara replies, "Oh no, it's no more financial in character than anyplace else, and Budapest is just as financial. I don't think that has anything to do with anything." The difference is only quantitative, not qualitative. "Enthusiasm for art, after all, is always involved with any number of interesting attitudes. Everybody wants to have a jewel":

L-S: You think that this is a kind of ownership thing as well, this enthusiasm?

O'H: Of course . . . Now that's silly to even talk about because the basic human motive is acquisitive.

L-S: That's a terribly American thing to say.

O'H: Well, it's not American. . . . What about the Elgin Marbles? (1975b: 15)

Far from oppositional, O'Hara's experimentalism repeatedly invokes the values informing the larger economy. It aspires to the personal "signature" of one "individual" who wants to do something different. In an early journal, O'Hara defines "greatness" as, "quite vulgarly," the "realization of personality" (1977: 110). This concept of the artist and art is as "bourgeois" as you can get, and surely such "auristic" art (see Benjamin 1969) participates in a consumer economy and commodity fetishism. Since O'Hara's individualism, or "personism," can accommodate both capitalism and avant-garde values, his poetic will not fit into the oppositional framework that postwar poetry has been fitted into: academic verse (upholding what Antin [1972] terms the "moral-metrical tradition") versus avant-garde writing (signifying a moral-metrical-political revolutionary stance). Those aligned with academic values and those moved by Olsonian poetics alike will find O'Hara lightweight. For his part, O'Hara dismisses both camps: a poet like Robert Lowell can get away with "just plain bad" things because the "metrics" are supposed to be so good, and someone like Olson is too hung up on the Pound heritage and the "important utterance" (1975b: 13). As Ashbery remarks, O'Hara is "too hip for the squares and too square for the hips," and that puts him in "a category of oblivion which increasingly threatens any artist who dares to take his own way, regardless of mass public and journalistic approval. And how could it be otherwise in a supremely tribal civilization like ours, where even artists feel compelled to band together in marauding packs, where the loyalty-oath mentality has pervaded outer Bohemia, and where Grove Press subway posters invite the lumpenproletariat to 'join the Underground Generation,' as though this were as simple a matter as joining the Pepsi Generation which it probably is" (in Perloff 1979: 12).

In the last twist of Ashbery's sentence, we see the dilemma of the experimental poet. Locating experimental arts within the functioning whole of the cultural economy, O'Hara is skeptical that art can command a critical stance outside the game. "Europeans," he remarks, "always talk about commitment in the singular, but they always seem to have two: esthetic and political. The American artist is much more likely to have put all his eggs in one basket." For "the only force" the American artist "can bring to bear on society, the only way he can be heard, is in (not through) his work" (1975b: 97). O'Hara casts his distrust of tendentious art and his awareness of the rhetorical, persuasive, and political power of aesthetic choices themselves as an American difference. Indeed, his stance resembles his "great predecessor" Whitman's — "Both in and out of the game and watching and wondering at it" (1965: 32). If Whitman challenges English and European literary traditions and institutions, he is not — indeed, cannot be — oppositional to American political values and cultural experience, since the very ground of his work is its alignment with such experience. Hence Whitman's agony, as his century rolled on. Williams's career provides another example. His political and cultural values oppose England, personified half by his father and half by T. S. Eliot, by appealing to American political and cultural experience; since the gap between the ideal and the real is too glaring to be ignored, however, he turns increasingly reformist. O'Hara resists the reformist temptation; his aesthetic values are inseparable from his culture's vices. In this admission lie the historical specificity and force of his work.

•

I

                    The
really stupid things, I mean

a can of coffee, a 35¢ ear
ring, a handful of hair, what

do these things do to us?
    (O'Hara 1971: 55)

A number of early O'Hara poems are programmatic surrealist experiments that often rely on a form–content opposition, and unfortunately
they have influenced the tone of much of O'Hara's criticism. "Tar-
quin," for example, juxtaposes the form of a Petrarchan sonnet with
a disjunctive grammatical and narrative syntax that does not deliver
what the sonnet form leads us to expect. Here an authoritative form
"artificially" gathers discordant imagery, diction, and syntax, and the
poem remains a set or conventional piece of avant-garde poetry. "Second Avenue" exemplifies the other major strand of his surrealist verse,
where the explosive material presumably gathers at some level of subjective experience: "Actually everything in it either happened to me
or I felt happening (saw, imagined) on Second Avenue" (1975b: 39–
40). O'Hara adds that "the life in the work is autonomous (not about
actual city life)" (40). Both of these paradigms cast the artist in opposition, whether to conventions of poetry and reasonable discourse
or to historical and empirical experience.

    But I am interested in a different kind of poem – in some ways
"about actual city life" – that neither signifies through its opposition
to conventions of discourse nor claims a purely autonomous (subjective or linguistic) life. Although such poems may seem vaguely surreal,
and the parts or details may not function symbolically to compose their
wholes, their seeming randomness resolves into an order nonetheless.
The details, "interchangeable" only from a metaphysical viewpoint,
carefully compose the textual surface as the superstructure of an economic and sociopolitical base. Cultural and historical connections
make for what O'Hara calls the "design" of such poems, maintaining
a tensile surface that resists both "formal smothering and emotional
spilling over" (1975b: 35), and such poems have a political charge,
because they exploit the tension between poetic and cultural "orders."
What O'Hara observes about Grace Hartigan's paintings applies
equally to his own compositions: "heterogeneous pictures which bring
together wildly discordant images through insight into their functional
relationship (their 'being together in the world')," which is an insight

into their "nature." She proceeds not by elimination but by "inclusion," "a continual effort to put more into the picture without sacri-
ficing the clarity she loves in Matisse nor subduing the noise of the
desperate changes she perceives in the world around her" (45).

Functioning relationships found existing "together in the world"
provide the compositional logic of O'Hara's best poems, so that
their violent or discordant surface is not resolved, like modernist discordance, into a universal unity on another plane "behind" it. Nor
do their disjunctive textual surfaces represent only a self-referential
engagement with poetic or grammatical conventions or "refer back
to the artist" (1975b: 44). Rather, these poems signify extratextually,
and their textual discordance meshes with another network of
equally violent relations, whether social, historical, or political.
"Europeans often find contemporary American art violent," O'Hara
remarks. "I don't, but violence is the atmosphere in which much of
it is created and which makes its commitment extreme and serious.
New York is one of the most violent cities in the world" (97). Certainly the pervasive imagery of visceral violence in O'Hara's poetry
attests to this fact. If law and order – in the city, the psyche, the
poem – are established and maintained by repression and exclusion,
violence – violation, invasion, disruption – is in fact their "natural"
bond. Given O'Hara's insight into the "nature" of New York life,
he is interested less in judging particular political and social arrangements, since all order is maintained by violence, and more in showing what "these things do to us." His compositional "violation of
our ingrained assumptions" (1975a: 35) harmonizes with his culture
at large and cannot be critical – except accidentally – unless it is also
critical of itself. Such textual violence does not claim the luxury of a
superior aesthetic vantage point, promising "to destroy something
but not us" (1971: 149).

Indeed, O'Hara views the artist as a self-destructive, sacrificial figure. He writes: "There is more sheer ugliness in America than you
can shake a stick at. And it is the characteristic of the avant-garde to
absorb and transform disparate qualities not normally associated with
art, for the artist to take within him the violence and evil of his times
and come out with something" (1975b: 98). He ascribes such a sacrificial role to Jackson Pollock, whose inclusiveness is, once again, a

virtue. O'Hara realizes that the "culture is capable of entertaining more than one truth simultaneously in a given era" (1975a: 12), yet few artists are capable of sustaining more than one truth. American culture comes with negative capability, and the rare artist who can let his ego be "absorbed in the work," who can give "himself over to cultural necessities" and uphold "a multiplicity of truths," can become a cultural "occasion" – a celebration to be celebrated (12–13).

"Memorial Day 1950" (1971: 17–18) is an early poem that locates avant-garde technical experimentation in the cultural mainstream. Art is violent and destructive all right, this young poet has learned, but not of the dominant political and cultural institutions:

> Picasso made me tough and quick, and the world;
> just as in a minute plane trees are knocked down
> outside my window by a crew of creators.
> Once he got his axe going everyone was upset
> enough to fight for the last ditch and heap
> of rubbish.
>   Through all that surgery I thought
> I had a lot to say, and named several last things
> Gertrude Stein hadn't had time for; but then
> the war was over, those things had survived
> and even when you're scared art is no dictionary.
> Max Ernst told us that.
>   How many trees and frying pans
> I loved and lost!

Picasso, the "crew of creators" knocking down the "plane trees" outside his window, and World War II cohere in one whole. Picasso's razing of perspectival illusions to a flat "plane," the destruction of nature ("plane" trees) in the name of progress, and the burning "airplanes" that make the world safe for democracy are all linked by wordplay and placed on the same plane. Since the connections are established by microrhetorical puns rather than by polemical rhetoric, they remain on the textual plane.[1] New techniques ("tough and quick"), new machinery (more efficient – "in a minute" the trees are knocked down), and new weaponry all subscribe to the values of a progressive history of technical and technological advance. Thus Picasso's brush becomes an "axe," which links him to the tree surgeons, who recall the "surgery" of the war and the education of the poet: "At that time all of us began to think / with our bare hands and even with blood all over / them, we knew vertical from horizontal, we never / smeared anything except to find out how it lived." Different kinds of "surgery" (root: "handwork" or "handicraft") belong in a functioning whole, a complex collusion of artistic innovation, technological advances, and scientific experimentation.

And O'Hara's relation to this complex is itself complex, for he insists he is "made" by these forces – created, seduced, and betrayed all at once. While he acknowledges his artistic education under the "Fathers of Dada," he recognizes that the oppositional dynamic of the avant-garde of 1918 – a response to World War I – is history. After World War II, even Picasso's *Guernica* signifies differently, and O'Hara has seen what mines can do: "spewed feathered fans of earth trees bones skyward in the most abstract of designs" (1977: 126). In a sense, "Memorial Day" memorializes the death of an innocent or oppositional avant-garde and traces its death to World War II, which has equally "made" the poet and rendered both destruction and moral certainty suspect. The "Fathers of Dada" he invokes are, after all, fathers – not good figures for O'Hara in general or in this poem in particular; they had a hand in "all that surgery." As O'Hara writes in a different context, "It is impossible for a society to be at war without each responsible element joining the endeavor, whether military, philosophical, or artistic, and whether consciously or not. The perspectives may be different, but the temper of the time is inexorable and demanding for all concerned" (1975a: 69).

Without a doubt, World War II was the formative experience for O'Hara's generation.[2] "World War II was simply part of one's life," he writes. "One went to war at seventeen or eighteen and that was what one did, perfectly simple" (1975a: 68). But his disturbing piece on his war experience, "Lament and Chastisement: A Travelogue of War and Personality," suggests it wasn't that simple:

> Should one allow oneself to become involved?
> What is the proper spirit?

If I killed Yasuo Kuniyoshi could I sleep? Even if he told me
    to?
If I should die would anyone care?
Am I really me? (1977: 114)

How can you be right if you kill everyone who is wrong?
I admire Walter Gieseking.
I admire Richard Strauss.
Does the artist do enough for humanity to obviate his fascism?
Can you fight ideas without ideas?
BUT
Is there ever a good without evil?
Can I detach myself from Stalingrad?
Can I rationalize Franco?
Could even the greatest symphony drown out the screams of
    Jews? (125)

. . . and the planes struck Japan and the bomb struck
Hiroshima and the war was over.
    Well, the war was over.
    . . . we killed the great Japanese architect the great German
scientist the great Italian musician dropped death on Hiroshima
killed killed killed and yes I hate us for it killedkilledkilled
    we saved our not-worth-saving world rampant with the
injustice cruelty and hate which bred us;
    we owe ourselves
    what?
    nothing?
    nothing;
    we are guilty?
    no
    guilty?
    no
    guilty (as the heart bleeds dawn-grey with the only killing
remorse *the pain for that we could not not do*)?
    yes. (128–29; emphasis added)

This painful self-questioning and acknowledgment of responsibility also reveals O'Hara's political side, which might help revise some misconceptions of him. In 1966, for example, he offended many by refusing to sign a petition against the war in Vietnam. Andrew Ross cites O'Hara's refusal as proof of his "blithe disregard for politics" (1990: 383); this interpretation actually signals Ross's disregard for O'Hara's politics, with which he may not agree.

As his writings on World War II show, O'Hara is anything but uninvolved with political issues; it's just that he will not take refuge in self-righteous polemics – of the Right or the Left – to evade personal involvement and deflect personal responsibility. And, for O'Hara, the issues are especially complex. "Modern artists ideologically, as the Jews racially," he writes, "were the chosen enemies of the authoritarian states because their values were the most in opposition" (1975a: 69); in his war memoir, however, he recalls that, from the navy's point of view, artists are "all queers" and all "queers" are cowards – they have "no guts they never do" (1977: 113–14). For O'Hara, then, fighting in the war (as an artist) also meant fighting against himself (as a homosexual). Fighting the "authoritarian states" through conscription in a different set of totalitarian exclusions, which inform the values of the military he was expected to kill for, complicates any simple opposition of the artist and the state, of "us" and "them."

If the war destroys illusions of an oppositional avant-garde, how can the artist have any critical distance or efficacy? "O Boris Pasternak, it may be silly / to call to you, so tall in the Urals, but your voice / cleans our world, clearer to us than the hospital: / you sound above the factory's ambitious gargle." It may be "silly" to call to Pasternak, but "Soviet society is not alone in seducing the poet to deliver temporary half-truths which will shortly be cast aside for the excitement of a new celebration of nonlife" (1975b: 103). And the reason he is invoked and stands "so tall in the Urals" is that his writing has a different "efficacy" than the other models "Memorial Day" invokes: "To Pasternak the artist is the last repository of individual conscience, and in his terms conscience is individual perception of life" (100). For Pasternak, "life is not a landscape before which the poet postures," and O'Hara cites Pasternak's statement that this Romantic conception of the poet " 'needs the evil of mediocrity in order to be seen, just as Romanticism always needs philistinism and with the disappearance of the petty bourgeoisie loses half its poetical content' " (102). Unlike the Romantic poet, "who imagines himself the measure of life" (101), Pasternak's poet is at once more firmly rooted in his historical context and acknowledges greater moral responsibility: "The human individual is the subject of historical events, not vice versa; he is the repository of life's force. And while he may suffer, may be rendered helpless, may be killed, if he has the perceptiveness to realize this he knows that events require his participation to occur" (106).

Pasternak's direction also contrasts with the technological route to an art with social force via functionalism, efficiency, radical surgery, and so on, all chiming with the "factory's ambitious gargle." "Poetry is as useful as a machine!" immediately follows this phrase and points up O'Hara's distance from Olson's "Projective Verse": "Verse now, 1950, if it is to go ahead, if it is to be of *essential* use, must, I take it, catch up and put into itself certain laws and possibilities of the breath" (1966: 15); for this project, the poet can exploit "the advantage of the typewriter," "its rigidity and its space precisions," and use "the machine as a scoring to his composing" to "bring into being an open verse as formal as the closed, with all its traditional advantages" (22). Formalizing process for reformist goals, mystifying aestheticism with functionalist rhetoric, applying technological criteria to artistic forms, and arguing for the utility of art all inscribe Olson in the myth of progress. Or we might consider Williams in contrast to O'Hara: defending poetry in wartime (1944), Williams comes up with "A poem is a small (or large) machine made of words" and "there can be no part [of it], as in any other machine, that is redundant" (1954: 256).[3] O'Hara, however, was schooled in the war and learned to be prodigal, to exceed mechanical functionalism: "And airplanes are perfect mobiles, independent / of the breeze; crashing in flames they show us how / to be prodigal." The efficiency of the "factory" system necessarily breeds the excess of war, and the link between progress and death, which should have been clear to all by the time of the Korean War, teaches *this* prodigal son his poetics.

"Memorial Day" technically aligns O'Hara with the avant-garde tradition. But the "wasted child," who returns when the war is "over," finds modernist functionalism and avant-garde oppositional agendas equally foreign to his purposes. O'Hara places himself inside a functioning systemic whole and does not lay claim to a perspective uncontaminated by the logic of his culture. His distinction lies in his ability both to convey a sense of being enmeshed in the texture-text of postwar life and to signal his distance from it by maintaining the moral clarity that "events require his participation to occur" (1975b: 106). His repeated praise for the Abstract Expressionists affirms the same value: "While the other protesting artistic voices of the time were bound by figuration and overt symbolism, [they] chose the open road of personal responsibility, naked nerve-ends. . . . Belief in their personal and ethical responses saved them from estheticism on the one hand and programmatic contortion on the other" (1975a: 69). This perfectly describes O'Hara's own stance of putting himself – his personal and ethical responsibility – on the line. And his "individualist" reading of Abstract Expressionism is perfectly consonant with the way the work of painters with radical and internationalist politics were co-opted for conservative agendas and reread, after the war, as icons of American individualism.[4]

"Music" offers one example of how O'Hara implicates himself in the cultural text. Its technical disruptions in fact articulate an underlying social, political, and economic complex. The poem registers the temper of the times, and the poet judges what he observes, but not from outside the system:

> If I rest for a moment near The Equestrian
> pausing for a liver sausage sandwich in the Mayflower Shoppe,
> that angel seems to be leading the horse into Bergdorf's
> and I am naked as a table cloth, my nerves humming.
> (1971: 210)

This seemingly surreal tableau is "found" rather than invented, yet the introductory "If" renders it the fictional find of a hypothetical perspective, both because "rest" is an abstract state only, what with everything changing, and because O'Hara carefully composes the scene with a rhetorical purpose in mind. The scene is 1951 America in miniature.

From his position in the Mayflower Shoppe – named for the Pilgrims' ship and recalling America's descent from its origin as a spiritual community to a "shoppe," whose archaic spelling pays ironic homage to this origin – The Equestrian's horse (associated in O'Hara with the primitive self, Native Americans, and sexuality) seems to be led by "that angel" (part of the statue) into Bergdorf's (for Christmas shopping?). The line "Close to the fear of war and the stars which have disappeared" frames this picture, linking commercialism, capitalism, the Cold (or Korean) War, and the disappearance of the stars – including, presumably, the Star of Bethlehem – outshone as they are by "all those coloured lights."

Other judgments are similarly specific to O'Hara's perspective: "I have in my hands only 35¢, it's so meaningless to eat!" and "If I seem to you / to have lavender lips under the leaves of the world, / I must tighten my belt." These judgments are not made from a morally or ideologically superior or external viewpoint but are colored by the speaker's position in this functioning economy; for example, he might feel eating was more meaningful if he had more than "35¢." If he seems marginal to the excesses he observes – indeed, if he seems to be on the outside ("lavender lips" under dead "leaves" could signify various types of exclusion) – he must "tighten" his belt and try to fit his given part in this text. "If I seem to you" – an apostrophe that directly implicates the reader – suggests that any reading of who is inside and who is outside is a question of perspective, a matter of where we find ourselves in this cultural text that is prewritten and prefigures us. And O'Hara's apostrophe, objectifying the lyric poet as a "marker" of subjectivity in a composition not entirely of his composing, puts the poem's observations in perspective and leaves the reader to decide whether to regard it as a serious critique of capitalism and commercialism or to buy into the ideology that would assure us "there is nothing *behind* these surfaces" (Perloff 1990: 176). "Here I am," O'Hara seems to say; "read me according to your lights." Unfortunately, his aversion to "important utterances" and his insistence that meanings and values are historically and personally specific have tended to encourage critical readings that trivialize and depoliticize his work.

Just as O'Hara's details work to historicize his judgments, his allusions serve not to universalize his experience but to alert us to his historical difference. First, although the alienated urban artist is a recognizable figure, O'Hara renders his alienation less a metaphysical problem than an economic issue – a matter less of "meaning" than of "35¢." Second, the title invokes the idea of a cosmic harmony, but the collusion of forces here – certainly global, if not in fact cosmic – is more "the music of the fears" (1971: 442), as the apocalyptic touch of "stars" and "war" hints. Finally, the Romantic figure of the poet, "nerves humming," recalls Shelley:

> Man is an instrument over which a series of external and internal impressions are driven, like the alternations of an ever-changing wind over an Aeolian lyre, which move it by their motion to ever-changing melody. But there is a principle within the human being, . . . which acts otherwise than in the lyre, and produces not melody, alone, but harmony, by an internal adjustment of the sounds or motions thus excited to the impressions which excite them. (1967: 1072)

For O'Hara, however, the "ever-changing wind" carries "impressions" that are not natural but culturally mediated, and his harmonizing does not articulate nature's babble but exposes the more (or less) than natural forces at work in articulating his composition and his self.

The relation between humans and nature has changed, O'Hara argues: "Modern life has expanded our conception of nature . . . for nature has not stood still since Shelley's day. In past times there was nature and there was human nature; because of the ferocity of modern life, man and nature have become one" (1975b: 42). Thus, while "adherence to nature, indifference to conventions" (43) are his values, his nature is thoroughly acculturated. Although "Music" is a recognizable seasonal poem, then, O'Hara's "fall" is inextricable from the cultural complex – commercialism, capitalism, impending Christmas, the Bomb – that packages it:

> But no more fountains and no more rain,
> and the stores stay open terribly late.

Likewise, the lines "It's like a locomotive on the march, the season / of distress and clarity" inflect seasonal and psychological changes with technological and military overtones and preclude their harmonizing. Shelley's "Ode to the West Wind" offers a relevant contrast to O'Hara's poem. His apostrophe "Clasp me in your handkerchief like a tear, trumpet / of early afternoon!" (occasioned by another Christmas decoration?) echoes Shelley's "Oh, lift me as a wave, a leaf, a cloud!" and "Make me thy lyre" (1960: 579). Like Shelley, O'Hara links the season's decline and the poet's dejection, but "nature" cannot speak or prophesy through him. "Be through my lips to unawakened earth // The trumpet of a prophecy," Shelley's poet implores the wind. O'Hara does not entertain this dream of a mutual regeneration: "If I seem to you / to have lavender lips under the leaves of the world, / I must tighten my belt." The progress of the poem and the poet's psychic adventure is not regulated by underlying natural cycles of return; the analogy no longer convinces.

Other poems allude to an organicist poetic but only to mark O'Hara's distance from it. "Adieu to Norman, Bon Jour to Joan and Jean-Paul" (1971: 328), for example, is recognizably a "depression before spring" poem, but it resists aligning human and natural processes and demystifies the "renewal" spring supposedly offers: "we are all happy and young and toothless / it is the same as old age." To buy into the myth of spring and all is to sink into senility. In this fix, "the only thing to do is simply continue." And O'Hara proceeds to give reassuring examples of continuing. The persuasive goal of this relentlessly paratactic and repetitious list ("continue" appears fourteen times in twenty-one lines) becomes clear in the concluding lines, whose syntactic continuity with the preceding passage fails to paper over their logical discontinuity:

> and surely we shall not continue to be unhappy
> we shall be happy
> but we shall continue to be ourselves everything continues to be
>   possible
> René Char, Pierre Reverdy, Samuel Beckett it is possible isn't it
> I love Reverdy for saying yes, though I don't believe it

The link between human and natural life cycles is only a trope and, therefore, a matter of persuasion and belief. In this poem, linear urban time and cyclical natural time are so out of synch – the ice that melts in the spring melts in the Ricard – and the rhythms of one's life and contacts have so little to do with natural rhythms, that any connection between the two is fanciful at best, as the patronizing last line hints. To jump from the paratactic syntax of human experience to expectations of real change violates the logic of its grammar. The paradigmatic rhetoric no longer suffices, and even Reverdy cannot make O'Hara believe in a *reverdie*.

II

In the modernists' recuperation of Romantic organicism, the continuity of natural processes, including cycles of return, at once validates past literature and authorizes its renewal, as in Pound's imperative to "Day by day make it new" (1981: 265). Modernist technical interruption and fragmentation cut through layers of historical and cultural contingencies to reveal abiding natural truths. O'Hara's technical discontinuities, however, do not appeal to the law and order of an underlying, universal natural process. Rather, his formal experiments only synchronize with a particular cultural moment and register a "consciousness of emergency and crisis experienced as personal event, the artist assuming responsibility for being, however accidentally, alive here and now" (1975a: 67).

O'Hara composes his poems on urban time, and his forms bear the signs of urban emergencies. To judge the poems as potentially "endless secretions" (Vendler 1990: 235) misses the mark, but not because the poems have formal orders. The necessities O'Hara operates under may not be formal prescriptions, but they are necessities nonetheless – external constraints that define what "freedoms" there are. His idea of "lunch poems" registers the effect of economic pressure on aesthetic production. The fiction of such poems is that the time limits of the lunch "hour" dictate their shape and length. Indeed, O'Hara always has a strong sense of closure, but the constraints shaping his composition are neither formal conventions dictating, for example, that four-teen lines make a sonnet, nor the internal necessities of "organic form," nor the psychological handicap of a "limited attention span" (Vendler 1990: 235). The necessities bearing on his forms are socioeconomic: his position in the economic system sets the limits of his freedom, process, and spontaneity, for poets, too, have to make a living. I "buy a strap for my wristwatch and go / back to work" (1971: 336) and "A glass of papaya juice / and back to work" (258) are strong enough closures. O'Hara's urban, institutional time has little relation to natural rhythms, whether seasonal, diurnal, or psychological; indeed, the un-natural units of clock time determine his accelerated compositional and psychological process.

In "A Step Away from Them" (1971: 257), for example, the time of the workplace frames something of a meditation on death, the limits of a lifetime. In the opening lines, the poet's lunch hour coincides with the laborers' and aligns O'Hara, who works for an elitist cultural insti-tution, with construction workers; the larger economy is democratic and prescribes the free time for both. Unlike Olson, say, O'Hara does not have to sweat through historical research to establish his bond with the working man. Yet while he is subject to the same laws of worktime as the laborers, O'Hara also knows that he is distanced from them as their literary and aestheticizing observer. His "free-verse" line breaks – so stylized as to signal their conventional status – in fact objectify, frag-ment, aestheticize, and eroticize the workers ("glistening torsos"), consciously marking both his different position in the economic "text" and his complicity with the power structure.[5] He can only "guess" that helmets "protect" construction workers from "falling / bricks"; else-where, helmets admittedly have aesthetic and camp appeal for him (335). The poet can take in the urban scene seemingly indiscriminately, without needing obvious formal orders, because, in Pound's words, "it coheres all right" (1981: 797) – but in a sense Pound could not have foreseen. It all "coheres" because an economic infrastructure positions each of the "details" on a larger canvas. The stylized "languorously ag-itating" black man–"blonde chorus girl" tableau (an "entertaining" conjunction), the "masculine" working classes, the "warm" Puerto Ricans, and the museum worker on his lunch break musing on the connections between "JULIET'S CORNER" and "Giulietta Masina" all compose one picture; they all "click" to the same clock and lock into place in the same economy: "Everything / suddenly honks: it is 12:40 of / a Thursday." The absence of symbolic or thematic connections among the details points up not the freedom of O'Hara's discourse but its prescription. He does not need to impose symbolic or formal orders to "articulate" his details into a whole, because they are already ordered, already articulated, with clockwork precision in a larger economic, social, and political order. An anagogic coherence articulates seemingly random details in a whole. Although O'Hara's is a profane version of Pound's "coherence" and Whitman's "form, union, plan" (1965: 88), it equally surpasses understanding.

In the end, nostalgia for a different role for art – what the Armory Show may have represented, the destruction of the very institution of art – is allowed to die. "They'll soon tear down" the building, the same or different "construction" workers; plus, the Armory Show wasn't "there" anyway. "Armory" lends an ironic touch here, like the literal application of the militaristic metaphor of the avant-garde in "Memorial Day." And O'Hara relinquishes this last illusion about the past as he heads "back to work" in an institution of art, whose very name is an oxymoron that says it all: "The Museum of Modern Art." In this poem as well, then, we see the poet in step with a system that calibrates his distance – his "step away" – from laborers and dead artists alike, and not only by virtue of his still being alive, either. For the historical configuration of the "details" has changed: the avant-garde, far from being oppositional, is safely institutionalized. And on a personal scale, O'Hara makes the same move, as the poem concludes: "My heart is in my / pocket, it is Poems by Pierre Reverdy." The paperback book and "pocket," the space of ownership, safely place his poetic "escape" back in the larger economy.

"Ode to Michael Goldberg ('s Birth and Other Births)" addresses the current state of "newness":

> . . . somewhere everything's dispersed
> at five o'clock
>   for Martinis a group of professional freshnesses meet

and the air's like a shrub – Rose o' Sharon? the others,

                                                     it's not

a flickering light for us, but the glare of the dark

                                   too much endlessness

stored up, and in store:

                     "the exquisite prayer

                     to be new each day

                     brings to the artist

                     only a certain kneeness"

                        (1971: 297)

"Kneeness"? A parody of Poundian "newness"? A meaningless phrase to deflate the "importantness" of all the pompous "-ness" words throughout the poem? A sign of the subjugation of the artist, brought to his knees in spiritual abjection or physical incapacitation – earlier we read about a movie hero whose legs are "cut off by a steam engine" (291) – before a greater, darker power? In a word, "newness" is an outdated creed, both because "freshness" has been so professionalized and because the poet lacks faith in the future, even in the diminished "little light" (1981: 795) of Pound's last cantos; "too much endless-ness / stored up, and in store" are certainly ominous lines. The past's faith in newness and the future no longer holds, because the future itself is packaged, and there is nowhere to get to. The oppositional efficacy of novelty is not an issue; novelty *has* a value, but it comes from partaking of the culture's economy of excess production and consumption. And if poetry is to be new and not boring, it has to guard against, as O'Hara nicely puts it, "nostalgia for the avant-garde" (Perloff 1990: 174).

For example, "The Day Lady Died" (1971: 325) replays certain modernist conventions but shows how they play differently in the current cultural economy. Although the array of names of writers, brands, and foreign phrases gives the poem a Poundian texture, O'Hara's poet comes across as a literal consumer in the Empire City's global marketplace – of "what the poets / in Ghana are doing these days," of Verlaine (chosen from among "Hesiod, trans. Richmond Lattimore," "*Le Balcon,*" and "*Les Nègres,*" a range of choices so dif-

ferent as to induce indifference), of Strega, Gauloises, Picayunes, and
the NEW YORK POST. The poet participates in this economy, for he,
too, has a product to sell – an aesthetic product (a fairly traditional
elegy, it turns out in the last stanza) endorsed by a "celebrity," Billie
Holiday. If O'Hara claims a special dispensation here – for the "uses"
of memory and art, say – he knows it is purchased in the currency of
his empire's economy. By contrast, when Pound denounces "Tò Κα-
λόν / Decreed in the market place" (1990: 187), he appears oblivious
to the fact that his own rhetorical strategy of quoting Pindar in Greek
script, for example, exactly parallels the marketing strategy of the cosmetic firm's giving its beauty creme a Greek name, for allusions to
classical beauty and classical poetry alike serve to sell modern or novel
products.

Since O'Hara emphasizes his complicity with the consumer economy in the first four stanzas, we could argue that he consciously exploits Billie Holiday to elevate his poem – both to aesthetic heights
and to political significance by dovetailing issues of sexuality and race.
Ross points to O'Hara's reliance in the last stanza on the stereotypi-
cal image of "the white intellectual worshipping a black jazz perform-
er"; as "a fond reader of O'Hara," he wants to find some irony or
parody in this scenario (1990: 386). I don't detect such a note; but as
another "fond reader of O'Hara," I want to believe that O'Hara's
consciousness of his cultural complicity absolves him of this form of
romanticized racism. Throughout the poem he portrays himself as a
discriminating consumer of tokens of cultural outsiders – whether
blacks ("poets in Ghana," Les Nègres), homosexuals (Verlaine, Genet), political radicals (Brendan Behan), or criminals (Genet, Verlaine)
– and the "stereotype" of the last stanza (another outsider, black
and an addict) is only another cultural "icon" O'Hara consumes. In
fact, he presents himself as a stereotype – a sophisticated, cosmopoli-
tan member of the "art scene," wined and dined by "people" on
Long Island.

"Rhapsody" (1971: 325–26) offers a complex vision of the position
and function of a poet in late-capitalist society. The different senses of
the title all apply to this improvisational composition that makes for a
chapter in the tale of the tribe and, in a way, celebrates it:

515 Madison Avenue
door to heaven? portal
stopped realities and eternal licentiousness
or at least the jungle of impossible eagerness
your marble is bronze and your lianas elevator cables
swinging from the myth of ascending
I would join
or declining the challenge of racial attractions
they zing on (into the lynch, dear friends)
while everywhere love is breathing draftily
like a doorway linking 53rd with 54th
the east-bound with the west-bound traffic by 8,000,000s
o midtown tunnels and the tunnels, too, of Holland

The opening passage presents a dense network: Madison Avenue, the hub of this economy and "portal" to its version of heaven, is sustained by the "myth of ascending," and the undergirding "realities" stop here – the "tunnels," the "jungle," violence, racism, and the repression of "love." And where does the poet, the chronicler of late-capitalist America, figure in this configuration? In a letter cited in *The Collected Poems,* Bill Berkson informs us that the "door façade is very beautiful" (543); O'Hara acknowledges its aesthetic value at the same time that he exposes the price of admission it exacts. The poet's ambivalent position becomes clearer as the poem progresses:

where is the summit where all aims are clear
the pin-point light upon a fear of lust
as agony's needlework grows up around the unicorn
and fences him for milk- and yogurt-work

The tapestry he stitches together weaves a constantly changing pattern of relations between exploiters and the exploited. All summits, clarities, and heights are achieved at the cost of repression. The entire civilization, represented by "Madison Avenue," erects itself by repression – by harnessing "the unicorn," the traditional figure of imagination and eros, to the work ethic. But the artistic "summit" of clarity and "light" – in the last stanza O'Hara allows how he has "always wanted to be near it" – also arises from a "fear of lust" or the repression of the instinctual life. "The pin-point light," "agony's needlework," the Empire State Building's "towering needle," and the higher vantage point of "we holy ones" are all heights reached at the same cost of exclusion, whether economic, political, sexual, racial, or aesthetic.

Poetic creation partakes of the whole economy of empire building, and the poet cannot be holier than what is around him. O'Hara folds himself into the "text" he observes and records, for he is a willing victim of civilization and its discontents: "while I cough lightly in the smog of desire / and my eyes water achingly imitating the true blue." His anecdote of the cab driver, for example, clearly reveals where O'Hara's loyalties lie:

> I am getting into a cab at 9th Street and 1st Avenue
> and the Negro driver tells me about a $120 apartment
> "where you can't walk across the floor after 10 at night
> not even to pee, cause it keeps them awake downstairs"
> no, I don't like that "well, I didn't take it"
> perfect in the hot humid morning on my way to work
> a little supper-club conversation for the mill of the gods

The black cabbie literally provides O'Hara with raw material for his poem; the episode is grist for his "mill." While the poet may live on the other side of the tracks from Madison Avenue, then, he is really not that far from it. Thus this passage loses much of its critical impact, because it depends on the same economy of exploiting certain classes and races as the system it would critique. This is "what you learn in the early morning passing Madison Avenue / where you've never spent any time and stores eat up light": O'Hara belongs to the class of workers who ride uptown in cabs driven by "Negro" drivers, whose very physiological needs – "to pee," for example – are in danger of being curtailed. Riding in the cab and listening to that story, he is himself one of the "gods," and not just as a "poet." He partakes of the empire's power, ironic though he may be about his position, since from a slightly different perspective he is an outsider, too.

Thus it is not enough to "smile," as in "Some inspiration! Some subject matter for the poet-who-would-be-god"; O'Hara has to "send" it all "out of" himself in a Whitmanic counteraggression (Whitman 1965: 54):

> it isn't enough to smile when you run the gauntlet
> you've got to spit like Niagara Falls on everybody

This violence of inclusion and what it does to the poet become the subject of "Spleen" (1971: 187): "I know so much / about things, I accept / so much, it's like / vomiting." As he insists throughout his work, poetry is "filthy"; there is no escaping this fact, and all superior vantage points above the cultural complex "historically / belong" to it:

> is Tibet historically a part of China? as I historically
> belong to the enormous bliss of American death.

Without a position outside the social text, the only social force the poet can command must come from within it; in effect, then, "Rhapsody" "celebrates" the "enormous bliss of American death" – the violent but creative displacement of instinctive and spiritual energy, the "rancid nourishment of this mountainous island." As Auden writes, "no one exists alone," but O'Hara, "composed" of "Eros and of dust" and belonging to the general "stupor," has little faith in "points of light" – "ironic" or not (Auden 1979: 88–89).

If O'Hara resists nostalgia for purity, he does not relinquish critical responsibility. In "Rhapsody," his literary memory – of Whitman and Hart Crane in particular – offers a perspective from which the difference of the present may be perceived. O'Hara's stressing such horizontal transportation links as passageways, tunnels, and surface roads revises the past's faith in spiritual transports rising above the traffic. Yet invoking the past brings into focus both O'Hara's complicity and his critique. For example, Crane's willing the Brooklyn Bridge of "shorter hours, quicker lunches, behaviorism, and toothpicks" (1966: 232) into an ascending transport to God is so anachronistic, so implicated in the "myth of ascending," and so deeply in collusion with Madison Avenue and its conversion of "quantity" (of material excess) into "quality" (of spiritual value) as to prompt O'Hara's parodic apostrophe concluding the first stanza: "o midtown tunnels and the tunnels, too, of Holland."

Similarly, O'Hara recalls Whitman in "a sight of Manahatta in the towering needle / multi-faceted insight of the fly in the stringless labyrinth." The "sight" of "Manahatta" in the Empire State Building – the "multi-faceted insight of the fly in the stringless labyrinth" – marks O'Hara's perspective: such an "insight" is not achieved at "the summit" of clarity, "the pin-point light," but within the labyrinth. And the labyrinth is larger than New York, the state, or the empire; it is global ("Canada plans a higher place than the Empire State Building"). O'Hara's multifaceted vision offers insight into his motives and place within this machinery, this functioning whole, so that he can be a rhapsode of his culture, to which he historically belongs.

And the proper procedure for a poem that stitches together a labyrinthine network of collusion is a paratactic series of discontinuous jumps without punctuation, subordination, "argument," or narrative. Such improvisational forms are immanent forms and signal less O'Hara's freedom from than his immersion in the cultural text. The violent textual juxtaposition of Madison Avenue and lynching replays the violent base of the cultural economy. What appears as a disorder bespeaks, to misappropriate Wallace Stevens, "a violent order." For all of the apparently haphazard and disjunctive movement of "Rhapsody," every detail falls into place as a piece of the puzzle to offer us a view of the "stringless labyrinth" that is, indeed, the height of artifice. O'Hara regards form as "proceeding" rather than "super-induced," but he is no "organicist," because the nature of "nature" has changed. The culture as a functioning political and economic system has colonized nature, harnessed the "unicorn" and trapped the "Minotaur." And it is this system – rather than natural process, which is in fact repressed and perverted – that guides poetic composition, which also proceeds by sublimation and substitution. Thus, while O'Hara works in experimental forms, he works against the organicism inscribed in them and registers his historical and ideological distance from modernist experimentalism and its late-modernist recuperation in oppositional stances resting on natural process and truth.

III

poetry's part of your self

like the passion of a nation
at war it moves quickly
provoked to defense or aggression
unreasoning power
an instinct for self-declaration
            (O'Hara 1971: 309–10)

O'Hara's compositional orders disrupt both traditional continuities and
modernist conventions and go to show that unconventional, open, or
experimental forms are as complicitous with dominant orders and cultural values as closed forms. For example, his poems freely string together seemingly random details, which are specific to a particular
social and historical moment and are in principle, or metaphysically,
interchangeable; they are not Pound's "Luminous Details" or Whitman's revelatory "types." O'Hara resists any ideology that would
"correct" or compensate for his practice and its necessary exclusions
on some metatextual ground. In the economy of any given poem,
however, the details are not interchangeable. Precisely because nothing
lies "behind" or "beyond" an O'Hara poem to authorize substitutions,
its particulars are unique. Ironically, then, any given poem becomes a
metaphysical structure in spite of itself, and eschewing symbolism or
the idealizing economy of any substitution does not absolve the poet
of the guilt of substitutive repression. Exclusion need not be motivated
by a specific ideology; it is systemic to writing a "poem," and a resolutely nonsymbolist poem is, in practice, as exclusionary as a symbolist
poem. For O'Hara, not just traditional formal or thematic coherence
but "the mere existence of emphasis" lends "An atmosphere of supreme lucidity, / humanism" (254). And since his "indiscriminate"
and "fleeting" eyes (197) make distinctions all the time, his promised
"death of literature as we know it" is "not more outside literature than
Bear Mountain is outside New York State" (499). But what distinguishes his disruptive compositions is that they expose the violence
that goes into their articulation.

O'Hara's particular lucidity keeps in view the idealizing operations of all representation and refuses to mystify techniques. His processual forms, for example, are no help in resisting the formal memorializing and freezing of process – whether historical, psychological, natural, or physiological. "Where will you find me, projective verse, since I will be gone?" (1971: 351), O'Hara asks, challenging any such confusion between poetic language and form – always a set of conventions, whether before or after the fact of their use – and process. All art formalizes and memorializes; no intimacy or immediacy is possible in language. And all "styles" are equally artificial, as he suggests in "Essay on Style." Whether aiming to purify language of all those logical-grammatical attachments – and, by implication, the larger familial-social demands for relation and reference – or "treating / the typewriter as an intimate organ" (394), writing always comes up against the irreducible mediation of representation. By contrast, Pound's notion that iambics "deform thought" (1981: 687) assumes a "form" prior to and independent of its representations; O'Hara's experiments do not uphold such a hierarchy.

Moreover, while O'Hara affirms the values of change and process, they are not all that positive. The imperative to change is less an essential or a historical value than a defensive response to a state of emergency; indeed, it signifies less a freedom than a necessity, following a strict logic: "A hit? *ergo* swim" (1971: 254). Anything that stops or freezes is dead – not only metaphorically speaking but, just possibly, literally. To resist a reified identity is necessary for survival – as a gay man, for example. But being a quick-change artist exacts a cost, as "In Memory of My Feelings" and other poems ("Poem Read at Joan Mitchell's," "To Hell With It," "Meditations in an Emergency") tell us. To borrow Plath's words, "there is a charge, a very large charge" (1981: 246), for O'Hara's performance; or, to quote O'Hara, "you are amusing / as a game is amusing when someone is forced to lose as in a game I must" (1971: 351). "One of these days there'll be nothing left with which to venture forth" (197), O'Hara seems to threaten, but ends up capitulating yet again: "I'll be back, I'll re-emerge" (198).

Processual verse in the Pound–Olson tradition puts the poet in control of the textual process: "if you . . . set up as a poet, USE USE USE the process at all points," Olson writes (1966: 17), and for him the question is how process must be used, how objects "are to be used" (20), and what "the use of a man" (25) is. And the one who "sets up" as a poet does the using, which, again, aligns such experimentalism with technological values. Thus "getting rid of the lyrical interference of the individual as ego, of the 'subject' and his soul" (24), will not get rid of "humanism"; indeed, Olson's "objectism" only reaffirms and facilitates the deeper collusion of technology and humanism, without "interference" from such archaic notions as the "subject" and his "soul." O'Hara, by contrast, shows himself to be more used and abused by, than using, the "process." Without a metaphysics to back up process, O'Hara has nothing to go on but his "nerve" – "the lyrical interference of the individual." And such "interference" has a vital moral and political function. To ignore O'Hara's moral and political charge would be to romanticize him as a natural or free spirit, which would be as much of a distortion of his work as seeing him as a symbolist or technician.

O'Hara insists on casting textual and rhetorical operations in terms that are moral and political rather than aesthetic or technical. "In Memory of My Feelings" (1971: 252–57), for example, shows rhetorical operations to be necessarily violent and repressive. "The dead hunting / and the alive, ahunted" applies to more than the relationship between the living speaker and his familial, literary, and autobiographical "predecessors" ("My 10   my 19, / my 9,   and the several years"); the process of hunting and being hunted describes his compositional method itself. The "several likenesses" of his transparent self are presumably designed to protect it from the fixity of a singular identity: "My quietness has a number of naked selves, / so many pistols I have borrowed to protect myselves / from creatures who . . . have murder in their heart." But these naked, figural selves, armed with their nakedness as if with pistols, are themselves murderous, as the violent sequences of "sordid identifications" throughout the poem amply show. Any figuration of subjectivity – however fluid – is a subjection or subjugation of "myselves" to a larger text:

> . . . the scrutiny of all things is syllogistic,
> the startled eyes of the dikdik, the bush full of white flags
> fleeing a hunter,
>   which is our democracy
>   but the prey
> is always fragile and like something, as a seashell can be
> a great Courbet, if it wishes. To bend the ear of the outer world

In the poetic metamorphoses of this passage, the violence of the hunter and the hunted – of human against nature – is transformed into a military violence via the "white flags" and then sublimated, first under "our democracy" and further in artistic representation – of nature in painting and painting under one signature, "Courbet," a realist who painted from "nature" such subjects as hunts and deer, complete with "white flags." The deer hunter, "our democracy," and the artist all follow the logic of figuration, which is a will to power over "nature" and has a persuasive motive – "to bend the ear of the outer world."

Figuration subjugates a "thing" or "fact" to a text and a textual function so as to enable a particular use of the "fact"; in O'Hara's words, "the prey / is always fragile and like something." Because representational government operates with a necessarily repressive figurative substitution, "our democracy" is rhetorical at base. Its idealizing or typifying substitutions subjugate individual identity to a general identity, which defines subjects as types and places "things" in categories. Political, social, and military violence and repression all enable their "literal" procedures through such rhetorical persuasion and entitlement, for poetic or metaphoric substitution is the basis of their authority and, therefore, of their power. All figuration is also persuasion, and poetic language is a language of power over what it so articulates. The "prey" is not itself until it is "like" something – that is, until it is inscribed in a given economy as "prey" and plays its scripted part. All substitutive economies boil down to raw power – as of the hunter over the dikdik – once their rhetoric is acknowledged.

Similarly, the hunted selves have no core identity prior to their various figurations, which identify them as "likenesses" so that they can be recognized as figures in larger natural, political, and aesthetic "texts." When we return to the poem's opening lines after this passage, we see that the fragility and fluidity of the naked self are "naturally" expressed in a series of similes. The naked self is never itself; its figuration – its subjugation in likenesses – *is* its nakedness, which renders it vulnerable to "creatures" who "have murder in their heart." Since poetic figuration always has an agenda and operates within a larger text, such nakedness is not innocent; it is not "sincerity" but, in fact, the opposite – a lie. Like the "frankly" O'Hara is so fond of, it is only a rhetoric of sincerity, as in the figuration of a proper name ("Frank") as a generic marker of a proper name. "Honesty," however, is something else; it acknowledges this necessarily powerful insincerity and rhetoric.

In this poem, the snake is an unstable figure. It marks at once the live, "writhing" body – "my body, the naked host to my many selves," "the scene of my selves, the occasion of these ruses" – and the principle of formal and rhetorical conversion that precludes things' being themselves except in figures. The rhetorical conversion of specific into general experience, facts into figures, "feelings" into art, "against my will / against my love," necessarily loses "what is always and everywhere / present, the scene of my selves, the occasion of these ruses, / which I myself and singly must now kill / and save the serpent in their midst." The writing self must figure itself as multiple and keep generating "likenesses" by "killing" whatever threatens to "freeze," including "these ruses," and saving the "serpent," the erotic body and the principle of constant figuration, the fluidity of somatic and linguistic process – precisely what all figuration represses. Thus, ironically, the serpent he must save – "the ardent lover of history," "tongue out" – is also the most traditional Western figure of all that it signifies here: it is the figure of rhetoric as persuasive, manipulative, and repressive, as opposed to "truth" – where things are and are themselves. In a word, what must be saved is the opposite of "Frank."

Since poetic and political truths alike are rhetorical, the poet has a certain kinship with the "Dear father of our country, so alive / you must have lied incessantly to be / immediate" (1971: 234). As a poet, "Frank" must affirm "it is more important to affirm the least sincere" (197); that way, he can achieve the "clarity," the negative capability, of "a void / behind my eyes" (277). To yearn for sincerity and natural truths is only to enlist in someone else's lie. For example, he writes in "Meditations in an Emergency," "I have never clogged myself with the praises of pastoral life, nor with nostalgia for an innocent past of perverted acts in pastures" (197). Since the same poem also registers the need to "discourage" "inexorably approaching" "heterosexuality," it is the pastoral location that makes for the "perversion" (as in yearning for the natural). Here pastoral values, with their appeal to natural truth and "natural" norms, reinforce the marginalization of homosexuals and poets; a pastoral convalescence or "emergence" is very much the prescription of the dominant power system, as James Merrill also acknowledges. "To affirm the least sincere," then, goes to show that what we have is not nature but culture, not truth but rhetoric, and O'Hara's spontaneity, which requires constant lying, is not closer to nature, truer to the fluidity of experience, or more sincere.

O'Hara has no illusion that opposing dominant discursive conventions grants him "freedom" or absolution from complicity. Since all individuation is guilty of subjectification, different figurations of the self (whether as singular, consistent, and coherent or as fragmented, multiple, and various) simply have different persuasive goals. It is not that one is the conventional, humanist self – and therefore in collusion with the dominant ideology – and the other is free. The "free" figuration is equally bound to the cultural text. Throughout "In Memory," which affirms "Grace / to be born and live as variously as possible" (1971: 256), war imagery predominates, with a number of specific references to O'Hara's experience in the Pacific. His war memoir, which begins with the loss of a sense of a coherent self, provides a historical gloss for the more "sordid identifications" of the Whitmanic self in this poem:

> What there was to say and what there was in me to say or to express just any way to get it said; what anyone and everyone had done to make them marked and separate from the rest; for they had stripped and raped us all and given us cards so we could practice our new trades newly forced in a legal way now that we were broken in and we all looked the same so nobody could

tell anybody else from anybody else; everyone without an eye,
the mouth a line, and a stupid soul to stare on every face I'm
dead I'm dead; nothing to do but say this isn't really me because
the real me slipped away just before you got here; shit I'm no
dope I knew this was going to happen and I slipped away before
you got here I slipped away the real me. (1977: 112)

Thus it makes sense that O'Hara's series of selves, ranging geograph-
ically from Africa to China, historically from Hittites to Indians, and
psychologically from women to children (1971: 254–56), add up to
an imperial self, consuming all and being consumed by all. If he is
"used up" by "all this," he also uses it up – "the prey / is always fragile
and like something." At once hunter and hunted, he preys and is
preyed upon; such is the economy of his rhetoric. "There is nothing
metaphysical" about the critique of the humanist self in this poem, for
it partakes of the same economy and "colonizes" peoples outside the
Western humanist tradition – Hittites, Arabs, American Indians – to
serve as its "vehicle" for "saying" how it has been raped and dispersed
itself.

In a number of passages, O'Hara makes explicit the violence of his
"sordid" – with its roots in black, dirty, squalid, base, mercenary,
avaricious – identifications. The race scene in the first section, with its
hints of sexual humiliation, self-consciously replays Whitman. To say,
"I am the man, I suffer'd, I was there" (Whitman 1965: 66), does not
merely subjugate one's experience to others', painful as that democratization is; it also subjugates and colonizes others' experiences to
one's "omnivorous" self. There is no giving without taking, for "the
prey / is always fragile and like something." Since synechdoche works
two ways to say, "I am him *and* he is me," it preys on the self and the
other alike; it resists victimization and repeats it. Whitman's identification with the "hounded slave," for example, protests the hounding
yet repeats it by subjecting the slave to his rhetoric, as the designated
analog of his subject:

I am the hounded slave, I wince at the bite of the dogs,
Hell and despair are upon me, crack and again crack the
    marksmen,

I clutch the rails of the fence, my gore dribs, thinn'd with the
    ooze of my skin,
I fall on the weeds and stones,
The riders spur their unwilling horses, haul close,
Taunt my dizzy ears and beat me violently over the head with
    whip-stocks. (66–67)

Tonally and imagistically, O'Hara's lines echo Whitman's:

A gun is "fired."
                              One of me rushes
to window #13 and one of me raises his whip and one of me
flutters up from the center of the track amidst the pink
    flamingoes,
and underneath their hooves as they round the last turn my lips
are scarred and brown, brushed by tails, masked in dirt's lust,
definition, open mouths gasping for the cries of the bettors for
    the lungs
of earth.

By substituting a horse race for the race "race," O'Hara makes
explicit the victimization, the "sordid" basis, of Whitman's identifications. In other words, any Whitmanic identification or "sympathy"
with the oppressed is also a form of exploitation. For "sympathy" rests
on the trope of synechdoche, which is no more innocent than any
other figuration. This passage can be read almost as a parody of Whitman's rhetoric, except O'Hara's investment in it makes "parody" inappropriate. The poem both critiques and places itself within this
American tradition of figuring the self as possibility, fluidity, and process. If one purchases one's "grace" or freedom from being fixed at the
expense of others' fixed experiences, one is playing a power role, duplicating the "sordid" appropriations of more central powers, for there
is no freedom without enslavement. When Whitman in effect says he
is free because he can play the hunted slave, he overlooks the asym-
metry: the hunted slave cannot be him. Psychological, political, rhetorical freedoms are not absolute but functions of one's given position
in the social text. And to speak poetically, in figures, is to hold a

position with the power to objectify and colonize. In O'Hara's "identifications," democratic "equality" comes down to a network of rhetorical identifications deployed for practical exploitation by whoever
is in a position of power over the figurative economy in a given instance.

In other poems, where O'Hara figures the psyche as racially oppressed peoples – "I consider myself to be black" (1971: 468); "I am
really an Indian at heart" (296) – he at once judges his repressive
culture (as a homosexual in the fifties) and partakes (as a poet) of its
dominating appropriative strategies. Figuring the repressed erotic life
in racial and class vehicles, the poet "belongs" where he is and can
even find amusement there:

> you know how wonderful the 20th Century
> can be
> and the gaited Iroquois on the girders
> fierce and unflinching-footed
> nude as they should be
> slightly empty
> like a Sonia Delaunay
> .   .   .   .
> we owe a debt to the Iroquois
> and to Duke Ellington
> for playing in the buildings when they are built
> .   .   .   .
> apart from love (don't say it)
> I am ashamed of my century
> for being so entertaining
> but I have to smile (337–38)

Elsewhere, we read: "a coal miner has kind of a sexy occupation /
though I'm sure it's painful down there / but so is lust" (335). Poetic
figuration – here a "Poem" contemplating D. H. Lawrence on the
matter of lust – is not innocent and, in fact, invests in the classist and
racist associations that inform a wide range of cultural figurations and
stereotypes.

O'Hara's textual discontinuities do not aim for greater naturalism, or even a more adequate representation of cultural violence. But they do tell us something about how both literary texts and the cultural text are woven and interwoven. Thus O'Hara can be a "legend" in his own time – a cultural "hero," the type of an "individual," who is also a "text" written by and into his culture. His very self is a cultural and political subject, just as his individuals – with proper names – play the generic part of "individuals" to compose a text where "individuals are important": "See how free we are! as a nation of persons" (1971: 234). Proper names are the proper figures of this "nation of persons," for they signify persons who lose all that is personal in this metonymic reduction, the way "persons" are used up in the political economy of "our democracy."

Grammar is as politically implicated as figuration, for it, too, violently subordinates parts to wholes. O'Hara aligns grammar with religious authority ("Personism"), social authority ("Essay on Style"), logic ("Biotherm"), and poetic structure. It signifies the repressiveness of all structure, for the "mere existence of emphasis," which shapes sentences and poems alike, leads back to "humanism" once again. And "beneath" the violent orders of grammar and representation "hides," as "Biotherm" reveals, the somatic violence of a bodily produced language. For even at the most basic level of articulation of grammar and denotation – of meaningful phrases, words, and phonemes out of physiological sounds – meaning emerges by a violent repression.

"Biotherm" (1971: 436–48) shows how the physiology of speech, the somatic level, is repressed to produce articulate sounds, just as erotic and psychic energies are repressed to socialize discourse. The temporal violence of bodily language is violently repressed in the interests of larger historical orders, whether aesthetic, social, or political. O'Hara clues his reader into this process early on:

you meet the Ambassador   "a year and a half of trying to
        make him"
    he is dressed in red, he has a red ribbon down his chest he
        has   7   gold decorations pinned to his gash

A slip of the tongue exposes a "gash" under the "sash" – a ribbon with medals. In such slippage, a violent somatic base – a tongue that can slip – appears underneath linguistic decorum at the level not of figuration or syntax but of denotation or right naming. And this linguistic decorum aligns with political, diplomatic, and symbolic decorous cover-ups of the physical violence of war and with the social cover-up of the sexual body.

Unlike Pound, who proposes right naming as the cure for repressive perversions of natural force, O'Hara proposes that right naming is complicitous with larger sociopolitical repressions of the body. On the one hand, he wants to save an intimate bodily language from the external violence of politicization – of being reduced to representing a group. "Trying to live in the terrible western world // here where to love at all's to be a politician," where "one specific love's traduced / / by shame for what you love more generally" ("Ode: Salute to the French Negro Poets" [1971: 305]) – where, in other words, everything is already political – "the poem whose words become your mouth" becomes one way of holding off the "jackals" pillaging "our desires and allegiances." On the other hand, his very symbolic medium itself violently represses the internal violence of somatic-sexual language.

Yet to regress to presymbolic or "semiotic" language will not do, because the symbolic order would have to be reinstituted for such language to signify as "semiotic." Thus O'Hara at once reduces language to the tongue, underlines its irreducible literary nature, and points up its collusion with other power structures. For example, in this passage from "Biotherm," he anatomizes the deep articulation of a somatic language, literary language (with its conventions of rhyme, repetition, and allusion), and the "military–industrial complex":

> out into the desert, where
> no flash tested, no flashed!
> oops! and no nail polish yak
>
> > yak, yak, Lieut.
> no flesh to taste no flash to tusk
> no flood to flee no fleed to dlown flom the iceth loot
> "par exemple!"

This is not semiotic language but a "poetic" language positioned as "bodily" within the symbolic order, where linguistic and military operations rhyme: the flash of the tests in the desert and the taste of flesh alliterate, and the rhythmic base for this harmony is Coleridge's, whose "Ancient Mariner" is here transvested as the "Old Mariner" in "high heels." There is no ground zero to poetic language. For what purports to be transgressive, semiotic language keeps regressing to the symbolic order; what would challenge the symbolic order – the total package of reasonable discourse, grammatical articulation, technological "progress," and the authority of tradition – keeps reinscribing it in constantly emerging accords.

For O'Hara, all orders – whether the production of phonemes, words, and poems or social, political, and economic systems – exact the same price. Free forms enjoy no special dispensation; beginning with a redefinition of nature as already cultural, O'Hara's "adherence to nature" does not grant him a morally superior perspective on culture. But his insistence on the bodily origins of language affirms a temporal and physical scale that interferes with the historical social text. At once a physiological signature and a trope, O'Hara's voice "establishes" his "own measure and breath," his "own gesture apart from the established order." His distaste for "fitting your ideas into an established order, syllabically and phonetically and so on" (1975b: 17), is impelled by a bourgeois concept of the individual artist with his "instinct for self-declaration," his war against all enemies – whether external or internal to linguistic operations. While his voice is impure, implicated or "folded" in its culture, it is still the voice of an individual in a specific time and place, flaunting "I am lyrical to a fault" (1971: 351). The "lyrical interference of the individual" that Olson would rule out voices O'Hara's "individual conscience" or "individual perception of life" (1975b: 100), which at once necessarily critiques "our democracy" and affirms his citizenship in the same "nation of persons."

Elizabeth Bishop
"Repeat, Repeat, Repeat; Revise, Revise, Revise"

Costume and custom are complex.
The headgear of the other sex
inspires us to experiment.

Bishop (1983: 200)

Elizabeth Bishop's refusal to be classified and anthologized as a woman poet is well known; less well known, perhaps, is her statement "I've always considered myself a strong feminist" (1981: 80). Taken together, these positions suggest that her being a "feminist" – whatever she may mean by it, she is not evading the political issue – does not entail her perceiving her work as a woman poet's, and she demands to be read from this double perspective.[1] For in order to read Bishop as a feminist, we need to place her all the more firmly within a patriarchal tradition so as to see how her revisions of it signify politically as well as poetically. Formally, her work is traditional: her lines are usually metrical, her stanzas often have intricate rhyme schemes, and her forms range from blank verse and sonnets to sestinas and villanelles. Her conventional stanzas and meters, together with her grammatical syntax, place her within the symbolic order, and while she challenges its assumptions and hierarchies, her dissensions – including "feminist" revisions – register within this framework. However, given her historical position after modernism, her conventional forms and language themselves serve a critical function: by aligning herself with a patriarchal tradition and observing conventional verse forms, she can critique a different – and, from her position, more dangerous because more naturalized – set of assumptions that underwrite the investment of authority in the person and experience of the poet, who is historically male.

Bishop's work, with its complex negotiation of formal and historical imperatives, forces us to question the idea of a separate women's poetic "language" or "tradition" – even a foreshortened version that would align her with Marianne Moore, her primary woman predecessor. Granted, her descriptive strategies owe something to Moore,[2] and both poets play with scale and point of view in order to preclude consistent, totalizing perspectives and to signal the constructedness of the world they describe. A poem like "The Steeple-Jack," for example, clearly shows what Moore may have taught Bishop. Similarly, both poets question the alignment of women with nature, a dominant metaphor written into the very language they use. "Turn to the letter M," Moore writes, "and you will find / that 'a wife is a coffin' " (1982: 67; her note credits Ezra Pound for this insight). The "letter M" links matter, mother, and mortality – a literal given exploited by others, including H.D. But the initial M also doubles as "Marianne's monogram" (Bishop 1984: 156) and suggests that a woman poet finds herself already written up in a cultural sourcebook or dictionary. The dualisms of letters, woman, nature, and death versus spirit, man, mind, and life are engendered and gendered by idealism, which Moore and Bishop equally resist. Being a "literalist of the imagination" (Moore 1982: 267), who skews discourse by "arguments" based on literal accidents, is one strategy of subverting the symbolic economy of idealism that Moore – among other poets, male and female alike – sometimes follows. Moore tends to rely on a special linguistic, formal, and moral dispensation to attack the assumptions that make for a center, author, or poem.

But this is not Bishop's stylistic strategy. She avoids Moore's formal and syntactic eccentricities and denies herself the privileged perspective of such marginality. Although Bishop admired Moore's "true originality," she also acknowledged "the sort of alienation it might involve" (1984: 140). She is careful to distinguish her work from Moore's idiosyncratic poetry: "She looked like no one else; she talked like no one else; her poems showed a mind not much like anyone else's; and her notions of meter and rhyme were unlike all the conventional notions – so why not believe that the old English meters that still seem natural to most of us (or *seemed* to, at any rate) were not natural to her at all?" (139–40). Bishop's backtracking to stress "seemed" is telling and suggests that she is perfectly aware of what is at stake in employing traditional forms.

From the beginning Bishop never strays too far from "the old English meters," and her work increasingly addresses all that is involved in this "seeming" – this alignment with a tradition that is common property, with always a more or less loose fit on several counts. As Helen Carr puts it, "The complex of history and flesh that we each are can never be represented accurately in a shared discourse" (1989: 141). Yet to wander too far from this shared discourse is not to get nearer one's particular "complex of history and flesh," whatever that may be; at the risk of simplifying Moore and the historical pressures that shape her work, I would propose her as a case in point. In poetic language, not only one's particular history but "flesh" itself must register, if it is to register at all, in historically coded and publicly recognizable conventions of patterning the physical properties of a given language, such as rhythm, rhyme, and meters. In Bishop's words, "*the choice is never wide and never free*" (1983: 94), for poetry is not a matter of creating one's own subjectivity but of choosing how to reappropriate an already overdetermined subjectivity.

While Bishop stays with meters, her remark that they only "seem" natural seems also to resist the alignment of the physical, bodily, "natural" face of language with such poetic devices as rhythm, meter, and lineation. A version of this alignment informs, for example, Julia Kristeva's (1980) argument that rhythm in poetry resists the deadly repression of the physical word by the signifying function. Poetry (by men or women) cultivates the "semiotic" function – gendered female – and enables it to hold its own against the paternal, symbolic order. All poetry is thus subversive: it weakens gender divisions and challenges the symbolic order itself (Moi 1985: 165–66). For this reason, all who would stabilize a social order – from Plato to Stalin and the Fascists – must root out poetry: "The poet is put to death because he wants to turn rhythm into a dominant element; because he wants to make language perceive what it doesn't want to say, provide it with its matter independently of the sign, and free it from denotation. For it is this *eminently parodic* gesture that changes the system" (Kristeva 1980: 31).

Yet this "gesture" signifies as such only within "the system"; furthermore, the semiotic dimension has its own systemically determined margins and centers. The criteria that define certain kinds of semiotic language as "poetic" are historically and culturally regulated – if not by tradition, then by contemporary consensus. In other words, poetry's formalism is determined, and even if a poet rejects conventional meters, stanzas, or rhyme schemes, she still must set up *some* artificial, formal order, combining in different ways available patterns for organizing the material aspects of the signifier, in order to have a pattern – with "repeats" – to mark the special or poetic nature of her language. Moore is only one example. What seems to subvert the symbolic order, then, also duplicates it in another register by instituting its own hierarchies. For example, meter or what registers as rhythm is not a natural quality of the semiotic dimension; it is an abstract pattern that metonymically substitutes for the physical qualities of a given language. Whether conventional or experimental, forms only *represent* the semiotic, as it is figured and positioned within the symbolic order, to signify the "natural" face of language. Thus poetic language destabilizes and constantly reverses all simple oppositions like semiotic–symbolic and signifier–signified, as well as the metaphorical alignment of these formal and linguistic dualisms with hierarchical cultural distinctions. This systemic and unstable subversiveness, I would argue, is the larger, discursive function of poetry's formalism, one that Bishop fully exploits.

Any discussion of women's poetry in general from a feminist perspective is complicated by at least two other considerations, more historical than generic. The first is the cultural gendering of poetry itself. Especially since the eighteenth century, the increasing separation of subjective and material realms, together with the gendering of these opposites, has aligned poetry with the "feminine" realm of the imagination, the emotions, and personal experience as opposed to the "masculine" values of reason, utility, empirical truth, and public experience. Since the Romantics, the male poet's cultural position of authority has itself come into question. Thus the modernists' poetic anxieties – how to "make it new" – tend to get cast in gender terms – how to write "like a man." This anxiety affects someone like Moore as much as Pound or Wallace Stevens, whose complex of gender and poetic anxieties Frank Lentricchia examines in *Ariel and the Police* (1988).

Poetry is a special, sacramental language, a privileged hieratic discourse – historically, a jealously guarded male domain. Especially since the Romantics, however, it may focus on personal experience – historically, a female province. In other words, poetry is an elitist discourse that may deal with culturally disadvantaged material. Moreover, while thoroughly intertextual, it may articulate private experience. Again, poetry would appear to maintain *and* question cultural binarisms like elitist versus communal or public versus private. Yet, as Carr (1989) points out, while popular forms of prose are now subject to critical study by feminists, the hierarchical distinction between poetry and "mere verse" remains virtually unchallenged. Poetry maintains its privileged position – ironically, at the cost of becoming culturally marginal – partly because it already radically destabilizes oppositional thinking, including cultural typing not only of gender but of what constitutes individual versus public experience. These terms are neither oppositional nor identical: each is articulated through the other and can play the other's part. And poetry will not reduce to discourse any more than it will reduce to individual expression or formalist sacrament. Feminist criticism of poetry, then, is not well served by arguments for a separate women's poetic tradition or language, for reasons apart from the universalism of such a position that a number of feminist critics have objected to.

The second historical consideration involves the history of twentieth-century poetry. When the idea of an authoritative norm (the consensus of a literary generation about *the* way to write) disappears with modernism and all historical styles become equally usable, the political efficacy and charge of "deviant" styles become limited. Conversely, after modernism, styles that observe historical conventions are able increasingly to question the rhetoric of their forms and may indeed have greater rhetorical flexibility than organicist experimental styles, which cannot afford to question their own rhetoric. For the only authority organicist experimentalism can claim is that it is ostensibly non-rhetorical – that it can access truths and processes beyond those available to conventional forms, which alone are seen as rhetorical. Organicist experimental writers end up with less room to question the values (ethical, political, or natural) that they invoke to authorize their forms, for without the identification of forms with certain moral, political, or metaphysical truths, the poet has no authority save that of individual talent, which in poetry is no authority at all. Thus ostensibly free forms, which must invest in authorities "above" or "below" the historical, conventional, or rhetorical, may enjoy less rhetorical freedom than conservative forms. Bishop takes full advantage of the "narrow" freedom her conventional forms offer, including release from the authority of "natural" truths, and her work increasingly registers the complexity of a woman poet's historical position, not only post eighteenth century but post modernism.

I

"The Map," which leads us into Bishop's *The Complete Poems,* points up the complex ways gender operates in her formally conventional verse. Typically, her speaker here is a reader of a representational text. "*What is a Map?*" Bishop will ask much later and cite "First Lessons in Geography" for an answer: "A picture of the whole, or a part, of the Earth's surface" (1983: 157). More specifically, this "picture" is a visual text that combines various representational media, including topographical description, printing or writing, and color. What serves as geographic description changes through the history of mapmaking: early maps were partly landscape paintings and partly chorography, and they were produced and consumed also as aesthetic objects to be displayed on walls, for example. With the Renaissance discovery of the laws of perspective, mapmaking moved away from painterly to scientific and mathematical representations of space, and the mapmaker was removed from the landscape. As David Harvey writes, "Perspectivism conceives of the world from the standpoint of the 'seeing eye' of the individual" (1989: 245), which is located outside and above the earth's surface: "The fixed viewpoint of perspective maps and paintings 'is elevated and distant, completely out of plastic or sensory reach.' It generates a 'coldly geometrical' and 'systematic' sense of space . . . [and allows] the globe to be grasped as a finite totality" (244). Consequently, space – "though infinite" – appears as "conquerable and containable for purposes of human occupancy and action" (246).

Thus, Harvey argues, rationalized mapmaking, which changed the very conception of space, underwrote the Enlightenment project (1989: 249) and its practices of "surveillance and control" (253). He points out that a map is a "totalizing device," "a homogenization and reification of the rich diversity of spatial itineraries and spatial stories. It 'eliminates little by little' all traces of 'the practices that produce it.' While the tactile qualities of the mediaeval map preserved such traces, the mathematically rigorous maps of the Enlightenment" converted "the fluid, confused," experiential spaces of "work and social reproduction into a fixed schema" (253). And with rationalized mapmaking, geographic knowledge and maps became valued commodities – "They defined property rights in land, territorial boundaries, domains of administration and social control, communication routes, etc. with increasing accuracy" (249) – and were indispensable for economic, political, and military control of territories.

History and geography, scientific objectivity, political and economic utility, and aesthetic value are inextricably bound together throughout the history of mapmaking; they are not mutually exclusive considerations. Neither are the "rhetorical" mastery that perspective offers and the actual, historical control and conquest that it enables. Given the complexity of the cultural text Bishop chooses to focus on, is her speaker's reading "adequate"? Her speaker seems to read and respond to the map primarily as an aesthetic object, apparently unaware of the perspectival assumptions of cartographic representation, of the functions maps have served in the economic, political, and military control of spaces, or of the history maps objectify. If the speaker is contemplating a current map of Europe (the poem dates from 1935), history, at least, would be difficult to ignore in looking at borders drawn and "countries" created in Bishop's lifetime. But her speaker has removed this visual image from cultural "commerce" for purposes of "contemplation" (1983: 12), bringing to it aesthetic responses and philosophical questions that appear inappropriate to the text at hand, and judges it by an irrelevant criterion: "More delicate than the historians' are the map-makers' colors." Thus, from our perspective as readers, the speaker who is misreading this artifact *appears* naive – most likely a female, possibly even a child. Sensibility, feelings, a certain frivolousness, and even sentimentality are the "female" markers of Bishop's reader, who is presented to *us* as a cultural text, and we judge her on the evidence of her negotiation of another cultural text. Thus we read this speaker as "female" from a position above the text of the poem, which is also the poet's position.

Yet while the speaker may appear naive to us, her relation to the text she reads in fact represents an attempt at mastery that duplicates the cartographer's relation to the terrain mapped. She simply works with different conventions and criteria, which we find naive or inappropriate for reading a map:

> Land lies in water; it is shadowed green.
> Shadows, or are they shallows, at its edges
> showing the line of long sea-weeded ledges
> where weeds hang to the simple blue from green.
> Or does the land lean down to lift the sea from under,
> drawing it unperturbed around itself?
> Along the fine tan sandy shelf
> is the land tugging at the sea from under? (1983: 3)

Apparently unversed in representational conventions, she confuses the representation with the original – "Shadows, or are they shallows," she wonders. Since she seems to be looking at a political map (with colored countries), which does not aim for visual realism, her questions indicate a willful misreading, a willful effort to read a tactile landscape back into the map.

The tropes she deploys in the second stanza clearly aim at mastery. If the mapmaker theoretically stands above the globe he levels and reduces in size, the map reader physically stands above the map. And she reads it by ignoring or disrupting the scale and proportions its metaphoric size depends on; in other words, she reads it on another level. This reading generates different power configurations: the "moony Eskimo" is outsized in relation to the map, but "moony" reduces the Eskimo on another scale. The speaker condescends to the Eskimo even as she reasserts a human scale over the map. "We can stroke these lovely bays," she says, and "peninsulas take the water between thumb and finger / like women feeling for the smoothness of yard-goods." These are tactile images, images of taking in hand or comprehending: they aim to master the metaphoric size of the map, partly by working on a literal scale. The speaker steps out of the meta-phoric scale of the map to repossess the mapped territory imaginatively and master the mastering map. The metaphor maker, as much as the mapmaker, commands an elevated perspective and enjoys the imagi-nary mastery – complete with the attendant distortions – that it allows. The two only follow the conventions of different media – one appeals to metaphors of experiential texture, the other to scientific objectivity – to authorize their mastering representations. And if the mapmaker's scientific appropriation of the landscape serves worldly purposes, the map reader's imaginary appropriation also serves a cultural function, opening the way to fantasies of exotic places and touristic colonizing. Aestheticizing may look powerless from the perspective of those who know what maps are for, but it is not power-neutral, and mis-taking is another kind of taking-in after all.

Our perspective as readers of the poem yet again duplicates the cartographer's and the map reader's. From our "higher" perspective, the misreading reader reduces in size to a child or a female, since in *our* cultural text aesthetic representation and tactile metaphors register as female vis-à-vis cartographic representation. To stop here and judge the map reader as naive and female, however, we would have to be ignorant of or choose to bracket the conventions of poetic representation that have articulated our text. For Bishop insists on calling attention to poetic devices: she spins off fanciful speculations based on the literal similarities of words, juxtaposes the closure of rhyming quatrains – complete with identical rhymes – with the "freer" middle stanza, and mixes stanzaic forms to underline the conventions governing *her* representation. The speaker's appearance as naive and female may well be an effect of Bishop's foregrounding her formal conventions; alliteration and rhyme, for example, seem to control the speaker's thought process and the questions she brings to the map ("Shadows, or are they shallows"). We then need to ask what is the relationship between such poetic schemes and the "original" *they* figure and represent. Bishop's map reader, it would appear, is mastered and feminized by the formal conventions of poetic representation and is presented to us as an "exotic" text, very much as the map is to the map reader with her defamiliarizing metaphors.

In the text Bishop gives us, her map reader is a naive or willful "outsider" to the historical functions of maps as means of domination: she blocks out the "indelicate" history that not only drew the map but positioned her as a "female" spectator to this prewritten world text. At the same time, she is an insider, duplicating this power relationship in her metaphoric mis-taking grasp. Similarly, as readers we are at once outside the poem, aware of its naive misreading and evasion of history and politics, and inside it, duplicating the map reader's naïveté in our misreading amusement at and diminution of her. Only an awareness of poetic conventions, their history and their politics, would make for an "adequate" reading of our text and guard against our slipping into a "female" or naive position and misreading "nature" into conventions. For it is partly in relation to the highly formal arrangement of the poem that the map reader appears naive, just as in Bishop's "Sestina," for example, the form distances the poet from her female characters, whose moves are controlled no less by the requirements of the sestina than by the natural laws scripted in the almanac or by socially prescribed domestic routines. Here, too, we have to acknowledge the power politics of Bishop's choice of form, which positions her characters as females. In the economy of "The Map," to be aware of and in command of conventions of representation is to secure a male position, and to inhabit a male position means to face up to "indelicacies," one of which is that here the poet holds a male position over her map reader. For Bishop well knows what maps are for: elsewhere, her "virile," militaristic "roosters" are "making sallies / from all the muddy alleys, / marking out maps like Rand McNally's" (1983: 36).

"The Map," then, presents an infinite regress of reversing gender positions. The earth is female to the cartographer, who mathematically masters it; the map is female to the map reader, who aesthetically masters it; and the map reader is female to readers of the poem, who read her as a text inscribed with certain cultural markers of femininity. Given such a series of mastering readings – each of which appears as a misreading from a different or higher perspective – we must guard against any ignorance or repression of the representational conventions involved at each stage. Lest we stop with our misreading and be exposed to another mastering misreading in turn, we need to see how the conventions of cartography, poetic representation, and cultural representation function. Bishop could not achieve such a complex position on gender without foregrounding the schematic, formal, and rhetorical conventions of her medium of representation and how they indeed exercise power over the "material" they represent. We ignore the "indelicate" power politics of poetic representation at our peril; to do so would be to mistake our reading of the aestheticizing map reader as female for a truth about aestheticizing or about females and their powerless, emotional ways of reading. Such a misreading would ironically position us as "female" from a higher rhetorical perspective that factors in the poetic conventions at work in our text. Thus to read our cultural text correctly, to see how "femininity" is as much a construction as abstract notions of space, we need to occupy a male position and be in command of how representational conventions intervene rhetorically to redefine the "original" phenomena they represent and turn into cultural currency.

To speak from the cultural position of a poet, in a language that registers as poetic, is to invest in a patriarchal prerogative and its exclusionary history. But only by doing so and foregrounding the formal and rhetorical conventions of poetic representation can Bishop begin to examine positions and constructions rather than nature and reified truths. She could not achieve this positional destabilization if she were to take her forms as anything other than conventional; she can only question this discourse from within by emphasizing the conventionality of her representation or of any representation that claims to be poetry, whether in quatrains or free forms. In this way she can show how poetic forms function rhetorically and how poetic figures exercise power over what they represent – what poetry represses in its expression.

"12 O'Clock News" may be read alongside "The Map" for its complex reversals of gender and reading positions. Here a newscaster seems to be reading, and clearly misreading, the geography of a writer's desk. He or she commands a "superior vantage point" (1983: 175), relying on findings of others who enjoy superior vantage points – anthropologists, ethnologists, and military reconnoiterers. Such an aerial misreading is far from neutral and spells out the politics of all vantage points "above" the subject of study or observation: it makes a hostile report on a "small, backward country" of a primitive, "inscrutable," "childish" people – "our opponents." A reporter's conventions of objectivity, coupled with obviously "wrong" readings, show that observation and description take place within an ideological framework, and what counts as "objectivity" counts as such only within a given system. The poem appears to satirize "objective" reports from "superior vantage points," exposing the politics and construction of such culturally authoritative discourses.

Formally, the reporter's hard facts are presented in prose paragraphs, but Bishop's text also appeals to the poetic convention of italicized marginal glossing. This device forces us to question which is the prior text and which is the explanatory or interpretive commentary – the writer's desk or the news report, the italic or the roman text. Bishop thus undermines the hierarchies of observable facts versus interpretation, factual prose reports versus figural or poetic readings. The poem may give us either an anthropologist-newsman-what-have-you reconnoitering and misinterpreting the geography of a poet's desk, an object of cultural hostility – "one of the most backward [countries] left in the world today" – or a poet equally misinterpreting and misglossing a sociopolitical text from the superior vantage point of a writer, taking things personally and reading from a perspective defined by the tools of his or her trade. That is, if the "reporter" is reading synechdochi-cally, fitting disparate details into a totalizing picture, the "writer" is reading metonymically, fragmenting a systemic cultural text into its material and writerly components; each has a different rhetorical strat-egy and political agenda. And who is reading and who is being read constantly shift positions, so that each reading is also a being read, each reader's exercise at mastery also mastering him- or herself.

Such a disruptive fluidity is inescapable once we activate certain reading conventions and register the function of the marginal, italic gloss to this prose poem. For if we read the poem simply as satirizing the discourse of the reporter and the assumptions underwriting it, we have to conclude that Bishop simply duplicates the reporter's reading strategy in satirizing and thus mastering it from a superior vantage point. While such mastery would secure a male position, it would also expose the master to the possibility of mastery from a still higher van-tage point. If we register how the convention of marginal glossing functions, however, and allow that whoever is writing the italic col-umn is also being satirized, we will not be tempted to master Bishop as one who reads for mastery, and thus ourselves duplicate the repor-ter's "naive" assumption that reading is a one-directional mastery of a text. If we are to read "adequately" the problematic of reading that "12 O'Clock News" represents, we need to see how either column can occupy the position of center or margin, original text or com-mentary, fact or interpretation, reading or being read, male or female. Bishop's subversions are systemic: she does not simply reverse hierar-chical binarisms but destabilizes binarism itself. And to register her poem's radical subversions, we have to invoke a specific, pedigreed poetic convention, even though its function here is ultimately to prob-lematize the very distinction between poetry and prose and the powers invested in each.

"Visits to St. Elizabeths" treats the same problematic in terms of literary history. The poem's compulsive and regressive narrative form, borrowed from a children's rhyme, seems to aim to master Pound. Bishop's form is antithetical to everything Pound stood for – certainly to his commitment to free, organic forms and his ambition to write a poem including history, a poem for which "Time is not." Bishop's incremental narrative – progressively enlarging its frame, which progressively diminishes Pound – incarcerates "the poet, the man" within its closure and the larger necessities it articulates:

> This is the soldier home from the war.
> These are the years and the walls and the door
> that shut on a boy that pats the floor
> to see if the world is round or flat.
> This is a Jew in a newspaper hat
> that dances carefully down the ward,
> walking the plank of a coffin board
> with the crazy sailor
> that shows his watch
> that tells the time
> of the wretched man
> that lies in the house of Bedlam. (1983: 135)

"Time is, history is," Bishop seems to insist; it is the sailor's watch that tells the poet's time, and this sailor is no Odysseus. The history Pound would have mastered has mastered him.

Again, however, Bishop's own position is far from secure, for the form she has chosen itself signals a generic compulsion for mastery. Pound's obsessions are reduced because they are placed within the generic obsessions of her form: Pound is just one of the characters in *her* totalizing historical narrative, which relates soldiers, sailors, Jews, children, poets, and houses of Bedlam. Bishop's uncharacteristically wide range here almost duplicates Pound's "superior vantage point," as she also brings in war, politics, history, and poetry. In other words, by taking on Pound's ambitions to speak with a culturally central voice, she necessarily duplicates his errors. What is true for Pound is true for her: attempting mastery through poetry, both are mastered by their obsession for mastery.

But Bishop's choice of a form with strictly prescribed movements and repetitions distinguishes her from Pound by underscoring her awareness that no verse is "natural," or uncontaminated by a will to power. For the form that would critique Pound's will to mastery by diminishing him also masters Bishop by negating the very grounds of her critique, since it forces her to occupy a higher, mastering vantage point. From our perspective, in turn, the poet seems quite obsessed herself, as we are forced into a superior position. But her title acknowledges her implication in what she seems to be critiquing, for a "saintly" vantage point entitles this narrative and places her within the same house of compulsions and megalomanias, if only for a visit. The sequence of words describing Pound runs: "the man"; "the tragic man"; "the talkative man"; "the honored man"; "the old, brave man"; "the cranky man"; "the cruel man"; "the busy man"; "the tedious man"; "the poet, the man"; "the wretched man." In this series, "the poet, the man" breaks the pattern, for "the poet" is not an adjective describing "the man" but a grammatical appositive and substantive equivalent of "the man." Here, at least, the "man" and the "woman" – poets both – "lie" in the same house; after all, "*This* is the house of Bedlam," the poem declares at the outset (emphasis added).

II

"A Miracle for Breakfast," written during the Depression (1936), is as politically resonant a poem as we get in Bishop; indeed, she singled it out as her "Depression poem. It was written shortly after the time of souplines and men selling apples, around 1936 or so. It was my 'social conscious' poem, a poem about hunger" (1966: 13). It seems odd that a poem with an immediate social reference should be a sestina, and I want to explore the function of this form in the poem's rhetorical development. The poem begins with "waiting" – for sunrise and breakfast:

At six o'clock we were waiting for coffee,
waiting for coffee and the charitable crumb
that was going to be served from a certain balcony,
– like kings of old, or like a miracle.

It was still dark. One foot of the sun
steadied itself on a long ripple in the river.

The first ferry of the day had just crossed the river.
It was so cold we hoped that the coffee
would be very hot, seeing that the sun
was not going to warm us; and that the crumb
would be a loaf each, buttered, by a miracle.
At seven a man stepped out on the balcony.

He stood for a minute alone on the balcony
looking over our heads toward the river.
A servant handed him the makings of a miracle,
consisting of one lone cup of coffee
and one roll, which he proceeded to crumb,
his head, so to speak, in the clouds – along with the sun.

Was the man crazy? What under the sun
was he trying to do, up there on his balcony!
Each man received one rather hard crumb,
which some flicked scornfully into the river,
and, in a cup, one drop of the coffee.
Some of us stood around, waiting for the miracle. (1983: 18)

The "man" could be a political leader, a Roosevelt or a Mussolini, promising miracles "like kings of old"; he could be a capitalist, offering a miraculous trickling down of wealth, or a communist, foretelling the end of waiting and plenty for all; or he could be a religious leader, a bishop, promising a conversion of bread crumbs to spiritual nourishment "like a miracle." For while the "man" suggests worldly powers, the poem also alludes to the Eucharist, as well as to various biblical stories of miraculously provided food, and the more comprehensive reading might be the religious one, with the scene's worldlier resonances serving to place larger cultural and political economies – and the representational rhetorics that sustain them – under the rubric of the religious transaction of Communion.

In any event, the appearance of this civil or religious patriarch – "like kings of old" – with his promise of a miracle, or something "like

a miracle," is synchronized with the natural "miracle" of the appearance of the personified sun. Whether Bishop is critiquing a certain
political or religious economy, both of which appeal to "faith" in
"miraculous," metaphoric conversions – whether of labor to value or
of a crumb to spiritual life and riches – she aligns its spokesman with
the sun as the "type" of such a power that oversees qualitative transformations. Synchronizing the appearance of the "man" and the sun
suggests that the authority of a political and religious leader is backed
by an analogy to natural, organic orders and changes, so that various
authorities interlock in a kind of typological chain. Such figures of
authority are "like" kings of old, who typify or personify natural powers, so to speak, or vice versa, depending on whether our perspective
privileges natural or sociopolitical orders.

Yet Bishop's presentation itself relies on the same rhetorical strategy
the man employs in his promise of miraculous transformations. For
the poem forces us to read the man allegorically to make any sense of
the events at all. Bishop demands that we convert the literal scenario
to an allegory to release a plenitude of meaning, and she calls attention
to certain figures like similes and personification to point up the rhetorical construction of her allegory. Indeed, since the trope of personification underwrites the man's authority, her rhetoric becomes the
substance of the symbolic system established in the poem. Thus Bishop's representational rhetoric is clearly implicated in the cultural and
social operations of rhetoric – the persuasive functions of figuration –
which her poem may in fact be warning us to beware.

Bishop's switch to the first person in the following stanza distinguishes the events related here from those of the opening stanzas. Yet
what we have in this passage is also an allegory: it presents an imaginary
or poetic creation that seems actually to realize a miraculous transformation and thus exceed the model of allegory. In other words, Bishop
gives us an allegory of a symbolism that proposes to unite imagination
and nature, figure and fact, in a "miracle" the speaker says is "not a
miracle":

I can tell what I saw next; it was not a miracle.
A beautiful villa stood in the sun

and from its doors came the smell of hot coffee.
In front, a baroque white plaster balcony
added by birds, who nest along the river,
– I saw it with one eye close to the crumb –

and galleries and marble chambers. My crumb
my mansion, made for me by a miracle,
through ages, by insects, birds, and the river
working the stone. Every day, in the sun,
at breakfast time I sit on my balcony
with my feet up, and drink gallons of coffee.

Separated from the crowd awaiting miracles, a poetic I–eye or imagination seems to see or envision in or through the crumb doled out a "beautiful" mansion, miraculously built by natural, organic processes also overseen by the sun. Although "mansion" recalls the biblical figure of a heavenly mansion, this miracle is wrought not by the Architect on High but by insects, birds, and the river working the stone and invokes, rather, the Romantic revision of biblical history, which transfers the biblical new Eden – when "the earth / Shall all be paradise" (Milton 1993: 296) – "from a supernatural to a natural frame of reference" (Abrams 1971: 23) and promises it as "A simple produce of the common day" (Wordsworth 1981: II, 39).

Bishop's first-person speaker is a type of the Wordsworthian poet, who enjoys the power of imagination "to create out of the world of all of us, in a quotidian and recurrent miracle, a new world which is the equivalent of paradise" (Abrams 1971: 28). The Romantic poet's vision of history thus duplicates the biblical and political millennialism of the first three stanzas. Like our patriarch, such a poet deploys typological correspondences across time, promises future fulfillments of past prefigurations, and thus patterns history – religious or secular – from a perspective outside it. Typology and the rhetorical mastery of history it enables place the poet in the same economy the man presides over, as Bishop's situating her visionary "I" on another balcony in another mansion suggests. Both projects are idealist, investing in metaphoric transformations of literal, natural, or historical events into timeless patterns and abstract values. And, it seems, to traffic in such substitutive exchanges – bread crumbs to Christ's body, labor to value, nature to a visionary palace – is to situate oneself on a "balcony" and claim patriarchal authority – as priest, king, or poet – to oversee these transactions. Writing as a poet, investing in the transformational powers of imagination and figuration, means entering this symbolic economy and its rhetoric, its persuasive figuration. "In my Father's house are many mansions" indeed (John 14:2).

It would be a mistake, then, to read the poem as a critique of religious or political rhetoric out of preference for the sustenance offered by a "nature" reworked by the "imagination."[3] Such a reading would have to identify Bishop with the poem's "I," as Kalstone does, for one example. He reads Bishop as critical of the crowd's expectations of easy miracles and "a chicken in every pot"; for Bishop, he suggests, miracles are not "apocalyptic" but "something which may be as daily as breakfast" (1989: 49–50). This reading attributes to Bishop the position I term Wordsworthian. As I have suggested, however, Bishop's poet belongs in the same economy, and if she is indeed critiquing the rhetoric of the man, she would have to be equally wary of the visionary poet's rhetoric, which underwrites scriptural and typological thinking itself. Poetry is more than simply implicated in the procedures of Eucharistic or economic or political substitution and representation; poetic language is the very ground on which such substitutive, symbolic economies may be sustained. Bishop's poet, then, is hardly in a position to critique or offer an alternative to political, economic, or religious rhetorics. This author only mirrors other authorities represented by the man. Thus, if Bishop gives us a critical poet here, she also demystifies the poet's critical credentials, and the visionary poet is rightly placed on a balcony – with "feet up" and "gallons of coffee."

Further, as both the detail of the feet up and the colloquial "gallons of coffee" suggest, what might at first appear to be a figurative, imaginary poetic exemption from a metaphysical poverty is cast as a socially specific and literal exemption from work and poverty. The poet must be exempt from immediate poverty to engage in figurative economies; and to figuratively equate literal and metaphoric hunger – for belief, say – is to exercise the same power as the man and offer only substitutive satisfactions or mere rhetoric. The poem exposes visionary powers to be quite worldly after all: they are enabled by a specific position within the real economy, which they help sustain by reinforcing the symbolic economy. Even dissent or opposition to the symbolic economy reinscribes its rhetorical procedures and institutes the poet as a power – indeed, a "male" power – duplicating those very structures he or she would oppose. In all, no poetic speaking escapes being "elevated" and gendered "male."

Nor is Bishop herself exempt. In reading her visionary poet as prefigured by the man, she *also* reads typologically – her Romantic poet, who substitutes imagination for God, is the antitype of the priest – and thus repeats the strategy by which the man and the "poet" master history from the superior vantage point of typological thinking. Yet there is a difference. If Wordsworth's first Eden, for example, is not only the biblical Eden but the "imaginative constructions of poets who have portrayed a golden age" (Abrams 1971: 26) – pagan poets as well as Milton, who made ample use of his pagan predecessors and their myths of the golden age, "groves / Elysian, Fortunate Fields" (Wordsworth 1981: II, 38), Hesperides, and so on – his new Eden will surpass prior constructions of it (Abrams 1971: 26, 29). Not only will the natural paradise outshine Eden and the poetic imagination outdo God, but Wordsworth will outwrite Milton. Wordsworth's figuration of poetic history follows the model of biblical history; in folding this typological reading of literary history into *her* typology, which aligns religious, political, and poetic histories, Bishop at once duplicates Wordsworth and frees herself from the charge to outwrite him. Her rhetorical strategy locates his "progressive" poetic program firmly within a larger progressive history, which she oversees and writes as a sestina.

Bishop's choice of a sestina formally reinforces her visionary poet's alignment with other patriarchal authorities by constraining him or her within the same limited vocabulary (*coffee, crumb, balcony, miracle, sun,* and *river*). Just as her allegorical figuration grants us a critical distance from her visionary poet's symbolic figurations, so does her choice of a medieval and ritualistic conventional form, which suits her allegorical figuration but is at odds with the organicist premises of the poem's visionary "I." When the promise of renewal and the rhetoric of natural supernaturalism are couched in a conventional, anachronistic, and even decorative form, the form in effect undercuts the model of poetic imagination that is its content. Her choice of form, far from privileging the metamorphic or transformational powers of the imagination, underlines the institutionalized power position of all poetic speaking and shows it to be of a piece with the other economies the man controls.

Like her allegorical figuration, then, Bishop's formal choice openly aligns her with a patriarchal tradition. By resisting naturalization, she achieves a distance from the equally patriarchal figure of the Romantic poet. The only way to gain a critical distance within poetic language is to play one traditional paradigm against another and bring out how both models are equally constructed and equally in collusion with larger cultural economies. Firmly aligning herself with the system, Bishop can show how a poetic imagination that positions itself against the system also belongs within it. If her poem critiques political and religious rhetoric as substitutive satisfactions for real hunger, its allegorical rhetoric and baroque form also work to resist the illusion that poetry can supply anything but symbolic satisfactions. Such a critique from within the system may be read either as a gender-specific challenge to certain models of poetic creation and rhetoric or as a more general political critique of the poetic "exemption" any poem always enjoys. Thus her ritualistic form both underlines this poetic exemption – Bishop herself speaks from a "balcony" of sorts, having time to play with sestinas – and does a kind of penance.[4]

Like "A Miracle for Breakfast," "Anaphora" also allows a socially and economically specific history to intervene in the melodrama of imagination and nature. Anaphora, a literary and liturgical device, serves in the first stanza to align the sun's rise to assume "his earthly nature" with the son-god's fall, "assuming memory and mortal / mortal fatigue." The second stanza, appealing to the device of homophony, aligns the sun's setting with the god's ascent: "the fiery event / of every day in endless / endless assent." Natural and Christian cycles – or, in more pertinent Wordsworthian terms, the cycles of nature and imagination, which awakes at sunset – run counter to each other. Yet they can appear to coincide – and each may be glimpsed through the other

– thanks to rhetorical devices like anaphora and homophony. If such
devices persuade us that natural processes and those of the imagination
are counterpointed and harmonized, they do so by performing the
political function of overlooking the historically specific setting. By
inscribing this specific history, Bishop distances herself from her en-
titling rhetoric:

> Each day with so much ceremony
> begins, with birds, with bells,
> with whistles from a factory

And then

> sinks through the drift of bodies,
> sinks through the drift of classes
> to evening to the beggar in the park
> who, weary, without lamp or book
>   prepares stupendous studies . . .
>   (1983: 52)

Once again, then, Bishop employs conventional schemes yet critiques
them from within, for just as "whistles from a factory" make the
"bells" less than pastoral, "the drift of classes" renders the "beggar in
the park" more than a poet-scholar figure.

"Brazil, January 1, 1502" likewise engages the politics of representation. This poem has received critical attention, because Bishop's political position here seems clear and correct. Her judgment of the
Portuguese colonizers seems unequivocal, and the poem allows us to
read it from a feminist perspective: the colonizers bring with them a
certain ideological framework, which already positions "nature," "natives," and "women" as available to conquest. Yet even here Bishop's
self-positioning presents a complication, and I do not mean only her
complicity as a tourist striking out, in "Arrival at Santos," for "the
interior" and immodestly demanding "a different world, / and a better
life, and complete comprehension / of both at last, and immediately"
(1983: 89). The important question within "Brazil" is: how do we
know the way Portuguese colonizers approached Brazil? The poem
begins with the assertion "Januaries, Nature greets our eyes / exactly

as she must have greeted theirs" – a statement that is hard to know how to read. Since nature surely would have changed between 1502 and 1952, these lines seem willfully to gear history to the present viewer's perspective; "exactly" is unnecessarily insistent.

But then Bishop is talking not about nature but "Nature," objectified and still gendered as "she" – the subject of powerful figurations by whoever cares to exercise such power from whatever political perspective. Indeed, the poem tells its story by emphasizing the mediation of its own figuration. In other words, the reader is presented with a "tapestry" – a figure that appeals to the specifically female representational medium of embroidery – that positions the colonizers within its visual "text," which the poem in turn re-presents. "Nature" does not greet *our* eyes here; what *we* see is a tapestry representing it, "fresh as if just finished / and taken off the frame": "every square inch filling in with foliage – / big leaves, little leaves, and giant leaves, / blue, blue-green, and olive"; "A blue-white sky, a simple web, / backing for feathery detail"; "Still in the foreground there is Sin: / five sooty dragons near some massy rocks" (1983: 91).

Bishop's manipulation of scale, one of her characteristic strategies for problematizing objectivity, serves here to call attention to *her* representation of landscape as tapestry and to alert us to *her* mediation. Our attention focuses on her representational surface, and we are forced to read the history of the encounter of Christian ideology with New World nature through her lens. Her conceit trains us to read the encounter between the colonizers and nature *allegorically,* before we meet the "facts," so to speak – facts we can judge only from her prejudicial perspective. If she condemns the colonizers for their allegorical preconceptions that enable their geographic conquest, she does so by duplicating their rhetoric exactly. She sets out to conquer, aesthetically and rhetorically, a historical rather than geographic "interior." Thus, while she takes a political position on the colonizers, she also positions her revisionary history as another allegory and leaves the reader room to ask: What motivates this poet's rhetoric and representation? Is this not a feminine or feminist "tapestry" claiming to represent history? What makes it a "truer" representation of history? Don't women's representations exercise the same male power over what they represent? Don't poets'? Read in conjunction with a number of poems that "condescend" – however self-consciously – to the "natives" of Brazil, such questions are not farfetched. "Arrival at Santos," for example, has statements like "I somehow never thought of there *being* a flag"; "Please, boy, do be more careful with that boat hook!"; and "The customs officials will speak English, we hope" (1983: 89, 90).

The poet as a maker of representations, tapestries, and poems necessarily occupies a "male" position, overseeing, colonizing, and mastering. After all, Bishop "authorizes" her feminist tapestry conceit by invoking Sir Kenneth Clark. And "conceit" – along with "unwanted love" and "war" – comprises one of the three evils in the world the "Roosters" rule (1983: 36). For even in that poem the poet, with her conceit and her gaudy rhyming triplets that insist on being heard, competes with the "uncontrolled, traditional cries" of the roosters, who may stand for Hitler or Peter, depending on how she deploys her conceit. Arrogance and allegory meet in "conceit," and the poet is the invisible "third" who always walks beside political and religious powers. Since speaking as a poet necessarily claims power for poetry, it necessitates foregoing simply oppositional stances. This recognition, and the humility it engenders, makes for the different power of Bishop's poetry.

III

Bishop's autobiographical narrative poem "The Moose" can show us how Bishop negotiates her strategic position in literary history as a woman poet. A number of readers have found a specifically female sensibility in this poem; I want to suggest that, far from showing a female sensibility, the poem situates itself firmly within the subgenre of Romantic and modern narratives of personal encounters with nature, observing its gendering of nature as feminine vis-à-vis the masculine-gendered experiencing subject-poet. At the same time, the poem also questions the gender framework of this subgenre, both because the subject is female and because the poem appeals to older

poetry. And her designating the work of glaciers as "scriptures" per-haps marks her comparable distance from an equally stony and "ad-mirable" scriptural history, a history of authoritative writing that is more than de-scriptive (literally, "derivative") and makes – or makes for – history. Further, Bishop's mother had spent time, lonely and unhappy as a young schoolteacher, in this Gaelic-speaking region, which is the subject of a story Bishop began in 1948 called "Home-sickness." Although she worked on the story for fifteen years, she was not able to finish it (Kalstone 1989: 119). Perhaps, then, the "interior" meaning the landscape withholds is also personal – the meaning of the equally illegible script of her personal history. In this poem, Bishop's descriptive reserve maintains her distance from personal and public history: it is an empowering powerlessness that keeps the historical scriptures undecipherable and voiceless, if at the expense of silencing her own past.

"The Moose" is a very different kind of poem. Here the past is retrieved momentarily, and the landscape yields a vision of its "im-penetrable" interior. "The Moose" is also distinguished by its sustained narrative, which gathers up and subsumes local descriptions to a tem-poral unfolding; here "everything" is not "only connected by 'and' and 'and' " (1983: 58), as it tends to be in Bishop's earlier travel poems. "The Moose" follows a carefully designed causal sequence of reversals that enables Bishop to move forward and backward at once. Leaving Nova Scotia in a repetition of earlier departures and reembarking on a journey west into the night, the poet enters "a gentle, auditory, / slow hallucination" induced by the bus, the very vehicle carrying her away "back to Boston" (a subtitle Bishop entertains through many versions).[6] In this auditory memory she returns to her childhood, where her grandparents' voices, reciting in turn a litany of losses, lull her into sleep or a dream state when the moose appears, "grand, oth-erworldly" (173). The forward movement of the narrative, repeating other departures, thus returns Bishop to her childhood and also accesses a larger vision, not unlike that of Wordsworth's "awful Power r[ising] from the mind's abyss / Like an unfathered vapour that enwraps, / At once, some lonely traveller" (1979: 217).

Moreover, when Bishop finally gives us a narrative in "The

Moose," her memory also assumes a literary-historical dimension, for
she remembers a lost childhood and even – in the hyperbolic terms of
"One Art" – a lost "continent" by recovering a scriptural history and
reclaiming a largely American and male poetic genealogy. By entering
a narrative syntax, which alone can open an approach to her past experience, she also enters a literary-historical syntax, which will transform and recast that very experience. Her grand narrative of all the
losses history and narratives effect and record both enables, and is enabled by, a recovery of "Grandparents' voices," poetic as well as familial. In "The Moose," Bishop is able to approach her personal
history because her narrative necessarily engages the historical record
of the genre, the "scriptures" of men. This "erring" detour places her
in a generic and literary-historical text that she can call "home." While
this "home" offers no protection and, indeed, costs her *her* experience
all over again, she is no longer an outsider describing and "admiring"
the "scriptures made on stones by stones."

The primal source the "female passenger" (Drafts) recovers in "The
Moose" is female, and Bishop emphasizes the moose's sex in even the
earliest versions of the poem. Yet the "strait" way to the moose runs
through a male poetic history, which should caution us against im-
puting a special significance to the moose's gender. What is at stake in
this poem is that by entering a narrative syntax, Bishop also enters a
historical syntax and, thereby, a traditional gender framework. The
logic of the historical terms in which she has cast her poem leads her
to its climactic recognition: "Look! It's a she!" In this copular metaphor, the moose changes from an "it" to a "she," and Bishop's word-
ing nicely calls attention to the transformation syntactic conventions
effect, a strategy she also uses in the lines "you are an *I, /* you are an
Elizabeth" (1983: 160) from "In the Waiting Room," to articulate the
paradox of identity. While her position as a subject genders the object
as "she" and thus repeats the male poet's traditional reading of nature
as female, her phrasing also exposes how subject–object relationships
are gendered within the larger syntax that governs this representational
system. The recognition of the moose's sex simultaneously places it
within both a linguistic syntax – in this case, a language with gendered

pronouns – and a literary-cultural discourse that syntax serves here to mirror.

Thus it would be a mistake to read the moose as a figure of a special female harmony with nature (Ostriker 1986: 118–19) or of a poetic source or community specific to women writers. To read Bishop's figure as a claim to powers specific to women writers would only reinscribe an organicism she – as a feminist – must resist. She only discovers that, *within* the symbolic economy she has entered, nature becomes female. What has brought her to this figuration is her contract with a particular tradition, written by men, of poems about journeys like the one she has made. Because this figuration is naturalized by the whole tradition of nature poetry, the moose stands out in Bishop's poetry as an uncharacteristic figure: there she "looms," an embodiment of primal nature. Primal nature, which elsewhere in Bishop dissolves into discourse, into metaphoric or linguistic effects, is here in the flesh, "roughly but adequately," (1983: 25) represented as a moose. And this vision exacts a political cost, as she well knows. Another poem in which Bishop presents nature as a "she" is "Brazil, January 1, 1502," where we are looking through the eyes of colonizers (and corroborating tourists), and the gendering of nature explicitly serves political agendas for mastery.

By consciously positioning herself within a poetic history and re-sounding the old "scriptures," Bishop in effect oversees the "assimilation" of her – in Adrienne Rich's term – "outsider's" eye (1986). *Assimilate* contains the built-in difference of *similis,* or likeness, and I am not suggesting that Bishop's vision is absorbed by or becomes identical with a male vision; she is, "above all . . . not that staring man" (1983: 205). I am suggesting, however, that writing has more than one allegiance.[7] If a writer attempts to revive meaning in a form recognizable as poetry, appropriating ordinary language for poetic use by appealing to its material qualities for special psychic effect, she necessarily consents to the appropriation of her experience by the history of such language use and its generic requirements and resources. To enter this special discourse is to enter a medium where the individual voice makes itself heard as such only by reviving a history of voices. It is

Bishop's re-sounding the "scriptures" of men that gives her – and us
– access to the meaning of *her* experience, at the moment it becomes
communal. This is her "ladder road" – to borrow Robert Frost's term
(1979: 378) – that brings her to the shared truth of communal experience: "Why, why do we feel / (we all feel) this sweet / sensation of
joy?" Despite the parentheses guarding her emphatic repetition and
despite the interrogative form, Bishop's assumption about her community with her fellow passengers and readers is uncharacteristically
confident. One explanation is that here she is speaking from within a
community of other poets, for this "joy" echoes through the tradition
of visionary writing, from Wordsworth's "access of joy" (1979: 218)
to Proust's musing "whence could it have come to me, this all-
powerful joy" (1982: 48).

Bishop speaks in the pronoun "we" throughout "The Moose,"
referring to the autobiographical self in the third person – a "lone"
female "traveller," marginal in more than one sense. Bishop abjures
"I," for the self that is the subject of the poem is not the "I" writing
it, who in fact holds a central position in this discourse. If the textual
meaning of personal experience can only be a shared meaning, it must
appeal to a tradition or history of what constitutes meaning within a
given discursive framework. If we start with experience and not metaphysics, truth can only be rhetorical and historical. And since Bishop
indeed begins postmetaphysically, with the absence of a home ground,
and regards origins as found, and founded, in temporal and historical
losses, she has little choice but to entrust herself to time and history.
This history is largely male, but there is no way out of it except into
metaphysics, which is exactly what anyone who would repossess her
or his particular experience must resist. If truth is to remain historical,
it must be communal and shared – a rhetorical truth accessible to all,
if in theory only. Individuals or groups can claim exclusive truths on
metaphysical or natural grounds alone, which Bishop firmly rejects
from the beginning; such a position would only mark the beginning
of the end, duplicating the errors of history.

"The Moose" audibly recalls a number of American poets, some
not heard before in her verse, and in the rest of my discussion I want

to explore the poem's native ground. Walt Whitman, Robert Frost, and Hart Crane provide models her poem may be read against, whether they are all consciously invoked or not. For Bishop's recuperation of these models is less a matter of "anxiety of influence" than one of entering a traditional narrative framework of journeys into nature and recoveries of origins, complete with the objectification and gendering of nature that come with the territory. Thus Bishop's narrative of recovering her past as "meaning" entails abdicating *her* past, and such a generic risk involves, for a woman poet, a political risk as well. Not only is narrative a patriarchal structure – as Edward Said, for example, has argued (1985)[8] – but entering the linear, causal time of narrative also means, in this case, entering the history (necessarily patriarchal) of how personal, temporal experience has been traditionally figured. And yet, for a woman poet, this strategy also explicitly dissociates the author, who is now an intertextual construct speaking in the first person plural, from the subject of the narrative, the "lone traveller" and her particular historical position, and such a revision of the Romantic-humanist identification of the poet with the (male) subject in effect empowers the female author. In other words, her narrative pattern of recovery through loss is not only the subject and strategy of her poem – its approach to meaning – but also the strategy by which she authorizes herself as a woman poet. And this pattern places her poem within the pervasive tradition of secular quest narratives studied by Abrams (1971). No revision can proceed without activating the history of the model, just as no repetition can be anything but a revision. As readers, we can access Bishop's meaning best by tuning into her literary past, by hearing and imagining as she hears and imagines

an old conversation
– *not concerning us,*
but recognizable, somewhere,
back in the bus:
Grandparents' voices

uninterruptedly
talking, in Eternity
(1983: 171; emphasis added)

The journey of "The Moose" begins with the poet repeating her
initial departure from home, and it begins with Whitman, whom she
distinctly echoes in her grand first sentence. While Bishop's repetition
of words – arguably, her stylistic signature – is quite marked, it is
subsumed by the repetition of syntactically parallel phrases and the
periodic sentence structure so characteristic of Whitman. Her first sentence especially recalls the opening of "Out of the Cradle Endlessly
Rocking," which establishes the link between narrative and memory.
The knowledge of loss enables the narrative syntax and opens up space
for memory, which returns Whitman to the initial experience of loss
and, farther back, to the source, "mother." Likewise, the knowledge
of time and loss, of "deaths, deaths and sicknesses" (1983: 172), authorizes Bishop's narrative, which in turn makes possible a recovery
(in memory) of the earliest loss and eventually leads back to a natural,
maternal source. While Bishop's journey is not on Whitman's scale,
and while her moose is no death mother, the two poems progress along
similar lines, and the temporal movement of their narratives follows
almost as a reflex of syntax – a movement native to sentences, an
impulse generic to writing.

Bishop's first sentence also echoes the fifth section of "When Lilacs
Last in the Dooryard Bloom'd," the imperial periodic sentence that
travels

Over the breast of the spring, the land, amid cities,
Amid lanes and through old woods, . . .
. . . passing the endless grass,

. . . .

Passing the apple-tree blows of white and pink in the orchards,
Carrying a corpse to where it shall rest in the grave,
Night and day journeys a coffin. (1965: 330)

Such a "continental" sentence – to use Allen and Davis's apt term
(1955: 232) – historicizes the landscape, and such syntactic mediation

enables Whitman to place the coffin and the violent historical event it represents within a natural order. The sentence performs a generic elegiac function of naturalizing and ceremonializing the unnatural death it mourns. Whitman tells us that a nation acquires a history through such violent experiences as wars and assassinations (1964: 508). If a national identity is gained by a historical "loss of innocence," so is poetic identity, and "Lilacs" is a crisis poem for the poet who had begun by declaring himself free of English verse conventions. The occasion by which the nation acquires a national history and identity calls for a recognizable elegy. Thus the event forces Whitman to engage a poetic past he had rejected as foreign – the history of the genre in English – before he can begin again to proceed beyond it, a course not unlike Bishop's negotiation with the poetic history Whitman represents.

"The Moose" also appears to be an elegy of sorts. Bishop's aunt, Grace Bulmer Bowers, was alive when she started the poem, and the first version carries the dedication "goodbye / to my one dear relative," with the last word crossed out and "relation" substituted (Drafts). The dedication disappears for a while and reappears, in its present form, in *Geography III* (1976). In the end, the "relation" lost is not only Aunt Grace but a landscape, even a "continent," and childhood. Like Whitman's sentence, Bishop's opening syntax stages the westward movement of the bus:

> From narrow provinces
> of fish and bread and tea,
> home of the long tides
> where the bay leaves the sea
> twice a day and takes
> the herrings long rides,
>
> where if the river
> enters or retreats
> in a wall of brown foam
> depends on if it meets
> the bay coming in,
> the bay not at home;

where, silted red,
sometimes the sun sets
facing a red sea,
and others, veins the flats'
lavender, rich mud
in burning rivulets;

on red, gravelly roads,
down rows of sugar maples,
past clapboard farmhouses
and neat, clapboard churches,
bleached, ridged as clamshells,
past twin silver birches,

through late afternoon
a bus journeys west (1983: 169)

Her periodic construction with its insistent repetitions superimposes linear and cyclical motion and places the bus's westward journey, which repeats a historical and continental movement west and away from a source, within cyclical natural time, represented by the setting sun. The sun, in turn, is synchronized with the tidal rhythms – the bay repeatedly leaving the sea and coming back "home," the river entering and retreating. It even evokes the internal rhythms of the bloodstream: the sun setting in a red sea "veins the flats' / lavender, rich mud / in burning rivulets." Earlier versions explicitly paint the sun "red as blood" and the sea "silted red as blood." The tides' pulse, as "the sea leaves the sea" (Drafts), answers to the human pulse and the course of history within this grand syntactic order.

Yet Bishop's first sentence does not end where it could grammatically conclude; it flows on for ten more lines as a loose sentence to take in the "lone traveller," whose destination and destiny remain outside the periodic unit and the Whitmanic harmony it establishes between natural-biological and historical journeys west. By continuing beyond the periodic closure and the harmony of cyclical and linear time it establishes, Bishop domesticates the tidal sweep of the opening stanzas and reduces the scene to a human scale, narrowing her focus to a group of "relations" and ending with "a collie supervises." In view of the aerial perspective of the beginning stanzas, "supervises" is an almost parodic revision of her opening lines. Earlier versions of the departure scene – "goodbye to the aunt," "female passenger," and "her seven relatives" (Drafts) – more explicitly identify the traveler as the poet. This retreat not only prepares for Bishop's *"narrow way"* (the phrase is Henry Vaughan's [1981: 289]) back to her personal past in the "narrow provinces" but revises the Whitmanic expansiveness she has invoked, marking her post-Romantic marginality to such an order. Thus Bishop acknowledges and repeats Whitman's "imperial" syntax only to place her traveler to the side of it. With a "Goodbye to the elms, / to the farm, to the dog," the passenger boards the bus, and from then on this metaphoric conveyance limits her perspective and the poem's. At this point, she moves on to another kind of syntax, more casual than causal, with a series of sentence fragments relaying the momentary notations of a specific observer, and concludes with the one-word sentence "Gone." Although such writing revises the opening sentence, Bishop's "narrower" experience still signifies within an established framework.

A similar tension exists between this six-stanza-long sentence and her short, intermittently rhymed lines of five or six syllables and three stresses. If, as she has suggested, her verse means to allude also to the ballad form, what better way to assimilate a syntax that carries Whitman's signature than in such a common, communal form in "old English meters"? The ballad functions as a common ground and rhythm – a generic, even anonymous, prepersonal narrative form – accommodating both Whitman's sentence and her improvisation, which, far from claiming originality, actually returns to a pre-text. Her "balladizing" of literary history makes room for her experience within an older "text" and resists Whitman's organicism and its bass tone of natural rhythms. Bishop's subjecting Whitman himself to a generic and historical pre-text, parsing his sentence along ballad lines, suggests that any ideas of correspondences between poetic and natural movements carry historical freight; by now they are "beat-up" vehicles that we would be ill-advised to mistake for natural transports. The very fact that Bishop can use Whitman's syntax in ballad lines emphasizes the conventional nature of *her* lineation, which here is metrical and does not coincide with syntactic units, and thus privileges a longer poetic history, protecting her from Whitmanic organicisms and sublimities.

The second American poet "The Moose" recalls is Robert Frost. I am thinking less of poems like "The Most of It" or "Two Look at Two," where it is "as if" we have face-to-face encounters with nature, than of "West-Running Brook" and "Directive," with their countercurrents against loss and entropy. As a figure of poetic transport, Bishop's "beat-up" bus is a temporal and historical, westward-bound conveyance. Yet because meter carries a historical memory and metaphoric substitution enacts both loss and recovery, the very vehicle that takes her away also returns her home. The entropic transportation of this temporal medium enables a transport out of time and delivers her to origins and sources in the very process of leaving them. Frost calls this a "backward motion toward the source": "The universal cataract of death / That spends to nothingness – and unresisted, / Save by some strange resistance in itself, / Not just a swerving, but a throwing back" (1979: 259). For Frost, it is this "tribute of the current to the source" that "most we see ourselves in" (260). In "West-Running Brook," saying, naming, and, above all, making moral analogies between human discourse and nature's course enable humans to resist the entropic movement they are carried away by and to pay tribute to the "source" they thereby locate.

"Directive" is even more to the point. The salvation it offers is both in earnest and ironic; while the poem instructs "you" to find "yourself" in nature, "nature" comes down to a species of metaphor. Backing out of a world "now too much for us" (1979: 377) is both a quest for self-purification, descending through layers of history to a natural, watery source, and a rhetorical quest through the "serial ordeals" of simile (l. 4), personification (l. 16), metaphor (l. 37), and allusion (l. 59), leading to the archetypal symbol of water as an unconscious source. The ritual of rhetorical purification – going "back" beyond legend, childish make-believe, and Gospel alike, beyond all rhetorical con-fusions, to a primal figure or archetype or original metaphor – *is* the moral and spiritual quest for wholeness "beyond confusion." Frost's ironic tone undermines his apparent resistance to poetic con-fusions, for while the vessel or "goblet" may be broken and stolen,

we will need it to drink of the "waters." Frost is dubious about search-
ing for origins beyond metaphoric language and questions the Romantic and modern versions of such quests that his poem ostensibly
reenacts. If we are to regain lost innocence, we must grow more sophisticated rather than less; we must be properly educated in metaphor
to recognize that the poetic "quest" only progresses from figure to
figure, from one kind of figuration to another.

Bishop's rhetorical progress is similar. Her bus trip is a simultaneous
metaphor for life's journey and for metaphoric conveyance itself. And
the entropic course of syntax, narrative, and analogical likenesses that
travel away from origins "runs down in sending up," in Frost's terms
(1979: 259), the memory of "Grandparents' voices," just as *their* conversation "in Eternity" about "deaths, deaths and sicknesses" sends up
the vision of the moose. This vision coincides with the narrator's falling
asleep or even dreaming, when the bus stops and turns off its lights.
Bishop's moose is seen as if dreamed, dreamed as if remembered: it is
a vision that crosses the categories of experience, imagination, and
memory. Although the moose, driven deep into the interior, can reappear and hold her own against Father Time, it is still "our quiet
driver" who returns us to this maternal source, if only to hear a "man's
voice" assure us she is "Perfectly harmless." In Frostian fashion, the
return is effected by the very poetic and rhetorical structures – the
"ladder road" (1979: 378) – that the vision purports to transcend, just
as male conveyances (vehicular and historical) bear the "female passenger" to her encounter with mother nature–mother memory. In this
move, Bishop masters much more than personal history. That her
journey and mode of travel are prescribed does not block but, in fact,
yields meaning. Yet such meaning as poetry discloses on its historical
and figural road can only be a shared meaning – that is, historical and
rhetorical. She writes her experience as it is written by the resources
– historical, formal, and figurative – of the common language of poetry.

Yet this coincidence of personal and communal experience may be
only a dream or vision sent up by the shared discursive resources.
Before Bishop settles on "otherworldly" to describe the moose, she
considers "half-seen," "night mare," "spectre," and "heraldic as a

dream," a line that survives through many drafts. While she means the experience to be visionary, she beholds the "otherworldly" through the bus window. She frames the sublime experience so carefully within the narrative of transportation and the metaphor of transport that it becomes a vision as much of poetic resources – again, not personal possessions – as of natural sources. Accordingly, she can describe this primal source only by means of another divagation from it – in similes like "high as a church" and "safe as houses," which repeat the "man's" "Perfectly harmless" in another register.

The substitutive logic that earlier had modeled the artifacts of civilization on nature (clapboard houses and churches "ridged as clamshells") now shifts into reverse: the moose is no sooner seen than lost again, assimilated by civilization, history, and the very rhetorical and syntactic processes that have enabled the vision. According to Joanne Feit Diehl, the moose, whose "unanticipated" appearance interrupts the "continuum of expectation" and "challenges our notions of a verifiable, ordered universe," "embodies a female strangeness that constitutes an inherently subversive notion of the Sublime" (1990: 107). As I have suggested, however, the moose's appearance is no more "unexpected" than her femaleness, and Bishop's subversiveness lies rather in her foregrounding the rhetorical processes that first conjure and then assimilate her vision of the female moose into the given discursive framework – with its polarities of civilization versus nature, male versus female, historical and narrative sequence versus the visionary moment – that shapes her entire journey and has already determined the moose's gender. The terms of Bishop's assimilation are not very subtle: her similes stand out because they aim not so much to efface themselves and describe her vision as to make it fit back into the world of churches and houses. Her similes openly exercise power over what they figure, because her point is to call attention to the rhetorical processes that "right" her experience and resublimate the Sublime.

At the same time that Bishop's journey repeats Whitman's and Frost's journeys, her historical difference also revises them. Whitman's way is the open road – even in "Out of the Cradle Endlessly Rocking" he goes back only to go forth – while Frost heads "back" in order to recover a lost origin. Bishop's narrative superimposes and disorients both journeys. She embarks on a westward journey, away from home ground, yet faces no new territory: she is only going "back to Boston," repeating original departures (hers as well as Whitman's). Given her different historical position, then, her repetition amounts to a redirection. Similarly, she revises a Frostian return when she backs out of origins and makes for "Boston." She resists Frost's nostalgia (however ironic) as much as Whitman's futurism (however strained). For Bishop, there is neither virgin territory nor an original source, but only repetition, which keeps revising and repositioning *arche* and telos. Nevertheless, this double and duplicitous road still affords a glimpse of the moose.

The "sublime" experience over, the last stanza returns to ordinary time. Once again, this return both follows and challenges the linear logic of narrative and metaphor:

For a moment longer,

by craning backward,
the moose can be seen
on the moonlit macadam;
then there's a dim
smell of moose, an acrid
smell of gasoline.

The remembrance of a poetic history that enabled the "backward glance" resumes and now leads back out of the vision. The poet the final stanza may be read against is Hart Crane. Many passages from *The Bridge,* like the first stanza of "The Harbor Dawn," find their echoes in "The Moose." Crane's project of seeking a "pardon for this history" (1966: 116) through an investment in memory, carrying "the reader into interior after interior" (251), prefigures Bishop's. In particular, I am thinking of the "Van Winkle" section with the "macadam" that "Leaps from Far Rockaway to Golden Gate," the poet as Rip Van Winkle "*not here / nor there*," and the personal and continental memory confronting an alien present. Here Pocahontas as "*time's truant*" represents Crane's American muse-memory of a primal

nature before history, and remembering this source amounts to envi-
sioning a secular salvation that would "justify the evil of our mortal
state" (Abrams 1971: 116). This Romantic revision of the Christian
paradigm of history that Abrams plots also informs Bishop's poem,
however "far gone in history or theology" (Bishop 1983: 57) she may
be. As in Crane, the New Eden glimpsed in "The Moose" assumes a
recognizably American shape; an enigmatic scribble on the margins of
one version of Bishop's description of the "moose" (from the Algon-
quin for an indigenous North American animal) seems to read "Plym-
outh Rock" (Drafts).

When we return to ordinary time, then, we recognize it by the
smell of gasoline in a violent Cranian juxtaposition with the moose's
smell. The gasoline that has brought Bishop to this encounter now
takes her away. Her last words remind us that an erring technological
progress has led her to her vision, a compensation comparable to what
the other temporal and historical movements in the poem offer. Yet
Bishop has nothing of Crane's transcendental impulse. It is only that,
"by craning backward," the sense of smell can hold on to the experience "a moment longer." After repeated injunctions to look –
"Look! It's a she!" "Look at that, would you" – Bishop ends with the
sense of smell. Like taste, it carries memory better than sight and allows,
in fact, for Crane's "*blood remembering*" (1966: 71); in Proust's words,
"when from a long-distant past nothing subsists, after the people are
dead, after the things are broken and scattered, taste and smell alone,
more fragile but more enduring, more unsubstantial, more persistent,
more faithful, remain poised a long time, like souls, remembering,
waiting, hoping, amid the ruins of all the rest; and bear unflinchingly,
in the tiny and almost impalpable drop of their essence, the vast structure of recollection" (1982: 50–51). Thus Bishop's concluding with
the sense of smell connects her to the moose's sniffing the gasoline
odor on the bus's hood – they are equalized here – and grounds her
literary recollection in an instinct for continuity, in the survival value
of "craning backward."

Such a regression within progress is what literary memory, narrative, allusion, metaphor, and meter all offer. The remarkable recognition of "The Moose" is that an original homelessness, a liberation

from metaphysics, binds the poet all the more not only to the common condition of mortality but to a shared history. In deploying the resources that are the legacy of this history, Bishop's work both challenges the models of an essentially or historically separate women's poetry and necessarily revises the figure of a universalist patriarchal tradition. Her position allows for both the error of our separate histories – which is, of course, their truth in the face of the dominant history – and for the truth of a shared history – which is, of course, its error from the perspective of marginalized histories. Indeed, the metaphysical binarism of margins/centers itself comes into question in Bishop's revisionary vision. In the elegy "North Haven" (1983: 188), her "White-throated Sparrow's five-note song" calls forth her hexameter, "*Repeat, repeat, repeat; revise, revise, revise*"; repeating by revising and revising by repeating, Bishop proves this is not bad advice.

IV

I will conclude with two poems, from both ends of Bishop's career, that address binary thinking itself. The critical power of these poems, which do not appear to be directly political, lies in their subverting and constantly confusing oppositional gender alignments, from whatever viewpoint they are proposed. In "The Gentleman of Shalott" (1983: 9–10) from *North and South,* hierarchical binarisms are leveled by an appeal to the fact of the body's bilateral symmetry, "a mirrored reflection / somewhere along the line / of what we call the spine":

> The glass must stretch
> down his middle,
> or rather down the edge.
> But he's in doubt
> as to which side's in or out
> of the mirror.

Inside and outside, originals and reflections, centers and margins are all impossible to distinguish. An original duplication or duplicity grounds the poem and renders any vocabulary that would hierarchize these doubles comically inadequate; that is the poem's deconstructive philosophical burden. But its title recasts the issue and brings in literary history and gender by invoking Tennyson's "Lady of Shalott." From *this* perspective, the poem's innocent proposal of coeval, nonhierarchical doubles seems comically inadequate. Now, such binary doubleness as the fact of two sexes is hardly neutral and signifies politically within a larger cultural and historical discourse. Without Tennyson, the poem might signify philosophically – but not historically or politically. Here allusion again serves a revisionary function; in order to signify politically and to question a gender-specific historical figuration of "poet" and "muse," Bishop must invoke Tennyson. Outside the "arena" of literary history and its politics, what would there be but our solipsistic gentleman, content with wishing "to be quoted as saying at present: / 'Half is enough.' "

The marvelous late poem "Santarém" (1983: 185–87) returns to the question of binary oppositions. Situated at the "conflux of two great rivers, Tapajós, Amazon," in a paradisal color scheme of blue and gold, Santarém seems another version of the New Eden, a dazzling vision of a "pardon" for a history of wrongs. Instead of the four rivers diverging out of the Garden of Eden, "Here only two / and coming together":

> Even if one were tempted
> to literary interpretations
> such as: life/death, right/wrong, male/female
> – such notions would have resolved, dissolved, straight off
> in that watery, dazzling dialectic

What dissolves is not the fact of two different rivers but the idea of binary oppositions; "such notions" that aim to fix and stabilize meanings are temptations to be resisted, lest Eden be lost all over again. Bishop's presentation of oppositional notions maintains cultural ratios – life : right : male :: death : wrong : female. Yet if binary-oppositional or patriarchal thinking is "wrong" in this setting, it slips into a female position. The "right" solution to these "wrong" notions is dialectics, which now becomes "male." And indeed it is, proceeding by sublimating differences from a totalizing "superior vantage point."

In turn, the female-wrong to this position is the "dialect" that survives within "dialectic." Dialect maintains "crazy" differences without opposition or the resolution of oppositions; it links to the "mongrel" combinations – the legacy of a history of "crazy shipping" – that she observes or, rather, remembers, possibly "remembering it all wrong." Right and wrong, male and female are unstable and keep changing places within this paradisal space.

And then "my ship's whistle blew. I couldn't stay." And we are back in the "real" world, with binarisms reinstituted in the final scene and the closing question of the poem: " 'What's that ugly thing?' " But perhaps we can "stay" after all: ugly/beautiful is only another binarism, and if we resist passing an easy judgment on her "fellow-passenger, Mr. Swan," we can remain in the protected garden of the poem and say that, in a sense, the thing *is* "ugly" once out of its "crazy" matrix, wrong once back aboard the "real" world, where one person's "exquisite" may well be another person's "ugly." These categories, too, are relational and not to be reified. The poem holds these reversals in "solution," resisting all attempts to resolve, dissolve, or solve them. For the poem *does* envision an Edenic garden, a home at the end of an "erring" history no less than an "erring" temporality: "That golden evening I really wanted to go no farther."

John Ashbery

"The Epidemic of the Way We Live Now"

All along I had known what buttons to press, but don't
you see, I had to experiment, not that my life depended on it,
but as a corrective to taking the train to find out where it
    wanted to go.
Then when I did that anyway, I was not so much charmed as
    horrified
by the construction put upon it by even some quite close
    friends,
some of whom accused me of being the "leopard man" who
    had been terrorizing
the community by making howl-like sounds at night, out of
    earshot
of the dance floor. Others, recognizing my disinterest,
    nonetheless accused
me of playing mind-games that only the skilled
should ever attempt. My reply, then as always, was that
    ignorance
of the law, far from being no excuse, is the law, and we'll see
    who rakes in
the chips come Judgment Day.

Ashbery (1991: 123)

The avant-garde values of risk taking, process, and novelty are also
John Ashbery's stylistic values, and his array of experimental techniques
– mixed tones and dictions, grammatical and syntactic inconsistencies,
referential instability, mixed metaphors, discontinuous forms – belongs
to the repertoire of avant-garde verse. What makes for the difference
– and the *real* novelty – of Ashbery's poetry is that he registers the
changing cultural function of such techniques and increasingly acknowledges, after the early sixties, that experimental techniques and
values are in fact consistent with the values of the larger cultural economy. And he turns his lateness to oppositional models of avant-garde
writing to his advantage by calling such models into question even as
he deploys them. While he does not exactly reject the framework of
"old," culturally conservative versus "new," culturally oppositional
art, he destabilizes the binarism, exposes the metaphoric nature of the
connection between techniques and values, and skews its analogical
ratios. Thus he is at once an academic poet who does not locate value
in the past and an experimental poet who does not assign inherent
value – epistemological, political, or cultural – to discontinuous compositions. Within Ashbery's texts, the Battle of the Books goes on;
while both conserving a tradition and avant-garde experimentation are
past models, they remain useful for demystifying each other and
thereby bringing into focus Ashbery's new historical situation, when
the borders between literary and cultural texts blur.

In his essay "The Invisible Avant-Garde" (1968), Ashbery writes
that in 1950 the avant-garde was "very exciting" because "there was
no sure proof" of its existence; in 1968, however, "there is no longer
any doubt in anyone's mind" that the vanguard is "a" tradition (1989:
389–90). The sense of the risk and danger of experimenting, which in
1950 gave "the feeling that one was poised on some outermost brink,"
is gone. Now "it might be argued that traditional art is even riskier
than experimental art; that it can offer no very real assurances to its
acolytes, and since traditions are always going out of fashion it is more
dangerous and therefore more worthwhile than experimental art"
(391). If the tradition of the new demands that "we all have to be
first" and "the experimenting artist does something first, even though
it may be discarded later on," it turns out that, "paradoxically, it is

safest to experiment" (393). When experimental art is thus institutionalized and the collusion of aesthetic novelty with commodity production in general becomes clear, the possibility that aesthetic
innovation can signify cultural opposition diminishes. How, then, can
the artist achieve any distance at all from the cultural "text"?

"What then must the avant-garde artist do to remain avant-garde?"
Ashbery asks, and the issue is more than an academic question of stylistic choices and complacencies. "For it has by now become a question
of survival both of the artist and of the individual. In both art and life
today we are in danger of substituting one conformity for another. . . .
Protests against the mediocre values of our society such as the hippie
movement seem to imply that one's only way out is to join a parallel
society whose stereotyped manners, language, speech and dress are
only reverse images of the one it is trying to reject" (1989: 393). Since
in the late sixties political, cultural, and aesthetic opposition becomes
institutionalized as a "movement" of "a group, a clan," "the artist
who wants to experiment is again faced with what seems like a dead
end, except that instead of creating in a vacuum he is now at the center
of a cheering mob" (394). And Ashbery wonders, "Is there nothing
then between the extremes of Levittown and Haight-Ashbury, between an avant-garde which has become a tradition and a tradition
which is no longer one? In other words, has tradition finally managed
to absorb the individual talent?" (393). As Ashbery's essay makes clear,
he holds the traditional values of the survival of the individual within
the social "text" and of "the individual talent" within the texts of
various "traditions." And the two projects are closely linked.

To survive both as an individual and as an individual talent now,
Ashbery resists any "Rigid binary system of inducing truths / From
starved knowledge of them" (1975: 56), whether the binarism of the
"old" and "new" traditions or of the opposition of literary and cultural
discourses. His work acts as a kind of switchboard for these "archaic"
oppositions and reflects a condition that Fredric Jameson, for example,
elaborates in "The Cultural Logic of Late Capitalism." Jameson also
argues that the avant-garde is now part of the "official" culture of
Western society: "What has happened is that aesthetic production today has become integrated into commodity production generally: the

frantic economic urgency of producing fresh waves of ever more novel-seeming goods . . . now assigns an increasingly essential structural function and position to aesthetic innovation and experimentation" (1991: 4–5). Thus modernism's "passionate repudiation by an older Victorian and post-Victorian bourgeoisie for whom its forms and ethos are received as being variously ugly, dissonant, obscure, scandalous, immoral, subversive, and generally 'antisocial,' " finds no parallel in how the new arts are received after 1950: "A mutation in the sphere of culture has rendered such attitudes archaic" (4). This "mutation" has abolished "distance in general (including 'critical distance' in particular)": "The prodigious new expansion of multinational capital ends up penetrating and colonizing those very precapitalist enclaves (Nature and the Unconscious) which offered extraterritorial and Archimedean footholds for critical effectivity." All kinds of opposition "are all somehow secretly disarmed and reabsorbed by a system of which they themselves might well be considered a part, since they can achieve no distance from it" (48–49). Jameson is left waiting for a new "map," an "as yet unimaginable new mode of representing" and clarifying the position of individual and social subjects within "the world space of multinational capital" (54), from which we have as yet no distance.

Ashbery, too, acknowledges some "vast change that's taken place / In the fabric of our society, altering the texture / of all things in it" (1975: 42), and much of the "novelty" of his work comes from his engaging this "historically original" (Jameson 1991: x) situation from the archaic position of a "poet" and with the archaic models a poet has at his disposal, which include avant-garde experimenters as well as the Romantics Ashbery invokes at least as often. For from his perspective, they are not all that different; Wordsworthian Romanticism subscribes to a model of progressive history as much as the avant-garde, and both are anachronistic in the present that is cut off from the past and the future alike. Ashbery repeatedly tells us that we must "stay" in the as-yet-uncharted present, which is not simply phenomenological time but a historically specific, dehistoricized historical time. When the model of a future-affecting literary memory and a progressive, redemptive history – an essentially Christian model that holds from the Renaissance through modernism – becomes implicated in the cultural values of technological progress, not only the possibility of any distance from, or clear view of, current cultural arrangements but the position and function of novel forms and styles – indeed, of poetry itself – come into question. More than "strong" predecessors, the disappearance of an earlier, "strong" figuration of history as the arena where truth unfolds makes for Ashbery's difficulties and anxieties, for predecessors are not exactly relevant without a history that would place him in some purposeful relation to them.

In Ashbery's historically unprecedented situation, "Nature" and the "Unconscious" have indeed been appropriated and colonized, so that these earlier "footholds" are reduced to mere signifiers of what they once were – actual forces outside the system. As such, they offered perspectives on cultural arrangements and constructions and enabled not only political but moral and aesthetic distance from them. By contrast, here is Ashbery's new landscape:

> Yes, friends, these clouds pulled along on invisible ropes
> Are, as you have guessed, merely stage machinery,
> And the funny thing is it knows we know
> About it and still wants us to go on believing
> In what it so unskillfully imitates, and wants
> To be loved not for that but for itself:
> The murky atmosphere of a park, tattered
> Foliage, wise old treetrunks, rainbow tissue-paper wadded
> Clouds down near where the perspective
> Intersects the sunset, so we may know
> We too are somehow impossible, formed of so many different
>   things,
> Too many to make sense to anybody.
> We straggle on as quotients, hard-to-combine
> Ingredients, and what continues
> Does so with our participation and consent. (1977: 50)

As nature goes, so goes the subject, Ashbery seems to say: both exist as each other's terminus through Romanticism and modernism, and neither is what it was. Nature is not a prior reality but already a representational text, and the subject is not a form-giving imagination or an integral "Mind of Man" but a "quotient." Ashbery often laments an "otherness" that infiltrates and "changes everything" (1975: 81; 1979: 74), turning it into a "caricature" of itself (1975: 80), and this otherness or simulacrum effect is a problem not only of artistic representation but of the cultural reproduction of "everything" into its image. Any number of passages in Ashbery suggest that the notions of "mind" and "nature," axes that once plotted poetic worlds, no longer hold. Yet a sense of moral responsibility for "our participation and consent" remains. No infrastructure supports the subject, and no position exists from which to speak, yet the poet is accountable; this is just one of the anachronisms that give Ashbery's work its pathos.

Folded into this cultural "text" – itself a discontinuous pastiche – from which there is no exit, Ashbery assumes the passive stance of "waiting" – and "waiting for the wait to be ended" (1975: 14) – for a clearing, a "deliverance" outside the system. But his is a "history of someone who came too late" (7), not only in history but to history, and his fantasy of a revelation remains just that. In the terms of "As You Came from the Holy Land,"[1] where the revelation takes on a religious cast, "that thing of monstrous interest" can "never come about / not here not yesterday in the past / only in the gap of today filling itself / as emptiness is distributed" (7). In this poem that rewrites Raleigh's "Walsinghame," the "holy land" could be Ashbery's literary past or his personal history in "western New York state"; the "house" that is "built in tomorrow" could be poetic "stellification" or personal redemption, following the "examination" and the "census" taking. But neither place can offer a clearing, a perspective on today and its peculiar, dehistoricized history. Because Ashbery thoroughly interpolates himself and his personal history in poetic and cultural history, his recurrent apocalyptic gestures suggest that any revelation is as much to be dreaded as to be desired and shades into visions of death or even of the Bomb, a final end to the whole thing rather than a selective end to the darkness that swaddles him. Even a "small" personal clarity can easily snowball into a "big" clarity because, "like the friendly beginning of a geometrical progression" (1970: 18), it sets in motion the model of a teleological, purposeful, future-oriented time and progres-

sive history, whether Christian, Romantic, or technological – all vari-
ations on the same model. Thus Ashbery must let go of the foothold
of utopian thinking – of bigger and newer "maps" – as well.

For "This movie deals with the epidemic of the way we live now"
(1979: 109), and Ashbery presents his texts not as offering privileged
clarities – or privileged obscurities, for that matter – but, indeed, as
continuous with other "texts" outside the poem, and he often ends
poems by referring us to "other centers of communication, so that
understanding / May begin, and in doing so be undone" (1977: 46).
We keep shuttling between poetic and cultural texts, both intratex-
tually and intertextually, and only an apocalypse could put an end to
this circulation: "I wish God would put a stop to this" (52), as he says
in "Friends," for only God can. Thus, while Ashbery repeatedly gestures toward some revelation or another, he repeatedly backs off. We
seem always to be led to the brink of a revelation, only to be "rescued"
(1970: 17) at the last minute; luckily, darkness forever obscures our
vision. Just as Ashbery's speaker repeatedly returns to his historical
"darkness," we repeatedly return to the "darkness" of his text. Ashbery
does not appeal to a "god-like" imagination above the historical text,
the permanent "mirage" (1979: 79). His stylistic and syntactic strategies
duplicate this kind of movement that gets nowhere, leading us on –
in a clear and coherent sentence or passage – toward some "revelation"
but just so far, and at the last moment turning away and collapsing the
whole structure, with a non sequitur or a deflation, as "The balloon
pops" (1975: 70): "The singer thinks / Constructively, builds up his
chant in progressive stages / Like a skyscraper, but at the last minute
turns away. / The song is engulfed in an instant in blackness" (1977:
71). The "song," "Syringa" implies, is – like Eurydice – impossible
to possess whole, for which we are and are not thankful. Whether in
sentences, poems, or the experiences they represent, Ashbery resists
the clarity of "The locking into place [that] is 'death itself' " (1975:
76).

In Ashbery, "darkness" has many shades, ranging from the sacred
to the profane.[2] At the sacred end of the spectrum, "darkness" offers
the protection of an uncolonized, unmapped dark continent, where
the self can carry on its romance with itself and nature:

The night sheen takes over. A moon of cistercian pallor
Has climbed to the center of heaven, installed,
Finally involved with the business of darkness.
And a sigh heaves from all the small things on earth,
The books, the papers, the old garters and union-suit buttons
Kept in a white cardboard box somewhere, and all the lower
Versions of cities flattened under the equalizing night.
The summer demands and takes away too much,
But night, the reserved, the reticent, gives more than it takes.

(1975: 2)

But this darkness shades into the metaphysical "utter darkness" (1977: 34) that stands behind the light of reason, the epistemological darkness of "No Way of Knowing" (1975: 55) that backs common sense, and the profane and profound historical darkness that shadows the "light of common day." To speak in a public voice, to be a bearer (barer?) of news, or to prophesy in a dark time would be to join the conspiracy of light – of reason, common sense, and "reality" – and expose, co-opt, or destroy "a darkness of one's own" (1977: 61).

Thus what prevents us from seeing "that thing of monstrous interest . . . happening in the sky" (1975: 7) may be read in many ways. Ashbery's resistance to revelation may be psychological or it may indicate ontological, epistemological, linguistic, or political limits to vision. Politically, what precludes clarity may be an "alienation" so pervasive and so naturalized that it no longer registers as alienation. Ashbery's figure of an office tower at night, "A slab of business rising behind the stars" (1977: 13), is a devastating image of this historically specific condition, where nature is overpowered by culture. The "slab of business" – a marker of historical "darkness" – eclipses natural darkness, whether a "darkness of one's own" (61), the foothold of the subject, or a darkness of the "American sublime," the foothold of Nature or Fate. This new base marks and illuminates the grave of sublime Nature and the self alike. "Business" crops up everywhere in Ashbery, permeating everything from personal and sexual relations to poetry ("this leaving-out business" [1966: 39], "the business of darkness" [1975: 2], "Business Personals" [1977: 18], and so on).

Ashbery's allowing business to infiltrate *his* business makes for his impure language, which disclaims the poetic privilege of clarity and a higher vision. Thoroughly interweaving literary and cultural representations and economies, he declines moral superiority. Jameson recalls Marx's imperative to grasp "the demonstrably baleful features of capitalism along with its extraordinary and liberating dynamism simultaneously within a single thought" and suggests that we must think the "cultural evolution of late capitalism dialectically, as catastrophe and progress all together"; "the lapse from this austere dialectical imperative into the more comfortable stance of the taking of moral positions is inveterate and all too human," yet must be resisted (1991: 47). For Ashbery, to think of catastrophe and progress as one is not particularly difficult; moreover, this "austere dialectical imperative" does not sound too different from Keats's "negative capability" or Yeats's imperative to hold "in a single thought reality and justice" (Heaney 1990: 108) – two examples of "aesthetic ideology." In his own way, Ashbery heeds these injunctions; what we end up with, however, is not a "single" thought holding oppositions in a dialectical or an aesthetic moment, but a diffusion – a "dust," to use another of Ashbery's favorite figures. For any such single thought would be a version of the "Logos" and would not quite "suffice," which is "A pity." But then "no one has seen it recently," and "To this day no one knows the shape or heft of the thing, / and that's the honest truth thrown out of court" (1991: 33–34). For Ashbery, any such ideological or aesthetic resolutions would in effect claim a position "above" the terms of the problem, and the solutions it would offer would not be to the problem we began with. Thus, even as he acknowledges – or, more precisely, because he acknowledges – individual moral responsibility, he resists assuming either moral positions or elevated vantage points.

The architecture of Ashbery's "landscapes" highlights this fact. Towers, traditional figures of elevated poetic posts, abound in his work, but so do skyscrapers, and the two tend to blend into each other, different "slabs" of the same "business." A poet who would position himself in a "tower" above the fray and aim to map the terrain below or offer moral judgments becomes a species of businessman, however "correct" his politics. For example:

We have to worry
About systems and devices there is no
Energy here no spleen either
We have to take over the sewer plans –
Otherwise the coursing clear water, planes
Upon planes of it, will have its day
And disappear. Same goes for business:
Holed up in some office skyscraper it's
Often busy to predict the future for business plans
But try doing it from down
In the street and see how far it gets you! You
Really have to sequester yourself to see
How far you have come but I'm
Not going to talk about that. (1979: 64–65)

Anyone who would "sequester" himself above the "street" and worry about "systems" and "the future" participates in the same power politics of city planning and economic blueprints. Utopian visions, business plans, and poetic reforms are, "plane upon plane," versions of the same bid for power, and Pound may well be the cautionary example here. Anyone following a course that leads "upward through more / Powerful forms of poetry, past columns / With peeling posters on them, to the country of indifference" would be implicated in the politics of power and would need to be reminded that "the little people are nonetheless real" (1977: 7). In fact, Ashbery's recurrent images of "dwarfs," "midgets," and doll-size people point up his concern for the diminution of the individual, given the deep collusion of any number of power-hungry agendas.

And poets enjoy no special moral dispensation. All structures are erected at an expense, and all substitutive representations exact the cost of repression. Ashbery's historical distance from someone like Pound, who aspires to the role of "legislator," is clear enough, but he is just as far from someone like W. H. Auden, who himself disavows such a Romantic and modernist ambition when he writes, "poetry makes nothing happen: it survives / In the valley of its saying where executives / Would never want to tamper" (1979: 82). Ashbery's cityscapes often recall Auden's; "These Lacustrine Cities" (1966: 9), for example, has the Freudian look of "September 1, 1939":

> These lacustrine cities grew out of loathing
> Into something forgetful, although angry with history.
> They are the product of an idea: that man is horrible, for
>   instance,
> Though this is only one example.
>
> They emerged until a tower
> Controlled the sky, and with artifice dipped back
> Into the past for swans and tapering branches,
> Burning, until all that hate was transformed into useless love.

Yet Ashbery's poet only duplicates such building:

> You have built a mountain of something,
> Thoughtfully pouring all your energy into this single
>   monument,
> Whose wind is desire starching a petal,
> Whose disappointment broke into a rainbow of tears.

By contrast, Auden "in one of the dives / On Fifty-Second Street" (1979: 86) claims a politically powerless and therefore morally superior vantage point on "a low dishonest decade" when "blind skyscrapers use / Their full height to proclaim / The strength of Collective Man" (87). Auden never clearly implicates his own rhetoric in what "Important Persons shout." One way to resist this economy from within would be to question the notion of "a voice / To undo the folded lie" – "the lie of Authority / Whose buildings grope the sky" (88). For such rhetoric, which exempts the univocal, "individual" voice and its truth, is itself "folded" in the "lie." When one wakes from this "dream," with "one's mouth full / Of unknown words" (1975: 55), we get Ashbery.

His "Decoy" (1970: 31) provides a model of a voice riddled with cultural (political) static. The rhetoric of self-evident truths, as in the "Declaration of Independence" – "We hold these truths to be self-evident" – is a decoy for agendas of exclusion ("ostracism") and control: "the perpetrators, / The men who sit down to their vast desks on Monday to begin planning the week's notations, jotting memoranda that take / Invisible form in the air, like flocks of sparrows / Above the city pavements, turning and wheeling aimlessly / But on the average directed by discernible motives. // To sum up: We are fond of plotting itineraries." So far, so good, but there's more: "And our pyramiding memories, alert as dandelion fuzz, dart from one pretext to the next / Seeking in occasions new sources of memories, for memory is profit." By now, who can tell the forward-looking "corporate vandals" from the backward-glancing poets?

Small wonder, then, that Ashbery can figure a poetic structure as a "skyscraper" (1977: 71). Auden's obscene, "blind skyscrapers," flashing "Imperialism's face / And the international wrong" (1979: 87), are easily incorporated into Ashbery's "pornographic masterpiece, / Variegated, polluted skyscraper to which all gazes are drawn, / Pleasure we cannot and will not escape" (1984: 17). Like the "many-colored tower of longing" that rises on "the earth" and needs "many ads (to help pay for all this)" (1977: 22), "*this* pornographic masterpiece" (emphasis added) is a monument to both a consumer economy and a poetic economy, the poet's "human haul": the "whole panoply of the past: / Landscape embroidery, complete sets of this and that" (1984: 17). Ashbery asks, "What need for purists when the demotic is built to last, / To outlast us, and no dialect hears us" – when there is no outside "wherever," where "the Just / Exchange their messages" (Auden 1979: 89). Ashbery's voice rings true in its recognition that it, too, is "folded" in the "lie." Of course, Auden also comes to the painful recognition that an author offering a political or moral "truth" that would expose the "lie of Authority" only duplicates it; "the whole poem, I realised," he writes in 1964, "was infected with an incurable dishonesty and must be scrapped" (Mendelson 1981: 326).

Yet even poetry that does not aspire to a higher vision falls within the system:

> . . . *it towers far above life, like some magnificent*
> *Cathedral spire, far above the life*
> *Pullulating around it (what*

Does it care for that, after all?) and not
Even aiming at the heavens far above it
Yet seemingly nearer, just because so
Vague and pointless (1979: 37)

All poetry – whether directed by clear "aims" or seemingly "pointless" – enters this economy when it is marketed as "poetry"; it is culturally "elevated," towering "far above life," and even approaches transcendental authority, nearing "the heavens far above it." Thus Ashbery's disavowing moral judgments also entails resisting claims of a special moral or political virtue for his technical fractures of a coherent "voice," his polyvocality. Claiming that stylistic and syntactic subversions of authoritative, stable discourse enable a truer, "freer" vision, cleared of obscuring conventions, is as suspect as privileging the clarity of rational and grammatical control. Writing about the Surrealists, Ashbery points out that "*Liberté totale* in Paris in the 1920s turned out to be something less than total. . . . In literature it meant automatic writing, but what is so free about that? Real freedom would be to use this method where it could be of service and to correct it with the conscious mind where indicated" (1989: 5–6). He repeats this point in relation to his own practice; his poetry "probably starts out" in the subconscious mind, he offers, but is "monitored" by the conscious mind "on its way out," so that it reflects the "whole mind, which is partly logical and reasonable" (1983: 51). Ashbery accommodates both the unconscious and conscious minds, nonrational and rational discourse, but privileges neither. In general, he tends to pit different compositional paradigms against each other and lets each correct the "error" of the other, forestalling any consistency – whether of rational or nonrational procedures – that could be mistaken for "truth."

If the unconscious has no monopoly on truth, neither does nature. Unlike organicist experimenters like Pound and Olson, Ashbery does not challenge conventional forms in order to access natural truths. For Ashbery, any form may be used as long as it is estranged from itself; one may use either open or canonical forms, but always against the grain by appealing not to the truth each may claim to offer but to its possibilities for error. Thus he employs elaborate traditional forms like pantoums or sestinas, with their "really bizarre requirements," not for control but to encourage a new kind of baroque automatism (1974: 124), and he deploys experimental, discontinuous forms not for greater verisimilitude to process but to achieve the greater antinaturalism of mannerism. "Multiple corrections" (1970: 53) mark Ashbery's way as he cuts against the rhetoric inscribed in any given form (canonical or free) or stylistic norm (rational or nonrational composition).

Because Ashbery resists claiming oppositional efficacy for his experiments, he achieves a certain distance from the "fray" after all. By contrast, a self-righteous experimentalism, claiming superior clarities and greater epistemological value, ironically consigns itself – like today's Language poetry – to academic, aestheticist word games at best; at worst, its opposition can turn into a most insidious complicity. Again, the history of the Surrealists tells a cautionary tale. "The Communist adventure itself is one of Surrealism's unlikeliest non sequiturs," Ashbery writes. "The idea that total liberty could somehow coexist with Stalinism is a truly Surrealist notion, but if one accepts it from this point of view one must go on to excuse the inconsequential behavior of munitions barons and concierges as part of the surreal demiurge. The Communists understood this very well and washed their hands of the whole disreputable bunch" (1989: 6).

An entire poem in *As We Know* reads, "The Cathedral Is // Slated for demolition" (1979: 93), and gives a thumbnail history of modern experimentalism. The title erects an emblem of moral and metaphysical closure, and the poem that proceeds to forecast the structure's demolition is entitled by reference to its authority. And "Slated" suggests that the cathedral will fall to the agenda of another totalizing power, which has other plans. Between the entitlement and the demolition falls the shadow of another institution, another power structure. If a cathedral and whatever will replace it – an office building? a civic center? a ministry? – both belong in one continuous history of transferring power, and if poetic "towers" and skyscrapers converge in the "vistas" they both command, the deep collusion of such humanist discursive structures as teleological development and progressive history with hell-bent technology must be recognized and resisted, as best one can. And Ashbery does what he can by consistently undermining teleological models of composition and purposeful development, without ever claiming a superior clarity for his obscurities and thereby reinstituting the values he would resist.

I

So going around cities
To get to other places you found
It all on paper but the land
Was made of paper processed
To look like ferns, mud or other
                    (Ashbery 1966: 10)

I want to begin Ashbery's "late history" with "The Instruction Manual," his most "readerly" poem. Its very readability – a performance not to be repeated – is part of the specific, "archaic" aesthetic model that the poem reenacts and parodies. This "pleasant" model, which observes sequential development, positions the imagination as a force antithetical to "our technological society." This is a Romantic-modernist figuration of imagination and reality as opposites to be "reconciled" in the narrative of the poem, which represents imaginary activity as an escape to spaces exempt from the pressures of reality. In a different register, the entire poem with its internal opposition of reality and imagination, where these terms have distinct referents, itself is an escape from the pressures that face the post-Romantic and postmodern poet, for whom such reassuringly clear oppositions are no longer available. This readable and "pleasant" poem sounds naive because quotidian and imaginary experience remain distinct; it does not seem to register how the imagination has already been colonized by the economic sphere as a "leisure" activity made possible and defined by worklife – a "holiday" written into the calendar.

This figuration of the imaginary also connects it to the Third World, which at this very moment is being colonized by the powers commissioning the writers of instruction manuals on the "uses" of "new" metals. Progress and utilitarian values define the technical writer's "real" world, and this world makes room for a separate, imaginary space as an escape. The co-opted writer can let off steam by dreaming about places he has not seen but certainly can visit as a tourist, if he keeps at the money-making instruction manual. (Although Ashbery never worked as a technical writer, for a long time he made his living working under deadlines as an art critic, which he says he did for the money and not out of any special interest [1983: 34].) The imaginary space that allows for the "freedom" to dream of exotic places is pre-scribed by the economic system that has colonized both the imaginary realm and its cognate, the Third World.

Ironically, this dreamed-of place is exotic precisely because it has a centered, hierarchical social order clearly reflected in the plan of the city. In this city, everything has its place and holds a clear relation to its surroundings:

> . . . we must catch a view of the city, before we leave, from a
>   good high place.
> That church tower will do . . .
> The caretaker, an old man dressed in brown and gray, asks us
>   how long we have been in the city, and how we like it
>   here.
> His daughter is scrubbing the steps – she nods to us as we pass
>   into the tower.
> Soon we have reached the top, and the whole network of the
>   city extends before us.
> There is the rich quarter, with its houses of pink and white,
>   and its crumbling, leafy terraces.
> There is the poorer quarter, its homes a deep blue.
> There is the market, where men are selling hats and swatting
>   flies
> And there is the public library, painted several shades of pale
>   green and beige.
> Look! There is the square we just came from . . . (1956: 29)

The model of a poetic composition in which details are organized around a thematic center and "add up" to yield a "whole" recurs in the pictorial composition of "Guadalajara" organized around a church tower, and both compositional orders correlate with the sociopolitical organization of a hierarchical society. These systems authorize each other; such a sociopolitical system, for example, would legitimate such poetic and aesthetic models, and vice versa. Thus this kind of poem, with referential stability and consistency, is the analog of the metaphysically grounded, sociopolitically stable society it envisions.

Ashbery's Guadalajara presents a version of an "aesthetic society," modeled on poetic composition, with a "graceful but confined freedom" (de Man 1984: 289) – the kind of society Pound imagined, for example, as Confucian China. The represented city aesthetically reconciles the irreconcilables of the technical writer's imagination and his quotidian worklife in "our technological society." Ashbery's titling the poem "The Instruction Manual" identifies the poem and the technical writer's manual; "This manual" (l. 5) may refer to either. Indeed, the fact that the poet holds the "higher" position of "instructor" over his reader hints at the pedagogic use – to "instruct" as well as delight – served by this particular aesthetic model, which roughly observes Horace's requirements of unity and consistency. The figure of the poet as both formal technician and dreamer, instructing and delighting, aesthetically "articulates" or connects his two lives – the quotidian and the imaginary. Ashbery emphasizes his distance from the paradigm he invokes, however, by exposing the economic "articulation" that undergirds the aesthetic connection. And the "naive" tone of the poem casts this economically and historically specific model of the relation between the real and the imaginary as somewhat "quaint."

The poem may parody either Romantic voyages like Baudelaire's or modernist nostalgic returns to societies ordered on archaic preindustrial models, granting the poet aerial perspectives. The domesticated voyages of fifties tourist poetry may also be Ashbery's target here. For the entire history of poetic escapes from "our technological society" comes into play in this poem, which also reads as a manual on how to write such poems by reciting their conventions and clichés: "condescension" to the "other" ("I look down"); a romantic seeker with no "inner peace," hounded by time or deadlines in this case ("I fancy I see, under the press of having to write the instruction manual" [1956: 26]); the choice of "representative" detail ("How limited, but

how complete withal, has been our experience of Guadalajara!" [29]);
and closure, achieved by a return to "ordinary time" ("We have seen
young love, married love, and the love of an aged mother for her
son. / We have heard the music, tasted the drinks, and looked at colored houses. / What more is there to do, except stay? And that we
cannot do" [30]). "We" are already bored by this point, having used
up what the scene offers, and ready to move onward.

While the surface opposition of boring work and escapist dreaming
reaffirms the "bourgeois" notion of art as a leisure activity as opposed
to the productive labor that enables it, Ashbery plays the banal quotidian and the exotic fantasy on the same tonal register, leveling the
Romantic hierarchy of dream over reality and signaling his lateness to
clear-cut boundaries between subjective and objective lives. To Ashbery, a poetic model built on clear distinctions between the subjective
and the objective has become as incredible as the archaic social orders
imagined still holding in Guadalajara. Both the technical writer looking "down" on the street from his skyscraper and the dreamer sur-
veying Guadalajara from the church tower are versions of the same
powerful, humanist figuration of the subject, here ironized and disarmed by the naive perspective of the poem's simplifying language and
almost Bishopian tone.

A much later poem, "Landscape," returns to this oppositional
model and presents a sequestered imaginary space, an attic – still elevated, if not exactly a tower – with a view of factory chimneys and
steeples. And what the Third World offers in "The Instruction Manual," the power of the poetic imagination supplies in "Landscape": a
"dream of gardens, of bluish horizons, / Of jets of water weeping in
alabaster basins, / Of kisses, of birds singing at dawn and at nightfall, /
Of all that's most childish in our pastoral" (1984: 7). Ashbery's choosing to translate Baudelaire's "Paysage" is telling. The poem's "exotic"
landscape suggests that this model of poetic power historically belongs
to "the first phase of capital," as some would say, with its skylines of
factory chimneys. If this landscape is "archaic," so are the compensat-
ing imagination and the rhymed couplets that shape its product. To
cast Baudelaire's early-modern city as exotic gives us some sort of hazy
perspective on what has changed after all. Here translation preserves

the pastness of the past, rather than making it present again; with the past on the screen, we can see where we are – or, more accurately, where we aren't. For in Ashbery's glassy-eyed postindustrial city, nothing so concrete as factories meets the eye.

One mark of the "mutation" that has taken place between Baudelaire and Ashbery is that "the clarity of the rules" has "dawned" on us: "*They* were the players" and we "merely spectators" (1970: 18). "They" are the "unacknowledged legislators of the world" (Shelley 1967: 1087), and any given model of poetic speaking and power plays all too easily into "their" game. The poet of "Landscape" – holed up in his attic, dreaming of gardens and pastoral landscapes, and giddy with "the thrill / Of conjuring spring with the force of my will" (1984: 7) – exercises the power of the imagination to compensate for his cultural powerlessness. Yet the supposedly powerless, sequestered, and isolated Romantic imagination actually assumes its culturally assigned function: acting for "someone else's benefit" (1970: 17), it does the ideological dirty work of reconciling reality and imagination, object and subject.

Ashbery positions the poet quite differently. His civilization, too, has decided to "sequester" him, to remove him elsewhere: "Much of your time has been occupied by creative games / Until now, but we have all-inclusive plans for you. / We had thought, for instance, of sending you to the middle of the desert, // To a violent sea" (1966: 9). But, he realizes, his position as a "professional exile" (57) in fact places him comfortably at home and at the center of the larger economy:

> In reality of course the middle-class apartment I live in is
>   nothing like a desert island.
> Cozy and warm it is, with a good library and record
>   collection.
> Yet I feel cut off from the life in the streets.
> Automobiles and trucks plow by, spattering me with filthy
>   slush. (56)

Ashbery's refusal to believe that the poet is in any way "removed" from the cultural matrix, his insistence on demystifying the Romantic model of the artist who pays the price of "alienation" for his "superior" vision, and his recognition that myths of marginality paper over the artist's complicity with the system all add up to a small measure of clarity in the end. That is about as much as we can hope for when the poet is firmly planted within "our technological society"; such, indeed, is the "epidemic of the way we live now."

II

> you too are a rebus from another century . . .
>   (Ashbery 1977: 87)

The changing models and cultural role of individual experience – and, therefore, of a poetry that considers itself "romantic" (1974: 129) – preoccupy Ashbery early and late. Personal experience ("the glad personal quality / Of the things beneath the sky" [1977: 69]), a private vision ("I know that I braid too much my own / Snapped-off perceptions of things as they come to me. / They are private and always will be" [1975: 44]), and moral responsibility ("the exact value of what you did and said, which remains" [1970: 54]) are not moot points for him. His personal poetry has little interest in self-revelation, veiled or otherwise; rather, his work investigates the rhetorical questions of how to figure a self and communicate a private vision:

> Stellification
> Is for the few, and comes about much later
> When all record of these people and their lives
> Has disappeared into libraries, onto microfilm.
> A few are still interested in them. "But what about
> So-and-so?" is still asked on occasion. But they lie
> Frozen and out of touch until an arbitrary chorus
> Speaks of a totally different incident with a similar name
> In whose tale are hidden syllables
> Of what happened so long before that
> In some small town, one indifferent summer. (1977: 71)

If all goes well, writers miswrite and readers misread, but they meet after all in the "indifferent summer" they come to share. For Ashbery, it is the generic "personal" that matters and continues to matter, as he questions the conditions for the very possibility of personal poetry. On what grounds can experience still be figured as personal? And if the whole idea is "archaic," what is the point of writing "poetry"?

If individual experience remains at the heart of Ashbery's enterprise, it has not remained unchanged "like a gray stone toga as the whole wheel / Of recorded history flashes past" (1977: 69). "Definition of Blue" (1970: 53) sketches the recent history of the subject: "The rise of capitalism parallels the advance of romanticism / And the individual is dominant until the close of the nineteenth century." As Ashbery's programmatic tone suggests, this fact is of more sociological than po- etic interest. "In our own time, mass practices have sought to submerge the personality / By ignoring it, which has caused it instead to branch out in all directions / Far from the permanent tug that used to be its notion of 'home.' " These branchings or "different impetuses" are themselves included in the new script of "our own time" and do not offer any distance from "mass practices": "There is no remedy for this 'packaging' which has supplanted the old sensations" and "there is no point in looking to imaginative new methods / Since all of them are in constant use." While neither the Romantic model of a homed-in, centered individual nor the branched-out, decentered posthumanist person offers "footholds," they have their uses: "The most that can be said for them further / Is that erosion produces a kind of dust or ex- aggerated pumice / Which fills space and transforms it, becoming a medium / In which it is possible to recognize oneself." The "dust" produced by the historical erosion and the cultural demolition of the "person" makes for a kind of dark mirror and the possibility of self- recognition "now." In any case, the old and the new models of the "individual" are lines in the script the poet is handed; the tradition and the tradition of the new only offer different "packaging."

In a sense, Ashbery's poetry sounds an extended lament for the humanist figuration of the poet, whose exemplary "central" position rests precisely on his or her experiences and feelings. Of course, this figuration relies on a centered model of cultural experience, which rhetorically intercedes between the private and the public and enables the poet to speak at once personally and representatively. Yet Ashbery does not resist but, in fact, facilitates the erosion of this model. Indeed, if the personal can be *recognized* only as intertextual, overdetermined, and appropriated, then by some strange logic his "inconsequential" experience becomes by definition representative again. If no space remains outside the cultural "text," Ashbery must speak from within it, and his poems accurately transcribe what the individual sounds like now. If, in his new landscape, the poetic imagination and the culture thoroughly contaminate each other, the borders blur between fantasy and reality, past and present, imagination and "our technological society." In this fix, a "strong" Romantic imagination and a "powerful," unifying role for poetry no longer pertain. And the language the poet speaks speaks against him; it is the language of the Other, the discourse of the colonized.

"The One Thing That Can Save America" (1975: 44–45) likewise addresses the poet's difficulty today. Promising a solution or salvation that never arrives, Ashbery's title borrows the voice of a humanist poet, an unacknowledged "legislator" bent on improving our lives. The poem, however, proceeds to question central speakers, superior vantage points, and singular solutions; "Is anything central?" it begins, and we already know the answer. Without the myth of centered cultural experience, however, how can the poet speak? Even the Romantic poet, speaking against the public and for his private vision, is authorized by his culture to play the part of a symbolic center as compensation for his actual marginalization and loss of power. But Ashbery's doubly dispossessed poet relinquishes myths both of speaking centrally and of marginality, which is another kind of foothold. If Ashbery knows the speaker is overdetermined, however, he also knows "the juice is elsewhere" – in personal moods, emotions, and experiences. But without the "archaic" ideological and compositional models of self, poet, and poem, how can his experiences – "They are private and always will be" – command a public audience or say anything to anyone else?

> Where then are the private turns of event
> Destined to boom later like golden chimes
> Released over a city from a highest tower?
> The quirky things that happen to me, and I tell you,

And you instantly know what I mean?
What remote orchard reached by winding roads
Hides them? Where are these roots?

These questions sound archaic because they are phrased as quests in a landscape of "remote orchards" and medieval cities with central "towers." The final, Eliotic question reveals the gap between the poet, with his "version of America," and the models of poetic speaking available to him. Lacking an aerial perspective, he cannot even imagine a "salvation." Plus, to trade in commodities like "The One Thing That Can Save America" is to be a politician – part of the problem rather than the solution. Hence there is nothing to do but wait:

All the rest is waiting
For a letter that never arrives,
Day after day, the exasperation
Until finally you have ripped it open not knowing what it is,
The two envelope halves lying on a plate.
The message was wise, and seemingly
Dictated a long time ago.
Its truth is timeless, but its time has still
Not arrived, telling of danger, and the mostly limited
Steps that can be taken against danger
Now and in the future, in cool yards,
In quiet small houses in the country,
Our country, in fenced areas, in cool shady streets.

This passage weaves together a complicated series of anachronisms and suggests that wise, timeless messages – both too late and too early – tell what will save not "our" America, with "Orchards flung out on the land / Urban forests," "place names" "Beating themselves into eyes which have had enough / Thank you, no more thank you," but an already lost America of "quiet small houses" and "cool shady streets." This rural America exists only in memory, both personal and collective, for modernization has changed all utterly, wiping out community and nature alike. As "Pyrography" tells it, "In the cities at the turn of the century they knew about it / But were careful not to let on as the iceman and the milkman / Disappeared down the block . . . / The climate was still floral and all the wallpaper / In a million homes all over the land conspired to hide it" (1977: 9). In "The One Thing," the "steps that can be taken" are out of synch with today's thoroughly acculturated "landscape"; they are as archaic as visions of a public role for the poet.

Since past works of art and poetry still enjoy the "footholds" of "Nature" and "Imagination," they are both attractive and irrelevant. "Why can't everything be simple again?" Ashbery asks in "Business Personals" (1977: 18–20): "Could one return / To the idea of nature summed up in these pastoral images?"

> Yet the present has done its work of building
> A rampart against the past, not a rampart,
> A barbed-wire fence. So now we know
> What occupations to stick to (scrimshaw, spinning tall tales)

Cut off from the past, the poet's "occupation" shrinks to "craft" or "fancy"; he can neither address current cultural matters nor tell his personal history, without making use of how others in the "business" told their stories. Yet that is no cause for alarm, for one can't really escape the past anyway, though it is hardly relevant: "Floating heart, why / Wander on senselessly? The tall guardians / Of yesterday are steep as cliff shadows; / Whatever path you take abounds in their sense." Ashbery's speaker is alienated from, yet sepulchered in, this very past: "How to get out? / This giant will never let us out unless we blind him. // And that's how, one day, I got home." Even fantasies of getting "out" are scripted by past odysseys. The past may be no help, but Ashbery keeps rehearsing it: "So I cradle this average violin that knows / Only forgotten showtunes, but argues / The possibility of free declamation anchored / To a dull refrain, the year turning over on itself" (1). Natural law has come down to "a dull refrain," the burden of the "showtunes," for nature exists only in past texts; Keats's "poetry of earth" has, in fact, died. And taken the poet with it: "You are wearing a text. The lines / Droop to your shoelaces and I shall never want or need / Any other literature than this poetry of mud / And ambitious reminiscences of times when it came easily / Through the then woods and ploughed fields and had / A simple unconscious dignity we can never hope to / Approximate now except in narrow ravines nobody / Will inspect" (21).

Since nature has now been acculturated and the imagination packaged, the poetic past is only a nostalgic preserve, but its very irrelevance offers Ashbery a purchase on the present. Patching together fragments of the past, Ashbery's present is an anachronism; but such asynchrony offers an immanent perspective and allows him to make do without morally superior vantage points. His allusiveness, so wide-ranging and pervasive as to render his poetry as academic as it is innovative, serves this purpose. He aims not so much at "safekeeping" the tradition (1977: 34) – he always maintains a parodic dissonance between his sources and how he uses them – as at a pastiche that both invokes the past and renders it irrelevant, so that the historical novelty of his situation may be perceivable. In "Purists Will Object," Ashbery asks: "What need for purists when the demotic is built to last, / To outlast us, and no dialect hears us?" (1984: 17). But *we* still hear the "purer" dialects; these lines, for example, articulate the very dilemma of a "historically original" condition by alluding to Mallarmé's and Eliot's notions of purifying the language of the "tribe."

Ashbery characteristically invokes the literary past to orient himself in the present and to signal its historically unprecedented nature. The landscape of "Daffy Duck in Hollywood," say, is "new," yet Ashbery can approach its novelty only via the history of his medium, which makes his speaker an anachronistic crux always speaking in some sense against himself, his present, his presence. For "While I / Abroad through all the coasts of dark destruction seek / Deliverance for us all, think in that language: its / Grammar, though tortured, offers pavilions / At each new parting of the ways" (1977: 33). Although he speaks the language of the past – with a Pop Hollywood spin, in this case – and although "Everything / Depends on whether somebody reminds you of me" (32), any real continuity is ruled out: " 'It's all bits and pieces, spangles, patches, really; nothing / Stands alone. What happened to creative evolution?' " (33). Everything is in fragments, yet nothing stands alone; neither pure discontinuity nor a Bergsonian *durée* applies. Unlike the modernists, Ashbery does not use allusions to reestablish continuity and "resuscitate the dead art / Of poetry," in Pound's words (1990: 185). Ashbery's allusions only make for a historical dissonance, a break from the prison of the present.

If the literary past can be deployed to break the hold of the historical present, and if the present is allowed to render the past irrelevant, a personal space might be imagined and represented in the interstices of the past and the present, the literary and the cultural. Ashbery figures the self in and as the disjunction between past paradigms of the central, humanist subject and the city's "gibbous" eye – the postmodern present in the "logarithm" of all other cities. In reflecting his subject in the convex mirrors of both a humanist painter's self-portrait and a cartoon character's "mug's attenuated / Reflection in yon hubcap" (1977: 31), Ashbery raises the possibility that two wrongs might make a right – that, "Although the arithmetic is incorrect," the "balance" may be "restored," and "the man who made the same mistake twice is exonerated" (1975: 11). A central "major man," the author of his "life englobed" (69), and a dimensionless cipher, prescripted and trapped in plans laid for him by some "mean old cartoonist" (1977: 31), are equally alien models of the subject; if each is allowed to contaminate the other, however, we get a sense of how it feels to live "now," somewhere between the past that exists only in "cold pockets / Of remembrance" (1975: 83) and the equally alien "Civilized Lethe" (1977: 32) of the city.

In Ashbery's terms, keeping the "meaningfulness" offered by past paradigms of meaning and the "randomness" of the "urban forest" up to the "pace" of each other (1974: 121) may point up the asynchrony of what passes for "now" – both the personal and the historical present. The poetic past – from "what Wyatt and Surrey left around" (1975: 19) to the Romantics and the moderns – is in "error," since it is the humanist project that has landed us in the impossible city. But the city is also in "error," for the "person," whether individual or generic, does not compute in its program. And this person – to whom something "happened" (1977: 71) on "a summer's day" (34) "so long ago" (1970: 19) and who is marked for a "small, other way of living" (1991: 145) – refuses to be canceled or deleted. Resisting both the strong meaning of the humanist past and the weak meaninglessness of

the posthumanist city makes for the strong meaninglessness of Ashbery's poetry.

Thus the past offers, ironically, the only "foothold" in the unprecedented present; there is no other way to recognize the present than
in the distorting glass of the past. The absolute novelty of the present
renders it absolutely dependent on the past, which is doubly wrong –
in error and inappropriate – because it got us here in the first place
and landed us in a "now" with no relation to "then." The past can
teach us nothing, yet we can know nothing without it. Such is the
state of affairs when a strong figuration of history no longer persuades
and a useless memory confronts an unrecognizable present. Once the
progressive model of change is played out, the continuity of personal,
cultural ("Pyrography," "Decoy"), and literary history alike disappears.

Yet "Self-Portrait in a Convex Mirror" makes it clear that Ashbery's work takes on cultural significance only when read against the
past. Here he invokes a past example of Mannerist self-portraiture to
instruct us to read his revisions of the humanist tradition and canonical
norms "correctly" – that is, not as idiosyncratic but as culturally and
historically necessary. He means to "surprise" us with his novelties in
the same way that Parmigianino achieves his surprising effects, "bi-
zarria" oriented by "The consonance of the High Renaissance" they
disorient (1975: 74). Ashbery's poem, then, directs us to read him
academically, within an established tradition, and it is not hard to see
why this poem, which inserts his practice into a canonical history,
secured his canonization. The poem's blank verse norm and its med-
itative rhythms formally gesture toward the Romantic tradition. And
to interpret this gesture, we might recall Ashbery's disarming comment
on blank verse: "I have felt very uncomfortable with iambic pentameter ever since I discovered, when I first began writing poetry, that it
was not impossible to write acceptable blank verse. It somehow seems
to falsify poetry for me. It has an order of its own that is foreign to
nature" (1983: 53–54). Writing about time, art, and "the enchantment
of self with self" (1975: 72) quite naturally requires "unnatural" blank
verse, the manner traditionally associated with such humanist matters.
Ashbery's citing prior authorities – Vasari, Freedberg, and so on – is
also an academic device meant, again, to align his poem with an es-

tablished discursive framework. After all, he begins his portrait with "As" – as a reflection on and off a prior "text" – and reinstitutes the model that he reads and that reads him. Wonderful though its meditations on the problematics of self-representation are, "Self-Portrait" matters more for its explicit bid for a place in the central humanist tradition. Like Wordsworth and Eliot, Ashbery asks us to read his distortions and deviations as historically necessary revisions of tradition.

As I have argued, "the clarity of the rules" that dawns on Ashbery as early as *The Double Dream of Spring* is that all avant-garde opposition is already co-opted, and he opts not for any "offensive" strangeness, where "the message . . . seems to be merely aggression" (1983: 36), or a defensive shoring up. Instead, he prefers "fence-sitting," questioning various options "in an orderly way that means to menace / Nobody" (1975: 76). Indeed, in "Self-Portrait" he chooses to invoke – and question – the progressive model of tradition as a constantly reinvigorated center, a record of the constant changes of what does not change. "A breeze like the turning of a page," Ashbery writes, "Brings back your face"; an inspiriting breeze like Wordsworth's brings back Parmigianino. Ashbery's breezes only turn "pages." The authority of a poet who begins to draw his self-portrait "As Parmigianino did it" lies not so much in "Nature" or "Imagination" as in past figurations of these powers; as Ashbery elaborates:

> it is certain that
> What is beautiful seems so only in relation to a specific
> Life, experienced or not, channeled into some form
> Steeped in the nostalgia of a collective past.
> The light sinks today with an enthusiasm
> I have known elsewhere, and known why
> It seemed meaningful, that others felt this way
> Years ago. I go on consulting
> This mirror that is no longer mine
> For as much brisk vacancy as is to be
> My portion this time. (77)

Thus Ashbery depends on the past with little faith that it has anything to say to us. The portrait "has no secret," its "soul is not a soul," its eyes are "empty," and its techniques are archaic ("Secrets of wash and finish that took a lifetime / To learn" [1975: 79]; "Turns out you didn't need all that training / To do art" [48]). Irrelevant as it is, the past remains the only mirror in which the poet can see himself – though, naturally, as an "other." The otherness that pervades Ashbery's self-representations derives as much from the present straits of the poet as from generic falsifications or misrepresentations. Generic representational distortions are his vehicle; his tenor is the subject's radical alienation, the unprecedented cultural preemption of the personal that makes him perceive himself as an "other" in the absence of relevant models. When the past is dismissed, however, the present freezes in "cold pockets." "You can't live there" (79) applies equally to "today" and the "museum." For the sequestered, ahistorical space of "today" is also something of a museum. Only the historical difference or the "distance between" the past and the present offers a "straight way out" – of both the enclosed museum of the past and the historical solipsism of the present, the "bubble chamber" "where everything gets programmed."

Ashbery presents, in all its complexity and pathos, the poet's dependency on the "second-hand knowledge" of a past that is no longer his: "Once it seemed so perfect. . . . This could have been our paradise: exotic / Refuge within an exhausted world, but that wasn't / In the cards":

> And we have really
> No time for these, except to use them
> For kindling. The sooner they are burnt up
> The better for the roles we have to play.
> Therefore I beseech you, withdraw that hand,
> Offer it no longer as shield or greeting,
> The shield of a greeting, Francesco:
> There is room for one bullet in the chamber:
> Our looking through the wrong end
> Of the telescope as you fall back at a speed
> Faster than that of light to flatten ultimately
> Among the features of the room . . . (1975: 82)

"Our looking through the wrong end / Of the telescope" flattens Parmigianino against the wall, and this passage is usually read as Ashbery's final dismissal of the past. But it is Parmigianino who is looking through the "right," or shooting, end of the telescope. Since he exists not in his room but in the room of our attention ("its room, our moment of attention" [69]), and since the poet's room is measured by his attention to Parmigianino, there is only one room. The "chamber" of their meeting is actually something of a "long" sepulchral "corridor" (78), the passage of their passing each other, and "one bullet" will hit both. The past will not reduce to "it was all a dream"; "Its existence / Was real," compared to the "waking dream" in "the gibbous / Mirrored eye of an insect." And if Parmigianino's portrait – "The diagram still sketched on the wind" – enables this vision of the city, it grants a perspective on the "urgency" of the present after all. Neither the painting's "life englobed" nor the "carousel" of the present "going faster and faster" until "no part / Remains that is surely you" alone offers distance; while "the chaos / Of your round mirror . . . organizes everything," the carousel reduces all to "one neutral band that surrounds / Me on all sides," boiling all "down to one / Uniform substance." The past and the present each need the other's prison to exit its own. The distance between them, the history that connects and severs Ashbery's city and the sixteenth century, grants each its random meaning. There is neither timeless Art nor authentic historical presence; each exists at the other's expense, with "room for one bullet in the chamber." And the relation between the personal past and present only duplicates the relation between the cultural past and present; the severence is systemic.

In the "chamber" of Ashbery's poem, where past and present representational models collide, we glimpse the particles that discursively compose a self. His "subject" is neither a "pure" innerness nor only a "cultural construct"; it is an innerness always seen as an otherness, mediated by both literary and cultural models of the self. "Houseboat Days" describes this kind of subjectivity:

> To flash light
> Into the house within, its many chambers,
> Its memories and associations, upon its inscribed
> And pictured walls, argues enough that life is various.
> Life is beautiful. He who reads that

As in the window of some distant, speeding train
Knows what he wants, and what will befall. (1977: 39)

Ashbery's speaker becomes a spectator of his own subjectivity. The sequestered "house within" is a mausoleum, decorated with inscriptions quoting Matthew Arnold on "life," "so various, so beautiful." And it houses both the "beautiful," "various" inscriptions of a poetic past and the "memories and associations" of a personal past, for the figure of a personal past is preserved only within the poetic house of memory and imagination.

But this house is no homestead: "You can't live there." It can only be glimpsed in a flashing light, as if it were another's house seen "in the window of some distant, speeding train" – the traditional emblem of the Industrial Revolution, the beginning of the end. Ashbery envisions the now-alien inner sanctum of the personal and poetic as distanced and carried off on the wheels of technology, which has left the train itself behind as an emblem of speed. While the inner appears as archaic and static, the figure of the train links to other figures of temporal and historical movement in the poem like the "weather and the certainties of living and dying," the end of summer, the dissolving "parliaments," and "new elections." Trafficking in both archaic consciousness and historical identity, the poet lives in the "interstices" between them, "Rooted in twilight, dreaming, a piece of traffic" (1981: 40) – as Ashbery describes himself elsewhere. He finds and founds his privacy, his personal identity, on the threshold between the poetic and the cultural, the past and the present, for the inner chambers are no more private than a train compartment. Indeed, their "pictured walls" are "inscribed" with the legends of poets past, themselves seeking a hedge against mortality, time, change, and history. Hence the Egyptian feel of Ashbery's "house within," which he figures elsewhere as the "divine sepulcher / Of life" – the "long sepulcher that hid death and hides me" (1962: 25, 27). This is the house of poetry, of the "long" art, both a tomb and an altar for the safekeeping of relics.

Ashbery's viewing the humanist inner house as in a train window again acknowledges the deep collusion of humanism and technology. This recognition admits the "error" of technological-humanist history but proposes that error as our "truth," which we can neither accept nor afford to ignore. The opposition of the imagination and "our technological society" is a Romantic and modernist paradigm; in Ashbery, however, the imagination and the historical "text" invade and pollute each other, as the "long sepulcher" of the inner "chamber" and the "speeding train" transform each other beyond recognition. This kind of "fence-sitting" enables Ashbery to write in avant-garde, experimental forms yet make such "progressive" techniques serve conservative purposes historically alien to them. Accordingly, he articulates his inner life in technologically inflected, impure discourses historically alien to its presumed universality. Thus he achieves an intimate voice through depersonalizing techniques and conveys a sense of cultural overdetermination by writing obsessively about himself. He does not reduce the private and the historical to each other but blurs the borders between them, for he does not question a sequestered imagination from a populist or politically radical perspective and still gives us an elitist, "high" art.

In other words, historically unprecedented mixtures become available to him, which skew the traditional political alignment of experimental forms with cultural criticism and lyric subjectivity with cultural conservatism. He does not observe the ratios between certain poetic techniques and ideological positions that are the norm – hence his success in a period defined by this oppositional framework. Alluding to both traditions and eluding both frameworks, he allows each paradigm to be infected by its opposite. He marshalls a language "Steeped in the nostalgia of a collective past" to point up the dissolution of collective norms and the irrelevance of past models; conversely, he deploys discontinuous techniques to reinscribe the past. He cannot appeal to the old, and he cannot appeal to the new, for by now the very ideology of the new is part of the old, the ideology of progress that landed him – and us – in this fix in the first place.

III

        . . . What brio in your chat, how
do you keep going next time?
    And I told him for half a dime I'd quit and screw

you too, only that's not done, the very
pillars of our civilization would crumble . . .
                                    (Ashbery 1991: 57)

Since Ashbery's texts are impure mixtures – of conservation and innovation, of poetic and cultural discourses – and thus exceed the critical framework of culturally oppositional experimental art versus
culturally conservative academic art, the politics of his verse eludes
easy classification. For example, Keith Cohen reads Ashbery's technical
disruptions of referential and reasonable discourse as challenging bourgeois discourse: "What some may relegate in his early work to the
area of language games and gratuitous surrealistic effects is an integral
part of a very serious attack, through language, on basic assumptions,
institutions, and modes of thought in contemporary America" (1980:
128). Yet Ashbery also recognizes the co-option of such critical strategies themselves; even Cohen admits to a problem in deciding how
to read Ashbery: "The voice of the poems seems at one moment to
be mouthing the [bourgeois] discourse, at the next moment to be
mocking it. It is often difficult to pinpoint where the rote repetition
stops and the critical distancing begins. . . . It is like trying to differentiate between a well-molded graduate from Harvard Business School
and a comedian's impression of a businessman. Indeed, throughout
Ashbery's work there is this problem of determining exactly where
the ax falls" (138–39). Paul Breslin picks up on this problem and suggests that Ashbery's resisting clear reference to "external occasion or
context" can be understood "either as political protest against a corrupt
externality or as aesthetic disdain of a vulgar externality" (1987: 215).

To ask "where the ax falls," however, requires an either/or choice
between political and aestheticist verse, and this opposition does not
hold in Ashbery's "epidemic" way of living, where everything is its
simulacrum, politics is already aestheticized, and aesthetics is already
politicized. Breslin, for his part, concludes that Ashbery is somewhat
adversarial to "bourgeois discourse" but is also "at home" within it
and "his own style is partially of it" (1987: 216). Breslin wants a poetry
that engages the external world yet remains conscious of itself as artifice: "One can reject neither artifice nor experience; each needs the
other if poetry is to offer anything beyond shallow elegance or blun-

dering sincerity" (235). But if the external world is no longer seen as a solid "reality" – if it is a tissue of representations – even referential language can no longer be itself. In other words, if "Nature" and "Imagination" are already commodified and no longer the referents that orient poetic language but mere signifiers or representations of nature and imagination, even referential language cannot be simply referential, because the referent is already a commodity. Indeed, while Ashbery resists a transparent language, he also insists that he aims for a "greater naturalism" (1974: 124), and this suggests we consider how the nature of "nature" has changed. His resistance to reference signals neither an oppositional politics nor a formalism. If the signifier plays a stable part – whether referentially or formally – in the symbolic economy of substitution, it ensures the stability of what is outside it. By denying the signifier any consistent substitutive function – again, whether reference or formal patterning – Ashbery shows that the referent is not a "thing" but another signifier, an acculturated "thing."

Thus, on the one hand, to regard his discontinuous techniques as a "serious attack" on "contemporary America" would require a serious misreading of "contemporary America." In fact, Cohen's analysis follows Roland Barthes's catalog of the "earmarks of bourgeois discourse as it infects Balzac's prose. Not surprisingly," Cohen continues, "these traits have not changed much since Balzac's time" (1980: 133). Ashbery would not agree. On the other hand, to characterize his poetry as "bourgeois discourse" is just as outdated. Breslin's version of it involves the "predication of a world in which *not much happens,* apart from the private events of falling in and out of love, forming and dissolving friendships, and eventually having to face one's own death. . . . This privatized world . . . rests on very large exclusions. Within it, one is unlikely to encounter hunger, violence, or injustice, the elemental suffering that makes the lives of the poor seem a rebuke to middle-class comfort" (1987: 215–16). Ashbery's honesty lies in acknowledging that the poet has no other space to speak from. And neither does Breslin, for that matter, for his list of the masses' afflictions has the hollow sound of commodified markers.

Of course, Ashbery's holiday syntax is exclusionary – what else could it be? But he takes no "comfort" in his "exclusions"; they do

not absolve him from moral responsibility or let him forget his sinful
immersion in the "grand galop," as he passively awaits deliverance:

> Someone is coming to get you:
> The mailman, or a butler enters with a letter on a tray
> Whose message is to change everything, but in the meantime
> One is to worry about one's smell or dandruff or lost glasses –
> If only the curtain-raiser would end, but it is interminable.
> But there is this consolation:
> If it turns out to be not worth doing, I haven't done it;
> If the sight appalls me, I have seen nothing;
> If the victory is pyrrhic, I haven't won it. (1975: 18)

"And yet / The groans of labor pains are deafening." The sinful state
is not mortality ("dandruff" and so on); rather, it is the poet's cultural
position, forced at once to be marginal (consigned to "worry about"
minor personal inconveniences) and to live off the labor of others, for
whom he can no longer pretend to speak. Ashbery presents this "world
in which *not much happens*" in an entirely different light than Breslin
casts it, for Ashbery's "consolation" has little to do with complacency
or comfort.

Indeed, "middle-class comfort" depends on the reification of objects – the " 'effacement of the traces of production' from the object,"
as Jameson describes it in a tone reminiscent of Ashbery's. "The point
of having your own object world . . . is to forget about all those in-
numerable others for a while; you don't want to have to think about
Third World women every time you pull yourself up to your word
processor, or all the other lower-class people with their lower-class
lives when you decide to use or consume your other luxury products:
it would be like having voices inside your head; indeed, it 'violates'
the intimate space of your privacy and your extended body" (1991:
314–15). Again, Ashbery forgoes such "comfort" by allowing his privacy to be violated; his "head," his mouth, is filled with these other
"voices." For his "private" world is not all that private, composed as
it is of "external phenomena": "your only world is an inside one /
Ironically fashioned out of external phenomena / Having no rhyme
or reason, and yet neither / An existence independent of foreboding

and sly grief. / Nothing anybody says can make a difference" (1970: 81).

Ashbery's review of a show called *The New Realists* makes explicit the nature of these "external phenomena": "The artist's work on this as on other occasions is not preaching or even mediation, but translation and exegesis, in order to show us where the balance of power lies in the yet-once-again altered scheme of things. Today it seems to repose in the objects that surround us; that is in our perceptions of them or, simply and once again, in ourselves" (1989: 83). In the "continuing effort to come to grips with the emptiness of industrialized modern life," the "most successful way of doing this seems to be to accord it its due," which means recognizing that "machines and machine-made objects" are "not phenomena, but part of our experience, our lives – created by us and creating us." If in the 1920s "a poet such as Eliot couldn't evoke a gasworks without feeling obliged to call the whole history of human thought into play," the artist today does not need to speak in metaphors, for "in today's violent reaction to threadbare intellectualism the artist has brought the gasworks into the home" (81–82). Ashbery's recognition that poets can no longer distance themselves from "modern life" – that neither ignoring it nor passing judgments on it is an option – accounts for the white noise in his work. To ask for an explicitly political poetry or some aesthetic efficacy – as in a reconciliation of "art" and "reference," in Breslin's terms – is to buy back into the mystifications of "aesthetic ideology" and its fascistic drift. Yet maybe even de Man's paradigm of Romantic poetry no longer holds, given – in Jameson's words – the "immense and historically original acculturation of the Real, a quantum leap in what Benjamin still called the 'aesthetization' of reality (he thought it meant fascism, but we know it's only fun)" (1991: x). In this situation, how are we to distinguish the ideological work that the "category of the aesthetic" performs from the aesthetic function ideology performs? Aesthetic reconciliations of historical reality with justice and value, and ideological reconciliations of the same, are equally imaginary resolutions.

In light of this "historically original" situation, a kind of gag rule applies: least said, "Soonest Mended"; stay in the "early lessons" (1970:

18); do not "grow up" (19); do not "argue" for your "Sincere
convictions" (1977: 38); stop making sense; remain impotent, innocent, blind – a "dwarf" though "possessing a normal-sized brain"
(1962: 26). For at this point the poet's "alienation" no longer
authorizes him to pronounce from outside the system; there being no
communal center, one cannot even speak of marginal positions, for
these privileged suburbs, too, have disappeared in the new urban
blight. Since Ashbery cannot claim the compensations of such power
as the cultural marginalization of the poet once offered – like the power
of speaking universal truths, however ineffectual in the "real world"
they may have always been – his vocation does not offer a guilt-free,
suburban exemption, and he can only avert his eyes from the "ap-
palling" sights, without any justification for doing so – without the
myth of "the poet," "art," or "marginality." Avoiding the "stench of
knowledge" and the "pain" of reasoning (1977: 38), he can keep his
hands clean but not, of course, his conscience clear, for everything
exacts its price:

> That's why I quit and took up writing poetry instead.
> It's clean, it's relaxing, it doesn't squirt juice all over
> Something you were certain of a minute ago . . . (1981: 25)

For his bourgeois subject is itself an image, only a simulacrum of a
"bourgeois subject."

I want to conclude my discussion of Ashbery by looking at *Flow
Chart*. A late chapter in his "history of someone who came too late,"
the poem rehearses the issues that inform his work from the beginning
and presents a moving account of "how it feels, not what it means"
(1977: 29), to experience one's time as the interface of autobiographical, literary, and cultural histories. A relentlessly discontinuous long
poem, *Flow Chart* has no illusions about technical novelty: "one is
doomed, / repeating oneself, never to repeat oneself, you know what
I mean?" (1991: 7) accurately reflects its kind of exhausted experimentalism. And it explicitly states the cultural position Ashbery's poetry occupies:

What right have you to consider yourself anything but an
    enormously eccentric though
not too egocentric character, whose sins of omission haven't
    omitted much,
whose personal-pronoun lapses may indeed have contributed
    to augmenting the hardship
silently resented among the working classes? If I thought that
    for a minute I'd . . . yet,
remembering how you didn't want to get up today, how
    warm the bed was and cozy, you
couldn't really begin with a proletarian, accustomed as they are
    to backbreaking
toil and so (you'd like to think) don't feel it that much.
    Besides they never read Henry James' novels.
Just for the sake of argument let's say I've never done an
    honest day's work
in my life. It's hardly heartbreaking news, not
a major concern. (150)

His "experiments" come without the authorization of "political correctness" or "science," the other traditional appeal of the "new":
"And as for me, sad to say, / I could never bring myself to offer my
experiments the gift of objective, scientific / evaluation. Anything
rather than that!" (151). One can think here of the rhetoric of Pound
or Olson or any other kind of "heroic" experimentalism – Ashbery
pretty much covers the field.

The ironies of the long passage I have quoted are not substantive;
it presents Ashbery's position more or less accurately. Not only do his
"experiments" play into the system, but their "newness" is something
of an anachronism. While *Flow Chart* takes liberties with notions of
"poems," this course is continuous with Romantic and modernist values, and Ashbery actually describes his poet as a wanderer "in the halls
of the nineteenth century: its exhibits, / talismans, prejudices, erro-
neous procedures and doomed expeditions": "I must shade my eyes
from the light with my hands, the light of the explosion / of the up-

coming twentieth century." Indeed, "Nobody asked me whether I
wanted to be born here, / whether I liked it here, but that's hardly an
excuse for cobbling a palace of mendacious *rêves* / into something like
existence" (151).

Whether Ashbery's "halls" are meant to hold the echoes of Wordsworth or not, Ashbery's historical and cultural dilemma becomes
clearer when we read *Flow Chart* alongside – and in the convex mirror
of – *The Prelude*. *Flow Chart* is an autobiographical poem, recording
"the origin and progress" of the powers of the poet's mind (Wordsworth 1981: II, 36) – although Ashbery duly registers appropriate sus-
picions about "progress," "poet," and "mind." It also reviews his
published books: " 'John's report cards' " (1991: 114). Wordsworth
could well be describing Ashbery's project, beginning with the "earnest longing" "To brace myself to some determined aim . . . either to
lay up / New stores, or rescue from decay the old / By timely interference" (1979: 35); drawing out "With fond and feeble tongue a
tedious tale" in the "hope" that "I might . . . fix the wavering balance
of my mind" (63); offering the "Song" – "which like a lark / I have
protracted" (479) to the "Friend" as a "gift," though "prepared" under the "pressure of a private grief, / Keen and enduring," in the con-
fidence that "the history of a Poet's mind / Is labour not unworthy of
regard" (481). Both poems give a minute account of subjective responses to events, whether cataclysmic or barely registrable by those
less "elevated" sensibilities who lack as large a capability of "being
excited without the application of gross and violent stimulants"
(Wordsworth 1981: I, 872). Ashbery's "egotistical" antisublime, consumed with "exquisite nitpicking" (1991: 158) and putting "too fine
a deconstruction" (205) on everything that may or may not have happened to "me," while days, seasons, and decades roll by "outside,"
reaffirms that "we moderns have to 'leave our mark' / on whatever
we say and do; we can let nothing pass without a comment / of some
kind" (158). In other words, despite Ashbery's unrelenting irony, and
despite the ironies that become apparent in juxtaposing him with
Wordsworth, *The Prelude* offers an instructive comparison to *Flow
Chart*.

Wordsworth's assumption that "each man's Mind is to herself /

Witness and judge" (1979: 457) holds for Ashbery: "Nothing is re-
quired of you, yet all must render an accounting" (1991: 164). Indeed,
legalistic terminology of trials, judges, and sentences abounds in his
poem, which is apparently occasioned by a "private sorrow" (8) and
a need for private accounting. Since Ashbery never specifies it, however, everything he says registers on a "higher" plane, as another attempt, complete with its attendant anxieties, to justify the ways of a
"Poet's mind." Certain details – the presence of "John," recurrent
plays on "Ashes," and vague references to family, sex, mourning, writing, history, and earlier poems – make for an autobiographical drift,
but as usual he denies us the "specifics" and even apologizes for his
lapses: "forgive us / our stitch of frivolity in the fabric of eternity if
only so that others / can see how shabby the truth isn't and make their
depositions accordingly" (167). We are left with the fact that "This is
a poem," for it does meet the minimum requirements of allusions and
line breaks: "be one of those / on whom nothing is lost. Organize
your thoughts in random lines and, later on / down the road, paginate
them" (159).

And we must turn to other poems, especially other poems that
provide instructive models of the "subject," as Ashbery claims to do.
Ashbery's "random lines" do add up to "something like / my autobiography," which "somebody" might "find . . . worth his while, i.e.,
exemplary" (1991: 135). The "exemplary" subject is presented in various terms: "I say 'I' / because I'm the experimental model of which
mankind is still dreaming, though to myself / I'm full of unworked-
out bugs and stagefright" (125). More, "I seemed to have turned into
a walking or / at any rate standing testimonial"; "I see I am as ever /
a terminus of sorts, that is, lots of people arrive in me and switch
directions but no one / moves on any farther; this being, in effect, the
end of the line, a branch-line / at that" (127).

Not clearly authorized to indulge in a more autobiographical reading, we must resort to a literary reading of such negative millennialism
and trace the fortunes of the humanist subject in postmodern times.
"Somebody dust these ashes off, open / the curtains, get a little light
on the subject: the subject / going off on its own again" (1991: 20),
Ashbery seems to plead, and we can only agree, but no such luck; he

and we are left with "This mound of cold ashes that we call / for want of a better word the past," which "inflect[s] the horizon," "calling attention to shapes / that resemble it and so liberating them into the bloodstream / of our collective memory" (27). As his autobiographical subject dissolves into a universal subject after all, our reading is deflected to an academic one, and there are enough allusions and meditations on writing to keep us going. Thus personal experience, self-accounting, and private trials are the subjects of the poem, but Ashbery treats them as irrelevant to the reader, a public audience, who is nevertheless asked to read it – to consume this product.

By now Ashbery clearly figures his writing as a product, which sells "personal experience" – regrettably incommunicable and perhaps not entirely consequential – and "poetry" – regrettably, only a luxury for those who can afford such conspicuous consumption: "the coat I wear, / woven of consumer products, asks you to pause and inspect / the still-fertile ground of our once-valid compact / with the ordinary and the true" (1991: 9). If we unravel this a bit, we see that we are asked to tailor Ashbery's "coat" to the canonical tradition, never mind the consumer products. Despite the present straits of the "poet," he is "asking" us to reconsider the same "compact" that Wordsworth, for example, invokes to legitimate *Lyrical Ballads:*

> It is supposed, that by the act of writing in verse an Author makes a formal engagement that he will gratify certain known habits of association. . . . but I am certain, it will appear to many persons that I have not fulfilled the terms of an engagement thus voluntarily contracted. They who have been accustomed to the gaudiness and inane phraseology of many modern writers, if they persist in reading this book to its conclusion, will, no doubt, frequently have to struggle with feelings of strangeness and awkwardness: they will look round for poetry, and will be induced to inquire by what species of courtesy these attempts can be permitted to assume that title. (1981: I, 868–69)

Here is Ashbery: "In the interests of not disturbing my fragile ecological balance / I can tell you a story about something. The expression will be just right, for it will be adjusted / to the demands of the form,

and the form itself shall be timeless though / hitherto unsuspected"
(1991: 185). Thus

> his literature will have performed its duty
> by setting you gently down in a new place and then speeding
>   off before
> you have a chance to thank it. We've got to find a new name
>   for him. "Writer" seems
> totally inadequate; yet it is writing, you read it before you
>   knew it. And besides,
> if it weren't, it wouldn't have done the unexpected and by
>   doing so proved that it was quite
> the thing to do, and if it happened all right for you, but wasn't
>   the way you
> thought it was going to be, why still
> that is called fulfilling part of the bargain. (185–86)

And he proceeds to present his un-Wordsworthian showpiece, a double sestina addressing, it seems, a tradition of organicist poetry that runs
from Wordsworth through Olson: "We're interested in the language,
that you call breath." This tradition dead-ends in the closure of Ashbery's form when "breath" gets its predictable rhyme: "the way / has
been so hollowed out by travelers it has become cavernous. It leads to
death" (186).

By interweaving Wordsworth and Ashbery at such length, I am
suggesting that, here as elsewhere, Ashbery practices his novelties with
one eye on the tradition. His defense of his novel manner is not that
different from Wordsworth's – or Eliot's, for that matter. In any case,
the "manner" of the writing should be distinguished from its "drift":
the manner could be different, "better written, with more attention /
to niceties of style and fewer obscure references," but "the concept, /
always, was beyond reproach" (1991: 117). Dressing his "stories" for
"the new financial age that offers better reception / to things of the
future, like mine" (184), is a marketing strategy, for he is interested in
selling: "For a dollar I could put it in the mail to you, / my little tract"
(155). *This* might sell better now than Whitman's "I do not say these
things for a dollar" (1965: 85) of more than a century ago. Indeed,

"To the 'newness' then, all subscribe" (159), and "All these officials
had a stake in the matter . . . So for / sixteen years I dazzled the con-
stituents with sayings of a country I had never seen; they knew I /
raved but thought it must always be so when men dreamed, but my
darker / purpose never surfaced" (161). "In fact," Ashbery continues,
"we never see all there is to see / which is good for business too: keeps
the public returning / these days of swiftly eroding brand loyalty":
"such / is the interesting climate we live in" (171). If he has a "darker
purpose" that is not merely teased into being by his evasive, marketing
strategies, it is the very old-fashioned one of keeping alive, by keeping
it in the dark, a private self: "But at times such as / these late ones, a
moaning in copper beeches is heard, of regret, / not for what happened, or even for what could conceivably have happened, but / for
what never happened and which therefore exists, as dark / and transparent as a dream" (12).

Flow Chart fully reveals the pathos of Ashbery's project, for it confirms the cultural marginalization of poetry by representing itself as a
kind of preserve where the subject – the endangered species – may be
kept alive. No more an "agent" than a cog in the machine, Ashbery's
poet tirelessly registers the rhythms of his inner life and, just as tirelessly,
enumerates the difficulties of writing. And his fashionable coat, "woven of consumer products," offers camouflage and better protection
than the entirely different "enterprise" of going naked. The intractable
nature of the poem – as of any Ashbery text – confirms the opinion
that poetry does not make any difference, unless, perhaps, it markets
difference. "The handwriting on the wall" says "return to your abstractions . . . life / has no need of you just yet." This knowledge
floods the poet with sudden clarity and reaffirms his charge: "I thought
I should / sharpen my appearance, for that way lies light, lies life, and
yes I am / talking about new clothes as well . . . As quiet as my / con-
tentment is the voice at my shoulder: make it over. Perhaps not a
total / from-the-ground-up rehab, perhaps only a few cosmetic
touches / would have an earth-shaking impact, in this instance" (1991:
49). One must admire Ashbery's ability to have his cake and eat it,
too, in these hard times. He himself keeps telling us that his poem is
only about himself and could matter less; he offers a product, novel in

cloth and cut, yet keeps apologizing that, in substance, it has no cultural function. For the substance he quixotically sets out to preserve is the humanist subject, the "holy remnants of the burnished / mirror in which the Almighty once saw Himself, and wept" (10).

Flow Chart is not merely a parodic simulacrum of a Romantic poem; it has a more serious undercurrent and a real investment in charting the fortunes of the subjective life, public as well as private. Yet he has neither "metaphysical reasons" (1979: 91) nor cultural imperatives for producing what he does: "I have the feeling my voice is just for me, / that no one else has ever heard it, yet I keep mumbling the litany / of all that has ever happened to me" (1991: 81). Similarly, we are impelled to keep reading – not because we expect some ultimate "high" of revelation but for the intermittent "buzz" we get. He goes on doing what he does because he has lost the "formula for stopping," as Jean Baudrillard remarks apropos joggers (1988: 39). After a while we lose the "formula," too, for *Flow Chart* attracts because it shows how "poetry" plays today, within the larger culture; in Ashbery's words, "You can't / can it and sell it, that's for sure, but it *is* a commodity, and someday all / will be wiser for it" (1991: 202). And for some "specialists," it plays as a nostalgic preserve, helping alleviate certain anxieties: "I will show you fear in a handful of specialists" (201).

This "fearful" specialist would like to think, however, that Ashbery remains committed to preserve, "produce," or "enlarge" the capability "of being excited without the application of gross and violent stimulants." That, in Wordsworth's terms,

is one of the best services in which, at any period, a Writer can be engaged; but this service, excellent at all times, is especially so at the present day. For a multitude of causes, unknown to former times, are now acting with a combined force to blunt the discriminating powers of the mind, and unfitting it for all voluntary exertion to reduce it to a state of almost savage torpor. The most effective of these causes are the great national events which are daily taking place, and the increasing accumulation of men in cities, where the uniformity of their occupations pro-

duces a craving for extraordinary incident, which the rapid communication of intelligence hourly gratifies. (1981: I, 872–73)

To keep alive the "discriminating powers of the mind" is, I would
argue, Ashbery's "darker purpose," a downright conservative aim that
finds models in Wordsworth and James. In other words, I do not buy
Ashbery's fashionable "coat"; while *Flow Chart* is dressed as a pure
product of its culture, it is also a conservative critique, which "darker"
and "worthy *purpose*" gives the author the "right to the name of a
Poet" (Wordsworth 1981: I, 870).

Or, at least, to the "label" of a poet. As I suggested earlier, Ashbery
associates "darkness" with the personal, "a darkness of one's own." If
his writing is designed to resist the erosion of the very idea of the
personal, naturally he can't deliver his "message" or give us the clue
to decode it. This is the "quite tiny key to success" he "hold[s] in [his]
hand" (1991: 171). He can leave behind only "clues . . . fated not to
be found this time" (66), a "trace / of his passing," or a "flicker of
ashes in the grate" (119). But here is yet another irony of Ashbery's
career: "Because in the dark / you knew something and didn't tell it,"
"the notion / became a battle-cry and soon everybody was trying to
disconnect his life and seal it / off, unsuccessfully" (44). Ashbery's stylistic strategies, aimed at preventing the commodification or "packaging" of private experience, once again play into the system and
render him a prized commodity – "Ashbery." He registers anxieties
about this commodification of his "desolation and solitude" (104), as
well as an anxiety of influence in reverse, lamenting the appropriation
of his stylistic signature – his way of not telling. In the end, even not
making sense is a strategy the poet must market. Ashbery's aim to
communicate without communicating anything of substance reaffirms
exchange value over absolute value and use value alike and is perfectly
consonant with a consumer economy. Although he resists commodified "messages," he still ends up commodifying his own strategies of
resistance – the products of "the talking engines of our day" (1979:
88), just right for "our own time." Since a flow chart diagrams a
manufacturing process, *Flow Chart* is an appropriate title for the autobiography of a poet who keeps processing his personal experience

into a mere signifier of what is most personal, so that it becomes cultural or literary currency, a simulacrum, a "guaranteed . . . label, which lasts forever" (1991: 6).

Flow Chart is Ashbery's greatest feat of self-analysis and self-justification. It demystifies the politics and economics of his "difficult" verse and blocks all compensations, all appeals to the "ideology of the aesthetic" or the aesthetics of ideology. It raises fundamental questions about poetry now: "What / if poetry were something else entirely, not this purple weather / with the eye of a god attached, that sees / inward and outward? What if it were only a small, other way of living"? (1991: 145). About the poet's function now: "if I am to be cast off, then / *where?* There has to be a space, even a negative one, a slot / for me, or does there?" (29). About the "unprincipled mire we walk about in today" (207): "where are the standard bearers? Why / have our values been lost? Who is going to pay for any of this?" (30). But *Flow Chart* offers no "big solutions," only big questions. Admittedly, it is only trying to sell a discourse with no use, a "dead" language in which a private person may still be imagined as speaking and sometimes, somehow, even heard.

James Merrill
"Sour Windfalls of the Orchard Back of Us"

No one has accused James Merrill of being postmodern. Yet his poetry most clearly flouts modernist poetic assumptions at the same time that his noncanonical use of canonical forms will not reduce to a reactionary formalism. His work challenges the dominant critical readings of the aftermath of modernism and demands that we rethink the models of literary history and change with which we have read American poetry since World War II. While Merrill inhabits conventional metrical and stanzaic forms without much anxiety, his verse also registers its historical position of coming after modernism, and its importance lies in its questioning novelty, progress, and modernity – the very possibility of new beginnings. Merrill's postmodernism, then, is not merely a late phase of modernism but represents a challenge to the ideology of modernity. His anachronistic gestures, which invoke traditional forms and subjects while rendering them problematic, resist progressive history and nostalgia alike and remain only gestures of tradition and form, rather than aiming for substantive recuperations of the past. Such formalism not only precludes any easy equation of a set of techniques with a particular politics but escapes any simple model of progressive literary history, which can only view the use of traditional forms as reactionary. Thus his work exemplifies the anachrony of a nonprogressive change that revises modernist models.

When an interviewer suggests to Merrill in 1967 that a period of consolidation set in after World War II in the wake of modernism, he responds: "As for consolidation, I'm not so sure. Anybody starting to write today has at least ten kinds of poem, each different from the other, on which to pattern his own" (1986: 25). Merrill's implicitly equating the "at least ten" different models acknowledges that each formal model, each technical option, represents a rhetorical choice, and this reading of postwar poetic history seems accurate. As Peter Bürger has argued, while the avant-garde movements of the early decades of the century failed to destroy the institution of art, they did destroy the possibility that any given school of art, any given style, could claim greater validity than another. The avant-garde has transformed "the historical succession of techniques and styles" into a "simultaneity" of "radically disparate" styles, none more "valid" or "historically more advanced" than another (1984: 63). Thus "today" (1980) a "realistic" and an "avant-gardiste" art can exist side by side, both equally valid (87), for the choice of any given style signals only a rhetorical stance and cannot make any claim to historical authority.

Merrill's formalism should be seen in this context as a *rhetoric* of formalism. His forms, posed as rhetorical gestures in their exaggerated artificiality, decorum, and anachronism, register his awareness of their marginality to what are in fact the prevailing modes of post–World War II American poetry. Such formalism questions the historical and metaphysical authority of conventions as much as it challenges free forms that appeal to "experience" – whether personal or sociopolitical – for their legitimation and authority.

Locating Merrill's work historically, then, involves the larger question of what exactly changes in literary change. In order to accommodate contemporary uses of conventional forms, literary change must be understood as more complex than a linear progress. For example, Antony Easthope's history of the iambic pentameter line in English poetry concludes: "In the aggressive early days of the struggle for bourgeois hegemony [and bourgeois figurations of subjectivity], especially around 1600, the pentameter had a novelty and glamour that was long gone in 1900. Now the pentameter is a dead form and its continued use . . . is in the strict sense reactionary" (1983: 76). This judgment follows from a progressive model of literary change: forms are at first novel, then grow old and die. That a "dead" form can still be used necessitates a historical modification of the organic paradigm: such use is "reactionary." With Eliot and Pound came new forms, which "foreground signifier over signified," insist on the poem as production, and assert the construction of the subject as "an effect of discourse" (134–35). Actually, this describes a rhetorical stance, which would characterize Merrill's work as much as the early modernists'. For Easthope, however, the issue is strictly technical, for the position he outlines as modern is an advance linked to the death of iambic pentameter, which is obvious to all but a few reactionaries. Easthope's model of progressive (evolutionary and revolutionary) literary history places his critical values themselves within the framework of modernism: formal verse in iambic pentameter can only be reactionary, because history marches on.

Formulating an alternative to such simple models of progress requires dissociating form from function, for forms are not what change. Iambic pentameter, for example, has not disappeared; nor is its use limited to the "reactionary" – to a habitual use that upholds the authority of custom and convention. For a more adequate model of change, we might consider the Russian formalist Tynianov's proposal. In Tzvetan Todorov's account, he distinguishes forms from functions, "which are understood as relationships between forms." Literary change involves a "redistribution of forms and functions": now "*the form changes function, the function changes form.* The most urgent task of literary history is to study 'the variability of the function of a given formal element, the appearance of a given function in a formal element, the association of the formal element with this function.' For example, a certain meter (form) serves sometimes to introduce 'higher' epic poetry, sometimes to introduce the vulgar epic (these are among its possible functions)" (Ducrot and Todorov 1979: 146).

Here literary change is not represented as an evolutionary or revolutionary process; it is not like technological history, in which forms may become permanently obsolete. Poetry, which emphasizes the signifier over referentiality, depends on a history of coding phonic and temporal relations and is at once more formal and more historically determined than more novel genres. In poetic change, chronology – the order of events – may break down into a network of anachronisms:

retrievals and reappropriations – of given forms for different functions, of given functions for different forms – and recombinations of various forms and functions. To be resilient enough to accommodate the varieties of twentieth-century American poetry and account for its discontinuities as well as its continuities, our model of literary change must be attentive to functional and rhetorical discontinuities within formal continuities and to formal discontinuities within functional continuities. Finally, we must also attend to the rhetorical varieties – to different tropological models or figurations – of temporality, precedence, continuity, and change that inform the work of different poets. With such a flexible approach, we can account for the fact that, in the postmodern period, closure (metaphysical, moral, or political) can occur within open forms, which have become only one more "tradition," and openness is possible within conventional, closed forms.

In their introduction to *The Line in Postmodern Poetry,* Robert Frank and Henry Sayre acknowledge that free verse, once conceived as a challenge to "repressive, academic traditions," has become, "especially in the eruption of the culture industry since the late 1950s, as writing programs and art schools have proliferated, part and parcel of the academy itself" (1988: xvi). "The point is," they remark, "both free verse and expressionist painting attempt to register the immediacy of experience, but both have been transformed into images. It is as if the prosody of free verse, the gestural brushwork of expressionism, are now used only as codes. We no longer see subjective expression, we see a signifier – i.e., the form of the poem itself – which stands for 'subjectivity.' " As free verse has come to *represent* authentic self-expression and sincerity, "the specter that its gestures might be masks, effects, the very signs of an inauthentic production, is raised" (xvii). The editors' dissociation of current free verse from organicist and experiential defenses of it is valuable, as is their acknowledgment that free verse can be "*conceptually* closed" (x). They question the contemporary viability of the Whitmanic identification of poetic, personal, and political liberty and admit the "ideological foundations" of free verse in bourgeois culture: it is "safe to suppose" that "as anti-aristocratic, bohemian, and avant-garde as free verse supposed itself to be, it was equally . . . thoroughly implicated in the rise of bourgeois culture as a whole and, particularly, in the democratization of leisure, and the attendant individual freedoms enjoyed by bourgeois culture, in the late nineteenth century" (xx). Yet Frank and Sayre have little doubt that the "postmodern condition" of the "loss of poetic authority and control" (xi) – however we evaluate this development – is addressed and observable in poetry in free verse; they do not consider the possibility of "conceptual" openness within a poetry "strait-jacketed by the 'closed' forms of rhyme and meter" (x).

Merrill's work calls for a model of literary change that is not based on contests between such binary oppositions as past and present, convention and originality, tradition and experiment. If the possible uses of the past are confined to the reductive models of iconoclasm, nostalgia, and reactionary recuperation, we cannot account for his project, which is rhetorically and functionally discontinuous with the canonical tradition his forms invoke. "An Urban Convalescence," which opens *Water Street* (1962), has been singled out by Merrill's readers as marking the beginning of his mature work. I propose, however, to cast this poem on a larger, historical stage as an exemplary postmodern "beginning" at the end of the modern idea of history as progress. To highlight Merrill's "lateness" to modernity and progress, we can approach "Urban Convalescence" by way of a detour and consider Paul de Man's remarks on the figure of convalescence. Discussing Baudelaire's and Nietzsche's "modernity" as a "forgetting or a suppression of anteriority," de Man writes: "The human figures that epitomize modernity are defined by experiences such as childhood or convalescence, a freshness of perception that results from a slate wiped clear, from the absence of a past that has not yet had time to tarnish the immediacy of perception . . . of a past that, in the case of convalescence, is so threatening that it has to be forgotten" (1983: 157). If this use of convalescence is "modern," Merrill's use of the figure is clearly different. He diagnoses "the sickness of our time" not as a Nietzschean "historical sickness" but precisely as forgetfulness, a series of slates wiped clean in response to a threat posed by the mere presence of the past. Of course, the "freshness," this modern erasure of history, is the postmodern poet's very sickness, his particular past, and Merrill's poem traces his "convalescence" from just such "modernity."

The poem begins with an emblematic modern scene:

Out for a walk, after a week in bed,
I find them tearing up part of my block
And, chilled through, dazed and lonely, join the dozen
In meek attitudes, watching a huge crane
Fumble luxuriously in the filth of years.
Her jaws dribble rubble. An old man
Laughs and curses in her brain,
Bringing to mind the close of *The White Goddess*.
                                        (1962: 3)

Luxuriating in the "filth of years," jaws dribbling "rubble," the crane is doing the work of demolition. While the scene suggests an unseemly overindulgence in the detritus of the past, the crane is also the agent of urban renewal. Making things "new" by tearing them up, it represents a militant commitment to change, which regards the "simple fact of having lasted" as a threat that calls for the swift retribution of a BLAST. And the mystification and even religious awe that attend the scene ironically hint at the spiritual mission of this breaking of the vessels.

With the allusion to Robert Graves, this devastation that leaves "not one stone upon another" reverberates with more specific historical and literary connotations. The "huge crane" brings to mind Graves's *White Goddess*, presumably because cranes were sacred to the goddess – a mother-muse figure who authorizes an Orphic model of a poetic language grounded in nature. Graves also links cranes to the invention of writing and cites a legend that Mercury invented the letters after watching a flight of cranes, " 'which make letters as they fly' " (1980: 224). In Egypt, Mercury was Thoth, the god who invented writing and whose symbol was the cranelike white ibis. Graves further suggests that the association of cranes with writing and literary secrets makes sense because "cranes fly in V-formation and the characters of all early alphabets, nicked with a knife on the rind of boughs . . . or on clay tablets, were naturally angular" (227). At the "close" of his book, he offers a poem imagining the wrathful second coming of the goddess at her "cannibalistic worst," in the form of *"A gaunt, red-wattled crane,"* to punish "man's irreligious improvidence" that has led to the exhaustion of the "natural resources of the soil and sea" (486).

Merrill's bringing in Graves effects an odd pun. If the reference to Graves suggests that the crane as goddess is punishing "man's" improvidence, its incarnation as a mechanical crane – an agent or, at least, an accomplice of "man's" sins against nature – is problematic. Further, the destruction wrought by the mechanical crane the "old man" operates is purely mechanistic, demystified, and urban and takes place in the linear time of *Time;* this crane is indeed an agent of forgetfulness. The crane as a goddess incarnate, however, is an elemental force, whose destructions belong to the cyclical time of nature and myth, and she threatens to avenge herself on those who forget. Merrill's conflation of historical and mythic forces and conceptions of change in a pun enables him to equate these mastering "ideologies" and thus to lightly sidestep both. His pun exposes the nostalgia underwriting a modernity that seeks to return to and recover a foundation through technical progress. By positioning himself at the margins as a "meek" bystander, he resists both progressive history and a regressive appeal to myths of return.

In this maneuver, the pun on "crane" becomes a textual "ground" that stages the conflict and continuity between progressive historical time and cyclical myth. Unlike a metaphor, a pun highlights a non-hierarchical, synchronic duplicity, doubleness, or difference internal to the signifier. The distance between the mythic crane, a symbol or reincarnation of the goddess, and the technological crane committed to an urban destruction and renewal is the distance between mythic-pastoral and technological-urban conceptions of death and rebirth. Merrill's pun compresses the conceptual and historical distance between two different systems in a synchronic doubleness and figures it as internal to language. Grounding himself in a purely literal and accidental resource, Merrill questions the claims of both the technological and the mythic "crane" – the Janus-faced deus ex machina of the modernist aesthetic. Thus "the close of *The White Goddess,*" with which Merrill opens, is not merely the conclusion of Graves's book but the end of a poetic era.

Discussing Elizabeth Bishop's "Visits to St. Elizabeths," Merrill remarks on her distance from Pound's poetics and praises her for not being "prey to . . . those (male?) drives, the one that produced the

Cantos' huge unruly text, the other that made its bid to change the map of Europe" (1986: 127). Elsewhere, Merrill associates the "monumental" impulse of the major modernist poets with a "male" drive. Speaking of Eliot, Stevens, Williams, and Pound as well as Robert Lowell, he observes that "these men began by writing small, controllable, we might say from our present vantage 'unisex' poems. As time went on, though, through their ambitious reading, their thinking, their critical pronouncements, a kind of vacuum charged with expectation, if not with dread, took shape around them, asking to be filled with grander stuff." The binary opposition of the gender metaphor is, of course, simplistic. While the monumental impulse does seem to afflict "men," Merrill goes on to remind us, "But that's too neat. Look at poor Anne Sexton who, submitting a poem to an editor, wrote: 'I realize it's very long, but I believe it is major' " (161). Merrill admits to having felt and succumbed to a "similar pressure" in his *Changing Light at Sandover.* While it takes Pound almost eight hundred pages to admit to "many errors" from a "newer" perspective, however, Merrill begins his own monumental undertaking with a demurral – "Admittedly I err" (1982: 3) – which, tonally and rhetorically, scales his "grander stuff" to human size. Unlike Pound, he does not try to "write like a god" (1986: 28).

If Merrill's poetry is marginal to a male will to power, it is equally marginal to an Orphic poetic that enthrones the master myth of the Mother Goddess, whose cult revolves around a heterosexual and reproductive center. According to Graves, "man's" offenses against the goddess follow from "enthroning the restless and arbitrary male will" and suppressing the female principle (1980: 486). Yet as Pound's grounding his male drive to power in fertility myths and cycles in his *Cantos* suggests, the two powers are not unrelated. The modernist project of the *Cantos* is to rewrite history as rooted in the natural laws the Goddess represents. This "rooted plan" authorizes formal discontinuities like the "breaking" of the pentameter, the "first heave," from which follow other breaks of other syntagmatic continuities like grammatical and narrative orders. Thus Pound's formal discontinuities are grounded in a substantive continuity with Romantic organicism. He can make it new, "Day by day," because *it* doesn't "wobble"; *it* is a pivot history turns on. And he deploys technical novelty to recuperate that foundation.

"Father Time and Mother Earth" in "The Broken Home" (1966: 28) are Merrill's personae of these master myths. As he explains, "That bit in 'The Broken Home' – 'Father Time and Mother Earth, / A marriage on the rocks' – isn't meant as a joke. History in our time *has* cut loose, *has* broken faith with Nature. But poems, even those of the most savage incandescence, can't deal frontally with such huge, urgent subjects without sounding grumpy or dated when they should still be in their prime. So my parents' divorce dramatized on a human scale a subject that couldn't have been handled otherwise" (1986: 72). Their familial placement in the poet's autobiography, as well as their histor-ical place in the "race run below," domesticates these master figures and acknowledges that the poet-child must obey them. But Merrill, unlike Pound, best obeys "inversely." The verse remains verse – that is, metrical. "The pentameter has been a good friend to me," he says; "you'd think I'd have noticed a little thing like a broken back" (25). And by remaining verse, his poems "invert" these power figures who would claim authority over his text. If the Father rules time and his-tory, the poet resists him by not subscribing to "newspaper" time, which is uncomfortably close to making it "new" daily. If the Mother watches over birth and death, the poet inverts her by growing and letting die his "gilt leaves." To be sure, his marginality to the master myths registers some guilt (see, for example, "Childlessness" [1962: 28–29] and "A Tenancy" [51–53]). Yet such psychological dramas, like Merrill's ideological and mythic contests, transpire within a framed aesthetic space: "the parents and the child / At their window, gleam-ing like fruit / With evening's mild gold leaf" (1966: 27). The gilt suffuses all guilt, for the stage of these dramas is always already a figure, a text, not a primal ground.

Similarly, while Merrill's mock-sublime "crane" makes light at once of an Orphic poetic and of a now-senile faith in technical re-newals, he also "obeys" both principles, if "inversely," for a pun is a curious hybrid. Its truth is, after all, technical, residing in its letters; at the same time, it gives of an uncanny double of super- or subliteral vision. For Merrill's relation to these master myths is not a progressive antagonism; he is not out to destroy them in order to install other, more valid myths in their place. From his postmetaphysical perspective, all truths are rhetorical, and all ideologies, whether mastering or marginal, are textual options. And he presents this rhetorical position not as a timeless truth but as indicative of the historical state of affairs at "the close of *The White Goddess.*"

Merrill's narrative of convalescence unfolds the options that the crane levels. The speaker remembers the figure of a garland decorated the lintel of the building being torn down. The iconoclastic destruction of received structures – specifically, structures of closure like buildings – is "inscribed" with a garland, "stone fruit, stone leaves, / Which years of grit had etched until it thrust / Roots down, even into the poor soil of my seeing." Again, the garland "sways" into "focus" as an emblem of the cyclical-mythic time that underwrites the modern project of catastrophic progress, of radical breaks with history. Next, Merrill moves to the memory of another representation of natural force – "a particular cheap engraving of garlands." The engraving evokes an equally fuzzy and belated avatar of the White Goddess, whose link to reproductive forces and "deadly" power still manages to register, just as the forlorn pastoral emblem of "garlands" still manages to be remembered – if at the expense of the history of the buildings and the people themselves, whose features "Lie toppled underneath that year's fashions." The engraving was

> Bought for a few francs long ago,
> All calligraphic tendril and cross-hatched rondure,
> Ten years ago, and crumpled up to stanch
> Boughs dripping, whose white gestures filled a cab.
> . . . .
> Also, to clasp them, the small, red-nailed hand
> Of no one I can place.

And this forgetfulness locates Merrill in his "urban" setting; in Graves's words, "The Goddess is no townswoman: she is the Lady of the Wild Things" (1980: 481).

By forgetting the goddess, Merrill both implicates himself in the modern urban "sickness" and turns away from a pastoral recuperation.

Following this episode, stanzas of drastic "exposure" underscore the poet's new clarity about his place on the margins of both progressive history and natural force, which are themselves only figurations of centers of power – emblems and chapters in the "massive volume of the world." Such knowledge of pervasive textuality, which is also "self-knowledge," delivers him "Indoors at last" to an explicitly and historically textual "house."

The speaker's move indoors coincides with a formal switch to quatrains. Merrill himself calls this poem "a turning point" for him and associates this turn with a return, with his staged formal switch: "I remember writing half of it and thinking it was going to be impossible to finish. Then I had the idea of letting it go back to a more formal pattern at the end" (1986: 45). Elsewhere, he tells us that " 'stanza' is . . . the Italian word for 'room' " and relates his fondness for regular stanzas to his attachment to "interior spaces, the shape and correlation of rooms in a house," rather than the vistas it commands or the "human comedies" it stages (3). Here the enveloping *abba* rhyme reinforces the enclosure of the quatrains. And the poem's resolution suggests that convalescence will involve remembering closures and interior spaces, answering a "dull need to make some kind of house / Out of the life lived, out of the love spent." Given the in-and-out movement that constitutes the poem's adventure, from "Out for a walk" to "Indoors at last," the repeated "out of" in the final line has an added resonance. "Out of" may mean not only "constituted of" but "outside" the lived life, the spent love. If we register both senses, the house-poem made out of the lived life moves out of the life lived.

Merrill here dedicates himself to his special brand of transpersonal autobiographical writing. For his move "inside," to the at least temporarily protected space of his own life, is modified by the fact that he also moves into quatrains. Subscribing to such marked conventions without any effort to naturalize his forms effects an impersonal, intertextual erosion of the personal, and Merrill's formalism, always sharply aware of this, does not offer protection but leaves him open to a different kind of history and loss.

Merrill often makes the textual dangers and "losses" – of signature and singularity, of authorship and authority – that are internal to writ-

ing his explicit subjects, but his conventional forms also work implicitly to efface the speaking subject, dispersing it in the drift of impersonal
time and history. Poetic conventions such as meter, rhyme schemes,
and stanza forms are timing devices that are also always more than
mere schemes, because they remember a past and carry with them the
burden of a public history. Thus Merrill's urban convalescence inside
quatrains represents more than an urbanity of manners that remediates
the natural or the oracular. A convalescence that identifies the "indoors" with formal stanzas dissociates the "inside" from the subjective
or the intuitive. As the architectural metaphor of "house" also signals,
Merrill is interested in public building, in transmitting a public history.
His conventions make for this historical dimension, while his artificial
staging of his forms registers their anachronism and thus divests them
of historical authority. Urban as well as urbane, Merrill can maintain
a critical distance from progress and historical authority alike, from
both Orphic, oracular, or intuitive speech and conventions.

For Merrill, change and continuity are not polar opposites; continuity is infected with change and change with continuity. For example, situating himself inside quatrains in "Urban Convalescence"
allows him to revise himself and question what are presumably his
authorizing values. He begins with a diagnosis of planned obsolescence
as "the sickness of our time" that requires things be "blasted in their
prime." Yet he immediately overturns this judgment:

> There are certain phrases which to use in a poem
> Is like rubbing silver with quicksilver. Bright
> But facile, the glamour deadens overnight.
> For instance, how "the sickness of our time"
>
> Enhances, then debases, what I feel.

This "revision" calls into question his "conservative" rejection of novelty, for his rejection itself joins "progress," or "the great coarsening
drift of things" (1986: 60). His second thoughts occur, however, in a
conventional form that would conserve the past. In this disjunction,
his conventional forms divest themselves of authority, for they are
dissociated from a conservative ideology that would judge the present

by taking refuge in the canonical authority of the past. If originality and novelty are outmoded concepts for Merrill, so is the expectation of a correlation between convention and authority. He employs conventions not because they carry a prescriptive authority but as if they did, at once remembering and transmitting a past and denying it any absolute vitality or validity beyond the fact of its being there – a shared, public past. For the anachronism of his forms in the time of *Time* and in one's own "life lived" and "love spent" is evident enough.

Moreover, to claim any inherent validity or recuperative efficacy for his forms would reinscribe him in the logic of modernity. Indeed, when he stages his more elaborate forms within larger pieces – as when he breaks into quatrains in the middle of a poem containing blank verse or even prose – he presents such forms as quotations cut off from their original contexts, functions, and "grounds." In his hybridizing use, the "quoted" forms both carry historical associations and assume new functions in their new contexts. Such functional discontinuity again subverts any claim to canonical authority, and traditional forms are, at the same time, technically closed and rhetorically open.

Merrill's distinction is his ability to register at once the textuality and the historical nature of writing. His polyvalent literalism and his fondness for "accidents" and puns in general foreground the play of the signifier and approach an internalization of history within poetic language. His conventional formalism, however, holds this tendency in check by placing poetic language within a public literary history. Thus he can be grounded in textuality, doing without historical or metaphysical foundations, yet stop this side of an ahistorical, self-reflexive subjectivity, for the textual inside is governed by publicly recognizable, historically coded rules, which transmit a past even if they do not carry any inherent validity.

Since Merrill's chosen subject is his personal past, his conventional forms, which recall an impersonal and intertextual past, serve to unsettle his entire project. If the "I" may be heard only through the chorus or con-vention of other poems and poets, the subject dissolves or is resolved into the textual medium. Merrill's writing is never naively personal; the writer's repertoire, poetic conventions, and the accidental resources of language always consume the personal source, leaving the poet to conclude "out of the life lived." The poet who would be saved from "more living" – the poet who would "fly" from Byzantium or Istanbul – has his wish granted only too easily and finds himself in another "Byzantium": "Far off a young scribe turned a fresh / Page, hesitated, dipped his pen" (1969: 31). There is no need to yearn, like Yeats, to be "out of nature" (1989: 194); the poet is always already a scribe, his source and destination strictly prescribed in a synchronic pun of Byzantiums and his very medium always already spelling out "what is past, or passing, or to come."

Nor is he naively conventional. Conventions, Lawrence Manley proposes, are animated by a tension and interplay between the "formal" and the "social" dimensions they encompass, since they derive their "quasi-objective and sometimes normative status from an underlying social dimension" (1981: 32). The history of conventions reveals another set of tensions, between the "social" and "historicist" phenomenon of "convention" and what is perceived, by contrast, to be objectively "universal," such as a "timeless" nature, or to be "unique," such as the concrete particularity of the "individual" (33). Merrill's use of convention stands outside this framework. To begin with, he refuses to place socially sanctioned conventions in opposition to individual or natural language. Speaking of "manners," he observes: "One could paraphrase Marianne Moore: using them with a perfect contempt for them, one discovers in them after all a place for the genuine." Not only are manners "more hospitable to irony, self-expression, self-contradiction, than many a philosophical or sociological system," but "manners for me are the touch of nature, an artifice in the very bloodstream" (1986: 33). "From my own point of view," he tells J. D. McClatchy in an interview, "voice in its fullest tonal range – not just bel canto or passionate speech" – would be "utterly unattainable without meter and rhyme and those forms we are talking about." These "obsolete resources" assume a new function in Merrill's work: they make possible a more "natural" tone of voice at the same time that they "breed echoes" and lend an "air of pastiche" to dispel the illusion of an "individual" voice (80). Yet Merrill's use of convention does not appeal to social sanction, either. Rhymed quatrains, for example, tend to be typical of the kind of convention Merrill relies on, and they cannot be said to carry any social or historical sanction in American poetry, least of all after 1960. That is, the necessity for their use cannot be inferred from "the habitual practice of other writers or . . . the prevailing opinion as to what ought to be done" (R. S. Crane in Manley 1981: 51), any more than from the claims of "natural truth" or individual talent.

The very anachronism of Merrill's particular conventions at a time when it is "too late" to "rely" on them – at a time when a reader can "hardly be trusted to hear the iambics when he opens *The Rape of the Lock*" (1986: 79–80) – situates his work in extraliterary history as well. In fact, his choice of traditional forms implies a social-class position, as suggested by a remark like

> Must I grow broad- and dirty-minded
> Serving a community, a nation
> By now past anybody's power to shock?
>   (1976: 12)

Robert von Hallberg notes this aspect of Merrill's style:

> During the 1960s, while some of his contemporaries, under the influence of Merwin, were pursuing styles that apparently dis-owned social relations, and others, like Lowell, were attempting to democratize, with free verse, low colloquialisms and brand names, the densely metaphorical styles they learned in the 1950s, Merrill held on to his meters and chose his phrases with a sense of class.
>
> So distinct a sense of class is implied by his style that he, at least as much as any of his contemporaries, has altered the politics of style in American poetry. . . . Merrill's distinction is his skep-tical view of that American *idée fixe,* the democratic or classless style. (1985: 112)

Yet von Hallberg does not consider Merrill a "culture poet" (116). "Culture" poetry "obviously involve[s] recent cultural history" (2) and engages "the feelings, experiences, and difficulties that are considered the irreducible center of public life" (4). The dominant tone and diction of Merrill's poems define a "camp" sensibility, which is limited and marks "minor" poetry: "By making a virtue of exaggeration, it cannot achieve justness, and a sane assessment of our most difficult experiences is part of what is asked of the greatest poetry" (112). I would argue that "our most difficult experience" at this time is precisely the problem of a "cultural center," and Merrill's ability to use – while questioning from within – the style and tone of a literature once associated with cultural centering makes his work very much "engaged." His exaggerations and parodic "edge" implicitly critique the power politics of any "central" discourse, and his anachronistic conventions, which point to the constructed nature of all styles and thus expose fictions of "classless" or "democratic" styles, also hint at the anachronism of the expectation that poetry engage centers, once the politics of centers has come into question. Whose center is *the* center? Whose history is History? By "centering" his work in an admittedly marginal formalism, by highlighting a degree of artifice that flaunts its disengagement from politics, by refusing to naturalize his forms – which might make for a pastoral convalescence but not an urban one – and by aestheticizing the political, his "camp" stance is perfectly clear about its historical position.

Merrill has no illusions about "central" speaking. Just as an aggressive disarticulation of articulate discourse partakes of the same economy of subjugation it would overthrow, any "central" speech is implicated in the very politics of power that establishes the center. In "Roger Clay's Proposal" (1962: 37) Merrill exposes the complicity of any opposition with the powers that be. The poem begins by invoking numbing news – "The bomb. The ultimatum" – and proposes it might help the cause of peace if "the leaders of a sobered world" would "submit / To execution." The recognition – "Ah, but those boys, their heads aren't in the clouds. / They would find reasons not to die for peace" – leads to the alternative plan of organizing the protestors to "die for peace": "I'd give *my* life. Each day I meet / Men like me, young, indignant. We're not cranks. / Will some of them step up?

That's plenty. Thanks. / Now let's move before we get cold feet."
Merrill makes this point explicit in an interview: "Every leader – president or terrorist – is responsible for keeping his ranks thinned out.
Good politics would therefore encourage death in one form or another
– if not actual, organized bloodshed, then the legalization of abortion
or, heaven forbid, the various chemical or technological atrocities"
(1986: 72).

As Merrill's equating president and terrorist and his blurring the
distinction between different options – for or against the "boys" –
suggest, the only way not to be implicated in the power politics of
making history is to keep well grounded in rhetoric. Thus: "In poetry
I look for English in its billiard-table sense – words that have been set
spinning against their own gravity. Once in competition with today's
headlines or editorial page you just can't sustain that crucial, liberating
lightness without sounding like a sick comedian" (1986: 38). The
"crucial, liberating lightness" that resists gravity sustains itself by doing
without the gravity of a foundation exterior to its own forms and
rhetoric. This is "English in its billiard-table sense."

Such "groundless" formalism signals Merrill's postmodern challenge to progressive history and metaphysical foundations alike. He
questions both experimental and conservative values, both of which
orient themselves in relation to a grounded, linear history, and thus
forces us to question a literary history figured on this model. At the
same time that he dismisses experimental techniques, "natural" or organic forms, and Orphic models of poetry, he demystifies his inherited,
traditional forms and calls into doubt the assumptions of closure, con-
tainment, protection, and control that accompany them. Similarly, he
dissociates the lyric from notions of a coherent lyric self with absolute
power over words and inscribes his "voice" and personal past as a convention of a variety of intertextual discourses – both literary and extraliterary. And he conveys his postmodern understanding of the poetic
self as textual, and all authority as rhetorical, in autobiographical writing in canonical forms. That his traditional, "old-fashioned kind of
poem" (1986: 39) is neither innocent nor ahistorical makes for work
whose timeliness lies precisely in its reluctance to lay claim to being
timely.

I

Merrill is an analogical poet, for whom all thought is within metaphor, but his stylistic signature is wordplay. He deploys the full range of paranomasias that work against naming and signatures, from puns to anagrams to etymological acrobatics. Such word use not only marks his surface texture but often shapes a poem's "argument" by eliding reasonable argument and undermining logical distinctions and categories. A pun may even function as the "center" a poem revolves around precisely by resisting centering and refusing to yield an unequivocal sense. Puns activate multiple meanings within the material signifier and exploit synchronic and nonhierarchical differences; they operate outside the substitutive economy of tropological language and the distinctions that it institutes. Metaphor, for example, works with diachronic and hierarchical substitution: the tenor precedes, in time and substance, the vehicle that substitutes for it. Consequently, metaphoric substitution opens up a space outside its substitutive transaction and projects a common denominator and value, with regard to which the comparison can take place, be understood, and be evaluated. Conversely, a common denominator outside the things compared must already be in place in order to enable their substitution.

For instance, to say "My love is a red rose" establishes a hierarchy between the tenor (love) and vehicle (rose), between the subject and its illustrative analog, and changes both: the "love" no longer has its own body but is embodied in a "rose," the body of the vehicle; the vehicle no longer signifies a "rose" alone but is informed by another meaning. In general terms, the subject and the analog or the abstract and the material are simultaneously altered; each is displaced onto the other. Moreover, in order to make or process such a comparison, we must first posit what "love" and "rose" share; for the substitution to work, we must appeal to a third entity, an idea that remains outside the exchange but legitimates the substitution – the idea of beauty, say. The double displacement or alienation of the two terms brings them into proximity with a third, abstract term, an ideal presence that emerges from this process to preside over and sanction the transformation each of the units undergoes. Jean-Joseph Goux has analyzed

how any substitutive exchange, whether linguistic, economic, political, or psychological, necessarily projects an ideal standard of value.
Any representational substitution of one thing for another must rely
on an ideal "ground" to legitimize it; representation necessarily creates
a value outside its transaction and thus both opens a history and founds
an idealism.[1] In rhetorical terms, no figuration exists without persuasion – without instituting a value and a standard of value.

Puns escape this economy of substitution, I would argue, and stand
outside the necessarily idealist history it opens and perpetuates. They
bespeak a pre-Oedipal language before the intervention of the third
party, the father, which symbolic substitution necessarily projects and
establishes as the overseer of its operations. As such, puns are untrans-
latable, because they do not enter a symbolic economy or recognize
the "metaphysical" values – the interposing father, monarch, logos,
gold – that monitor substitutive transactions and determine priorities.
The signifier itself holds two or more meanings simultaneously and
rules out a perspective from which to hierarchize them. Put differently,
puns are "motivated" figures; since they do not involve an "arbitrary"
exchange (of word for thing, of vehicle for tenor) or representation,
they need no metaphysical authority to justify the transaction.

Yet the rhetorical status of puns is problematic. Two sets of motives
– the poet's conscious, rhetorical motive in his word choice and the
"unconscious" motivation of language – cohabit in a pun, so that the
author's rhetoric is at once explicit and subsumed by a kind of "original" rhetoric that, in fact, subverts authorial control. Thus the signifier
performs two contradictory functions simultaneously – both reference
and production of meaning. As Oswald Ducrot writes, "Authentic
homonymy, or ambiguity, supposes that between the different meanings of the same expression there is neither a common core nor even
continuity; this makes it impossible either to explain any one by the
others or to derive them all from one basic signification. Consequently,
if an ambiguous expression has the two meanings a and b, its use in
sense a and its use in sense b correspond to two choices that are as
distinct as if two different expressions were involved. This makes the
divergence between the appearance and the reality of language all the
more flagrant. Choices that in reality have nothing in common lead

us, on the surface, to choose the same expression" (Ducrot and Todorov 1979: 238). Hence, in puns, the "growths" or ramifications of
meanings are "fatal" (Merrill 1972: 72), for they coincide with a reduction to the literal sign system and expose the divergence between
different kinds of motivation.

Reviewing Francis Ponge, another writer who "forfeits no resource
of language, natural or unnatural," Merrill (1976: 112) defends this
"lowest form of humor": the pun "is suffered, by and large, with
groans of aversion, as though one had done an unseemly thing in adult
society, like slipping a hand up the hostess's dress. Indeed, the punster
has touched, and knows it if only for being so promptly shamed, upon
a secret, fecund place in language herself. The pun's objet trouvé aspect
cheapens it further – why? A Freudian slip is taken seriously: it betrays
its maker's hidden wish. The pun (or the rhyme, for that matter)
'merely' betrays the hidden wish of words" (111). Here a pun is a
transgression – specifically, a sexual transgression – of established rules;
[2]it exceeds proper bounds of naming, meaning, property, and propriety; it accesses a "feminine" source, evading the father's law; and in
its "objet trouvé aspect," it seemingly lies outside the author's control.
Puns sound the unconscious of the language itself and link to other
poetic practices, such as rhyme, that exploit multiple meanings within
similar sounds. In other words, a pun threatens all rules that would
stabilize the signifier, and upsets the one-to-one correspondence of
word and thing and the correspondence theory of "truth."[3] The syn-
chronicity of puns subverts not only reference and rhetoric (as figuration and persuasion) but all modes of thought that proceed
diachronically, such as causality, induction, and deduction.

The rest of Merrill's defense of punning turns on why the device
might prove especially useful at this time: "It betrays also a historical
dilemma. If World War I snapped, as we hear tell, the thread of civilization . . . the next generation's problem was to create works whose
resonance lasted more than a season. A culture without Greek or Latin
or Anglo-Saxon goes off the gold standard. How to draw upon the
treasure? At once representing and parodying our vital wealth, the
lightweight crackle of wordplay would retain no little transactional
power in the right hands. But was it – had the gold itself been – moral?

Didn't all that smack of ill-gotten gains? Even today, how many poets
choose the holy poverty of some secondhand diction, pure dull content in translation from a never-to-be-known original" (1986: 112).

This passage will be my text for a comparison of Merrill's figurative
language – specifically, his attitude toward puns and paranomasias in
general – with that of my paradigmatic modernist Pound. In part, their
differences arise from their different sensibilities, which appeal to different structural tropes in their figuration of poetic language. Pound is
an anagogic poet, who seeks identities "beyond metaphor," and puns
should offer him great rhetorical support;[4] Merrill is an analogical poet,
who should be wary of puns. But in certain ways, each works against
his grain. Ostensibly investing in canonical forms, Merrill undercuts
the authority his forms imply by "freeing" the signifier. He pits history
as tradition against history as a disruptive, irrepressible present force at
work in language itself, a force not containable within the forms that,
in fact, activate it – by calling for rhymes, say. Thus Merrill's brand of
formalism is a distinctly postmodern subversion of formalism: he uses
canonical forms that would pattern and control the polyvocality of
words themselves to stage or set off what exceeds forms – the material
excess coded in the signifier. By contrast, Pound disrupts traditional
unities in order to disclose, in their breaks and cleavages, absolute
natural truths operative now as ever. Privileging "images" over metaphors and "names" over paranomasias, he invests in a processual
language and deploys unconventional forms to seize the precise ideogrammic image or the right word, to show its right meaning, and thus
to reveal universal truths. His modernist antiformal verse, then, represents a recuperation of the function of formalist verse to contain and
stabilize the process of signification – to submit the arbitrary signifier
to a governing code.

Aiming to purify language by radical surgery, Pound excises grammatical and logical connections and opens a way back out of discursive
structures, and the larger discourses they serve, to the "root" words –
words as rooted in nature. Similarly, breaking the pentameter and de-
railing the story line, he accesses natural process, the transfer of force
through forms. Purging poetry of its occluding historical accumulation
and rhetoric, Pound strives for right or proper naming – for the *mot*

juste or *ching ming* ("precise verbal definition"). In short, Pound insists "one must call a spade a spade" (1975: 41), for right names carry moral value, and moral values inhere in nature; they are not rhetorical, consensual, or democratic. We need only to be shown these truths, not to be persuaded of their truth-value. The "right" name and the "significant" fact – the fact that "signifies" by getting its right name ("call things by their right names" [85]) – stand in a relation of equity. Pound's ideal is a barter economy, where name equals fact in value and can morally, justly, substitute for it. It would be nice if we could get rid of letters, too, and signify in picture writing, a form of writing in fact homologous with the economic law of simple equivalence and equity Pound banks on.[5]

The evil that undoes this economy is "usura," all that exceeds the equity of bartering the right name for the thing or the ideogrammic image for the metamorphic process. Usurious uses of language include "ornamental" and "explanatory metaphor" (1975: 374), rhetoric, "contagious" words: any word use that is exorbitant and generates an excess "out of nothing." Pound wants *just* exchanges, not only of the right name for the thing, but of the precise "image" for psychological and natural processes and of the right money for human and natural productivity. Value does not inhere in things or words but in their relations, because Pound agrees with Fenollosa that "relationships are more real and more important than the things which they relate" (1936: 26). Since transformational process is Pound's source of value, usury becomes an endemic danger. The threshold between just interest, which promotes productivity, and excess interest that blocks it is not stable. And when metaphor becomes a rhetorical excess over metamorphic process, when words exceed things and claim value in excess of what they signify, when money claims excess value over the labor–goods transaction, we have usury, canker, "fatal growths" – dangers exacerbated by capitalist economies with their valuing representation over experience.

Usury, then, is a generic evil of all representational systems; it is the excess, abstract value that representational transactions create, which alienates each of the transactional units from itself. In Canto XLV, for example, Pound indicts usury for blocking productive relationships, as

"USURA" – a capitalized ideal value; a rhetorical, personified presence; Latin "capital" petrified into Tradition – comes between the embroiderer and her needle, the stonecutter and his stone, the young bride and her bridegroom. It is the abstract value that forestalls productive exchanges, and it corrupts concrete things and their Anglo-Saxon "names." "With usura," then, "is no clear demarcation" (1981: 229) but "lost contours, erosions" (62).

Moreover, in Pound's economy, not only metaphor but the signifier itself has an evil potential to deviate from right naming and to generate excess. While some puns may reveal nature's inherent design and clearly support anagogic identifications, there is no way of drawing a line between revelatory puns and those that are usurious. Certainly, their basis in letters inclines them to proliferate – to reproduce "out of nothing" – and thus makes them dangerous, as shown in anagrams. In "Azure hath a canker by usura" (1981: 230), for example, Ezra juggles a few letters, and "azure" yields "usura," which transgresses both the godly air and the seeds it carries – seeds that insure nature's "intention" to reproduce in kind. Sound play, the semiotic dimension of language, is gendered female in Pound and does link to nature, but male-gendered right naming must be ever watchful that such natural force does not get out of hand. Nature, the source of productivity, must not be repressed, or it will return to destroy, as Canto II warns us at the outset; but it must be channeled or sublimated. For example, when Odysseus "enlightens" Circe in Canto XXXIX and Pound gets "Fac deum" out of "fucking," he "properly" sublimates the "Thgk thkk" of Circe's loom, the sensual thickness of language and its drugging pull against reason. Letters and their accidental order are thus properly harnessed to reveal the "rooted plan." And Canto XLVII tells us that civilization building – from agriculture to poetry – proceeds by plowing, scoring, and measuring "dark" nature to make it yield to the light of "intelligence," which has "power over wild beasts."

Merrill, who observes Pound's gendering and borrows his language of economics, defends wordplay precisely on the grounds of its transgression. It does not sublimate but gives in to the excess that transgresses the bounds of propriety, justice, and moral equity. For him, culture and language have clearly gone off the "gold standard," whether a metaphysical guarantor of stable reference and metaphoric equity or an authoritative tradition of "Greek or Latin or Anglo-Saxon" that can substitute for metaphysics. And if puns are immoral or amoral in exceeding a Poundian equity or right value, Merrill asks, wasn't the gold standard also immoral? For a "general equivalent" of value was itself established and maintained by repressing the multiplicity and difference of the parties entering the transaction – by subjecting them to systematic transformations. The pun, as a synchronic excess of stable signification, can "represent" the metaphysical excess that is our "historical wealth" – if at the cost of "parodying" it by indulging in letters. Puns, which retain "no little transactional value" for destablizing transactional language, appreciate in value at a time when the postmetaphysical poet needs all the means he can muster to create works whose "resonance lasts more than a season." And poetic forms, including meter and stanzaic patterns as well as rhyme schemes, are also useful to activate just this kind of value in excess of referential language. The excess value that makes for poetry resides in the words one lives by, not in metaphysics – whether the gold standard of an authoritative tradition or nature.

Since Greece is where Pound begins, Merrill's "After Greece" (1962: 12–13) may be the place to begin to see what happens after the thread of civilization has "snapped" and truths have become "old ideas / Found lying open to the elements." The poem's opening lines sound downright Poundian, as they trace an elemental process in an elemental language, paradoxically so elevated in tone that it approaches biblical pronouncement. Godlike, they speak the world into creation and read like a translation: "Light into the olive entered / And was oil." In Pound's brand of classicism, this elemental basis of transformational energy enables the constant renewal of the "old ideas"; a foundation of natural metamorphoses supports and authorizes all other transfers, translations, and exchanges. For natural process is the standard of value that determines equity – equitable substitutions in proper writing, naming, and figuration, as well as justice in morality, politics, and economics. All transactions are measurable against this natural standard of value.

From Merrill's perspective, however, such a natural ground that

regulates processes of exchange and substitution necessarily moves outside the game of substitutions, in order to function as their standard of
value. Natural process as a standard of value becomes Natural Process
– a capitalized universal – and joins the "system" of "old ideas." What
appears in Pound to be an anti-idealistic stance resolves into a recuperation of idealism, with nature replacing the metaphysical ground as
universal value. In Merrill, the natural ground that would authorize
making it "new" itself falls into place as part of the "old" system. If
nothing "holds up heaven nowadays," if the gods have departed, Merrill's poem recognizes that an elemental nature must go with them.
When "heaven" disappears, the earth does not thereby become
accessible as a primal source, for nature cannot serve as a universal
standard without recuperating or reproducing the "old ideas." Organicism, then, lies firmly within metaphysical thought.

Merrill's Greece has fallen not only from the Edenic cultural origin
of Greece but from a Poundian grace as well, which grants right naming a special dispensation as a language that is more than currency, a
language of the elements that can recover essentials. For Merrill, the
very act of right naming exiles him from any natural origin; it enters
the economy of representation, reinstitutes the "old" history, and re-
initiates his exile under the "northern sky":

> how I want
> Essentials: salt, wine, olive, the light, the scream –
> No! I have scarcely named you,
> And look, in a flash you stand full-grown before me,
> Row upon row, Essentials,
> Dressed like your sister caryatids
> Or tombstone angels jealous of their dead,
> With undulant coiffures, lips weathered, cracked by grime,
> And faultless eyes gone blank beneath the immense
> Zinc and gunmetal northern sky . . .
> Stay then. Perhaps the system
> Calls for spirits. This first glass I down
> To the last time

I ate and drank in that old world. May I
Also survive its meanings, and my own.

The passage rehearses and closes a paradigmatic history: in the very act of original naming, the essentials solidify into "Essentials"; a "fecund" nature freezes in stony representations like "caryatids" and "tombstone angels," repeating the deadening history of idealism. And the poet backs out of such petrification with "spirits." Pound's cure for such blockage and petrification was right naming; for Merrill, naming is part of the problem, the disease and not the cure. The cure, or *pharmakon,* seems indeed to be a pun, for "spirits" is a slippage in right naming, an epistemological indeterminacy that refuses to solidify.

"Animal intoxication," Emerson writes, is one of the *"quasi-*mechanical substitutes for the true nectar, which is the ravishment of the intellect by coming nearer to the fact"; the inspiration we owe narcotics is "some counterfeit excitement and fury" (1990: 208). In Merrill's terms, Emerson's sublime, fatal fact becomes "Fact" or Nature, an Idea. Merrill's "facts" or "essentials" are no longer primal or fatal; already "Essentials," they belong in a "system" of signification already in place, and themselves fall into place in it, "Row upon row," as in the poem. The only way to connect to a primal inspiration appears to be through the quasi-mechanical substitute of a pun, in a "ravishment" by the "fatal growths" of its senses.

Puns escape the idealizing economy of referential and representational substitution, since their multiple meanings are coeval, residing in the letters of the word. Hence, as Merrill defends them, puns are immoral (there can be no question of "justice" or "equity"), cheap (their "wealth" has no measurable value and posits no standard for such evaluation), transgressive (of the naming father and the hierarchical structures of substitution, whether of name for thing or vehicle for tenor), and "unseemly" (they offer forbidden sexual pleasure and economize on psychic expenditure [Freud 1963: 118] by skirting the economy of sublimation).

Only a "counterfeit" standard, Merrill's pun on "spirits" represents and parodies "our vital wealth" by alluding to "Spirit," a metaphysical base, via the delusion of "spirits," a sort of ludicrous logos. Given the range of senses "spirits" carries, it writes large or capitalizes the mode of operations that characterize puns; in fact, it might serve as a paradigmatic Pun. "Spirit," from an Indo-European root meaning "breath," is both the essential "life principle" and the "mind," "intelligence," or "thinking, motivating, feeling part of man, often as distinguished from the body." As such, it follows the spirit or the "real meaning, true intention" of the law–Law of naming, the production of ideal value; at the same time, it questions this value, for it also spells profane "spirits." At once liquor and mind, animal intoxication and true inspiration, the pun "spirits" converts spirit and letter, ideal value and counterfeit value, into each other without end. Similarly, as a "distillation" or liquor, it is the "essence" of a substance, which is not substantial or hardened but a liquid (all quotes from *Webster's*). Thus the pun makes a complex detour back to the spirit of the law through an esprit, a play on letters that interrupts the essentializing process; it represents a return to essentials or essences through a liquidation of "Essentials" or Essences. "Spirits" is a word without a single essence, and its indeterminacy at once subverts the process of naming and recovers a base essence, which naming loses. This base device, the "lowest form of humor," is also basic — essential without being Essential, without the capital letter that in fact kills the spirit and raises the letter of the law into Law.

"Capitals" is itself a multivalent term. Architecturally, "capitals" may be said to balance "heaven":

Of the gods' houses only
A minor premise here and there
Would be balancing the heaven of fixed stars
Upon a Doric capital.

Since, Merrill explains, classical architecture was part of a whole "system" of values, capitals belonged in a network of other "capitals":

in that vast fire
Were other irons – well, Art, Public Spirit,

Ignorance, Economics, Love of Self,
Hatred of Self, a hundred more,
Each burning to be felt, each dedicated
To sparing us the worst; how I distrust them
. . . how I want
Essentials: salt, wine, olive, the light, the scream –

Yet poetic and grammatical conventions themselves belong in a system of capital values. The convention of lineation, for example, gives us "how I want / Essentials"; with the subsequent, midline capitalization of "Essentials," the essentializing and idealizing process of naming – of a referential, substitutive model of language – dovetails with the conventions of poetry and sentencing. The various "capitals" convene in one "system." And if this system lies in ruins "After Greece," where does one turn, without erecting another general equivalent or "gold standard" of value? "The system," Merrill concludes, "calls for spirits" or metaphysical authority. Just as he questions capitalizing from within the "system," while observing its conventions and imperatives, his pun on "spirits" brings down metaphysical spirits at the same time that it projects them. His spirits and his capitals represent and parody God's creative breath; the capital of the logos or words are our "vital wealth" indeed.

Thus Merrill can hope to survive "meanings," both to outlive the "old ideas" and to disarm his own meanings – the threat that *his* essentials will replace and replay the Greek capitals. By evading naming, he escapes a materialism that detours back to idealism, which negates the material life of subject and object alike. By dwelling in the materiality of the signifier, he enters a different economy of language. Merrill's puns signal a kind of metaphysical excess inscribed in language – an excess that also undoes metaphysics. Such a rhetorical ground exorcises the nostalgia for essentials and right naming. Merrill's source is an original rhetoric, before substitutions, which allows him to erect such meanings as he can survive.

"Economic Man" (1984: 298–99) also indicates Merrill's distance from a modernist recuperation of metaphysics through organicism.

Here, Merrill places poetry within a system of other, isomorphic economies based on substitutive exchanges and describes their present
straits:

> Perhaps it is being off the gold standard
> Makes times particularly hard.
> Dark brings the jingle and glint of waning coin.
> The Huntress pokes through a vast pantheon
> Of paper, each leaf sacred to someone
> Like Richelieu or Hamilton.

Being off the metaphorical gold standard, without a universal "general
equivalent" of value, we have the "jingle and glint of waning coin."
Without the one God, we revert to a pantheon, a waxing forest of
symbols or paper leaves, each consecrating a different and local politics
and history. The "Huntress" seems to be Diana or Artemis, whom
Pound also uses in similar contexts. The patroness of silversmiths, Diana was often represented on coins; for Pound, this is the beginning
of the end and a perversion of values, when a goddess of fertility hard-
ens into coinage – a representation of value that weighs heavier than
the real value it represents:

> coin'd Artemis
> all goods light against coin-skill
> (1981: 753)

In Merrill, too, the goddess appears overwhelmed by the usurious
increase of representation and pokes through this paper "grove."

For Merrill, however, as metaphysical authority goes, so goes nature:

> These days the people I know, like raccoons,
> Squat over streams to wash their hands
> In the clear thinking of John Maynard Keynes,
> And nothing clings to the pans.

One cannot mine nature or extract value out of it without positing a
"gold standard"; a "significant" or signifying nature both upholds and
is upheld by a metaphysical superstructure. Without it, "the heavens

fill with counterfeit / Bodies and lights, which seem to circulate," and all exchanges become unjust:

> The woman of the world puts on
> These trinkets with a frown.
> They poison her compliance and the love
> We had no other way to prove.
>
> The diehards cry: "Restore
> The monarchy! Our buried king
> Lent significance to everything,
> Made the desert bloom and the heart soar.
> Uranium the jet-black President is insane –
> Ah to be loyal subjects once again!"

A king would offer "significance" – capital that would guarantee equity in exchanges – and ensure growth, health, sanity, and light. Instead of the gold standard of a king we have the President, an elected representative whose rhetorical or consensual authority is unstable because he comes with a given half-life. This built-in self-destructive term of "Uranium the jet-black President" synchronizes with technological change, with its equally built-in obsolescence.

Where to look, then, for something whose "resonance" lasts?

> Personally I would leave him at Fort Knox
> And look for something better – yes, but what?
> Each time you butter bread
> Paid for with money that your money made
> The debt grows more prohibitive
> To those luxurious lives you didn't live.

Merrill would just as soon leave the President to his fortifications – military power now substituting for the divine authority of kings – to guard his gold reserves and preserve the very idea of reserve value, but what is "better"? The truth is, Merrill's bread is buttered by an economy of "usury." As a poet certainly, he lives on interest; indeed, his kind of poetry thrives on an *excess* interest. And this usurious life of a representational economy incurs debts to "reality"; it is farther and farther removed from the capital – the luxury of "real" life and the proprieties of naming. But he knows he will be "covered" in due time, when he reverts to his "original value in the vault" and Economic Man's debts to Eros are paid.

The poem's concluding stanzas equate poetic language with Freudian and economic substitutions and the history of religion and civilization that they institute. Freud as "Master" substitutes for "our king" and ensures equity in translating Eros into civilization and wealth:

> Infants (the Master said) in the erotic filth
> Of their own bodies first imagine wealth,
> Then sweat to purge it from the very bone.
> With shaven head and climbing eyes
> A priesthood grew. Soon Cities filled the skies,
> Of gold and precious stone.
>
> The next step was to build one here below.
> Less rich, conceivably, but no
> Less real, these concrete blocks
> Up from whose monumental bowels jokes
> Pharaoh's ghost: "Such interest we accrue,
> We might some day relent and cover you."
>
> Forty floors down is Wall Street; forty years
> Ago, the merger of Heart & Hurt
> That made me. Sunset. The gilt cages halt,
> Fill up with financiers,
> And sink. Not one of us but will revert
> To his original value in the vault.

Poetic, economic, political, religious, technological, and libidinal economies are all of a piece in this poem; they are all substitutive economies that progressively abstract "value" out of infantile "erotic filth," and all are mocked by the "Pharaoh's ghost" that still haunts the system's "monumental bowels." Despite Merrill's satiric edge, the "buried king" lives on now as death, which does make for a standard of value for the structures erected by "financiers" and poets alike.

Hence the ground of "original" values best be kept abstract, out of circulation.

The poet as Economic Man is a capitalist, for he does not work with metaphysical or use values but with exchange values. He is the postmetaphysical man, made of and by a network of economic exchanges and mergers. Economic Man keeps things flowing not by repressing usurious increase but precisely by resisting exact values. Merrill's vested interest in maintaining this vital status quo is also his interest to us, his readers. Disdaining a currency that has equity in nature and its truths and indulging in the luxuries of words as much by writing rhymed verse as by punning, he affords us the pleasures of his language. Merrill is able to use the resources of the past on grounds that question their very grounds. He draws on the poetic "wealth" by making the "capital" of the past work for him, returning "usury" to "use."

Although his privileging representation over presence is of a piece with consumer capitalism, his questioning natural truths and attending to constructions of truths, to rhetoric and history, enables a critical distance from within the systemic whole his work is part of and even complicitous with. His practices are far from the complacencies of the New Formalists: while his forms call attention to the historically determined nature of his language, he declines claiming authority on these grounds, which would substitute history for metaphysics. Merrill's self-conscious forms, with their eighteenth-century urbanity, are as historically anachronistic as they are "inappropriate" for natural processes. Merrill employs amazing technical and historical resources in a pervasive critique of all metaphysical thinking and restores to poetry what may well be its generic function – to engage the economy of figurative language itself and reveal its production at once of both proper meanings and metaphysical excess.

II

"Lost in Translation," one of Merrill's major poems, also points up his revision of modernist traditions, and once again I would like to approach the poem via Pound. As performance and as trope, translation is central to Pound's work; it informs his understanding of literary change as engendered by metamorphic passages between languages, which revitalize the target languages as they alter the originals. The fact that translation is possible and can even revitalize a given language implies that "no one language is complete," and in "our time" no "man" can "think with only one language." All languages are constantly changing, "churning and chugging," and the metamorphic process of translation liberates poets from the "paste-board partitions" and conventional habits of thinking in any one language (Pound 1968a: 36). An ideal, universal value backs up the metamorphic passages between languages, which liberate the poet from the conventions of any single language and access unchanging psychological and natural truths. Translation at once offers access to these universals and allows for changes in the formal and rhetorical practices of a given language, so that the universals can be presented in terms that convince us now and in English, say.

Historical continuity is not an issue for Pound; he plunders the past and a variety of literatures, without regard for historical contingencies, to cull whatever they offer him for current use. Pound's tradition may well be defined as what will translate, for it is not so much a given body of past literatures as a miscellany of past works that might prove useful now. They may teach the poet techniques other than those English offers – different metric systems, for example. Or they may carry "messages" that should be heard anew. By aligning present experience with past versions of such experience, a poet can provide historical proof of its transhistorical and transcultural universality. The possibility of translation, which is bound up with the very possibility of Pound's beginning as a poet, proves the existence of "cores" that are independent of "codes," whether of different languages or of different periods.

Early on, these "cores" are largely emotional or psychological experiences. "Only emotion endures," Pound declares (1968a: 14), and it endures through renewal and transformation: "My pawing over the ancients and semi-ancients has been one struggle to find out what has been done, once for all, better than it can ever be done again, and to find out what remains for us to do, and plenty does remain, for if we still feel the same emotions as those which launched the thousand ships, it is quite certain that we come on these feelings differently, through different nuances, by different intellectual gradations." The poet thinks from life, not books, but old books may offer new ways of getting at "life"; Daniel and Cavalcanti, for example, are useful because they offer "that precision which I miss in the Victorians, that explicit rendering, be it of external nature, or of emotion" (11).

The poet is the medium of the two-way passage that constitutes tradition. Making it new day by day also means making it old, because "it" – here, the process of natural change itself – does not change. "The Tree" exemplifies such a transformational passage of universal experiences:

> I stood still and was a tree amid the wood
> Knowing the truth of things unseen before,
> Of Daphne and the laurel bow
> And that god-feasting couple olde
> That grew elm-oak amid the wold.
> 'Twas not until the gods had been
> Kindly entreated and been brought within
> Unto the hearth of their heart's home
> That they might do this wonder-thing.
> Nathless I have been a tree amid the wood
> And many new things understood
> That were rank folly to my head before.
>   (1976: 35)

In this poem, the psychological adventure of an Ovidian metamorphosis also enables a historical understanding, for the poet now recognizes the truth of earlier examples of such stories, of "Daphne and the laurel bow." In repeating the psychological experience that is the source of this myth, he learns both a truth of nature and the truth of poetry, which meet in "the laurel bow." He becomes a poet, awakening at once to nature and tradition – specifically, the tradition of metamorphosis from Ovid's myths through Browning's masks, whose voice echoes in the poem's final line. Here the truth of tradition lies in its truthfulness to the nature it patterns, for the "laurel bow" links natural process, psychic fluidity, figurative language, and literary tradition. In other words, psychological universals validate tradition and tradition validates psychological truths; without this validating "translation" across languages and through history, the psychological experience is sheer "nonsense" (1968a: 431) and the tradition "rank folly."

As a trope, then, translation questions the status of the original as unique and unrepeatable, for it assumes the original text can be transmitted into another historical time and language. The possibility of translation also posits an ideal meaning that can comprehend both the original and its copy. Accordingly, as practice translation is "good training, if you find that your original matter 'wobbles' when you try to rewrite it. The meaning of the poem to be translated can not 'wobble' " (1968a: 7). "Meaning" is the Confucian "unwobbling pivot," the third term supervising the substitutive exchange between two sign systems; it is the ideal value that oversees the transaction from one language to another. Pound's enterprise must assume such an ideal value, for on no other basis can literatures of many different languages, cultures, and historical times be readable now in English. Translation and tradition are substitutive exchanges enabled by this idealizing, which Pound's multiplicity recuperates. His internationalism is backed up by the "gold" of "self-evident" natural and psychological truths, meanings that never change.

This modern reading of tradition, authorizing violations of historical and cultural continuities from higher perspectives, can be traced back to Keats's "On First Looking into Chapman's Homer" (1978: 34). Here, too, translation accesses a past that is not one's own; therefore, it is not a binding past but a realm open to future colonizing, projecting exciting imperial conquests of lands not already drained dry. Translation at once confirms the dependency of poetic experience on a given language and offers "vistas" beyond it. Keats had never breathed the "pure serene" of Homer's "demesne" until he "heard Chapman speak out loud and bold." Hearing Homer in this translation, however, he does not feel like an archaeologist who has reconstructed the past but "like some watcher of the skies / When a new planet swims into his ken." Thus translation enables mastery as much of the future as of the past; in Pound as in Keats, it promises imperial futures and "realms of gold." Violating the academic continuities of discrete traditions, translation can recuperate a useful continuity of past, present, and future, for Pound's progressive figuration of history places value not in the past per se but in its use for pointing to "tomorrow's water supply" (1970b: 57).

By contrast, Merrill questions the possibility of translation: riding on the symbolic function of words, it loses their semiotic dimension, which makes for the excess that is poetry. Since how one conceives of translation amounts to how one figures literary tradition and history – the relation between past, present, and future – different conceptions of translation would signal different figurations of history and language. The possibility of translation posits meanings separate from the historical and linguistic contingencies of their articulation; its impossibility challenges this metaphysics.

"Lost in Translation" (1976: 4–10) is ostensibly an autobiographical poem. While its title suggests the existence of an original that can be "lost," the poem in fact explores how origins and originals must be constructed by the divagations of translations, interpretations, and metaphors. Merrill approaches his personal past via a series of texts – jigsaw puzzles, fabulous oriental tales in quatrains, letters, poems, and their translations. In these displacements – composed, as he puts it, largely of pieces drawn from the "craftsman's repertoire" – the source experience dissolves into the craftsman's resources. And any given "piece" fits in a number of puzzles and plots a number of stories; one "scene" or letter sustains different readings or misreadings; and words or even letters carry various senses. Along the way, unequivocal meanings and experiences independent of codes come into doubt.

For example, one of the "pieces" in Merrill's puzzle "that shifts like sand" is "An inchling, innocently branching palm." Like the other pieces of the puzzle, it can be "put aside, made stories of," or "questioned / Like incoherent faces in a crowd, / Each with its scrap of highly colored / Evidence the Law must piece together." The piece of a sandalwood puzzle assembled in the "library" can reappear, as the "plot thickens" in a London library many years later, in a "tole / Casket" and be translated by a medium from a "freak fragment / Of a pattern complex in appearance only" to the "lumber mill" and even further back to "that long-term lamination / Of hazard and craft" that has "Made it matter in the first place." Or it can be translated into Valéry's "Palme" and read in Athens – that "sunlit paradigm" of a rooted poetry, which "Taps a sweet wellspring of authority." Or it can translate into Rilke's "leaf-carved capitals" or Merrill's "self-effacing tree" that "turns the waste / To shade and fiber, milk and memory." And we can interpret this last tree as providing welcome "shade" from "sun-ripe" originals, as offering only ghostly, textual substitutes, or as supplying the true sustenance of nature and memory. How to read this "piece" remains in question. Merrill's tree is not necessarily a natural fact, but it can play the part, among the others in its repertoire; it is not the crux of a single metamorphosis but enters any number of metaphoric and interpretive exchanges.

In the prose piece "Acoustical Chambers," Merrill recalls the period that the poem describes:

> By the time I was eight I had learned from [Mademoiselle] enough French and German to understand that English was merely one of many ways to express things. A single everyday object could be called *assiette* or *Teller* as well as *plate* – or were plates themselves subtly different in France and Germany? . . . At the same time, I was discovering how the everyday sounds of English could mislead you by having more than one meaning. One afternoon at home I opened a random book and read: "Where is your husband, Alice?" "In the library, sampling the port." If samples were little squares of wallpaper or chintz, and ports were where ships dropped anchor, this hardly clarified the behavior of Alice's husband. Long after Mademoiselle's exegesis, the phrase haunted me. Words weren't what they seemed. The mother tongue could inspire both fascination and distrust. (1986: 4)

Whether in translation or in homonymy, the only solids are the signifiers; their meanings are open to question or "wobble" and cannot be trusted. Thus Merrill will conclude, "Words might frustrate me, forms never did; neither did meter."

The crucial autobiographical puzzle in the poem is the absence of the child's parents; and their impending breakup, reflected on the historical stage, "With 1939 about to shake / This world . . . / To its foundations," comes to signify the eventual loss of all "parental" authority in the poem. Appropriately, the immediate origin of the poem, it appears, is textual – Merrill's reading Valéry's "Palme" and recalling its translation – as we learn from a parenthetical aside well into the narrative:

> (Thus, reading Valéry the other evening
> And seeming to recall a Rilke version of "Palme,"
> That sunlit paradigm whereby the tree
> Taps a sweet wellspring of authority,
> The hour came back. Patience dans l'azur.
> Geduld im . . . Himmelblau? Mademoiselle.)

This parenthetical explanation of the poem's origin follows a bilingual line in the story of the past that reading Valéry has conjured: "Mademoiselle," the boy's governess, is urging " 'Patience, chéri. Geduld, mein Schatz.' " Presumably, her remembered speech chronologically precedes the parenthetical lines; but these lines reveal that a textual experience in fact precedes the recollection of the spoken words and the lived experiences they recall in turn.[6]

Doubt shrouds the particulars of the recollected past as well. While Merrill plants "An inchling, innocently branching palm" in his jigsaw puzzle, he adds a parenthetical "(surely not just in retrospect)," alerting us to the possibility that the content of the past experience may also be an effect of his present reading. Since a "backward-looking" "pageboy" is one of Merrill's guises here, it is fitting that the poem's inspiration or influx is his reading a French poem, seeming to recall its German translation, and only thus, by way of these textual detours, remembering spoken words and a possible experiential context for them.

The "source" speech, moreover, is itself double; the "remembered" source is bilingual, an original translation. The poem's other bilingual line, Mademoiselle's " 'Schlaf wohl, chéri,' " nicely illustrates this root division. With her "French hopes, her German fears," Mademoiselle

– who is neither a mademoiselle nor French – fits into the poem's historical puzzle of the impending war and Germany's "bid to change the map of Europe" (1986: 127). She also fits into the autobiographical puzzle. English, though it is even Mademoiselle's mother tongue, plays no part in triggering the recollection that is Merrill's poem, for in the "puzzle" of the long-ago summer the boy's relation to his mother tongue is anything but secure; his parents absent, he has only Mademoiselle, mother substitute and surrogate mother tongue, who speaks French with a German accent.

No wonder, then, that "Lost in Translation" is "epi-graphed" by a translation – four lines from Valéry in Rilke's German. Epigraphs from foreign languages are conventionally left in the original to confirm their authority as sources that prefigure the later poem. Here, however, the authoritative textual source Merrill cites is itself a translation, a trope for an original source, and he will go on to judge what is lost in this metaphoric transmission. For his title also plays on Robert Frost's aphorism "Poetry is what gets lost in translation." The reason for this loss is the arbitrary and therefore, given a specific language, absolutely necessary nature of linguistic signs. Poetry's untranslatability questions the primacy of the signified over the signifier. Poetry, after all, emphasizes the sensory shape of words and the forms that have historically coded their physical properties – in rhyme, meter, and so on – in a given language. Translation substitutes one formal system or code for another; when the core of the original "wobbles" in translating a poem, it becomes clear that the core or meaning is not independent of the code but a function of it – of the specific phonic and grammatical properties of a given language or poem.

Hence, Merrill describes Rilke's translation as the ruinous German invasion of the French, hinting also that such appropriations and substitutions come down to power plays:

> I've seen it. Know
> How much of the sun-ripe original
> Felicity Rilke made himself forego
> (Who loved French words – verger, mûr, parfumer)
> In order to render its underlying sense.

Know already in that tongue of his
What Pains, what monolithic Truths
Shadow stanza to stanza's symmetrical
Rhyme-rutted pavement. Know that ground plan left
Sublime and barren, where the warm Romance
Stone by stone faded, cooled; the fluted nouns
Made taller, lonelier than life
By leaf-carved capitals in the afterglow.
The owlet umlaut peeps and hoots
Above the open vowel. And after rain
A deep reverberation fills with stars.

Translation is impossible. Both words in Merrill's phrase "underlying sense" do double duty: the underlying sense is both the abstract meaning that lies under the letters and the sensory qualities of language that underlie its abstractions. And "underlying" means at once a support and a lying or untruth at the base. In translation, the sensory life of the poem is sacrificed to its underlying sense; but this sense is not an absolute, the true meaning of the text. Instead, it is a lie; it "under-lies" the truth of the letters. It is just this complex, generative interplay between the code and the core that translation loses, effacing, as it must, one or the other aspect of the work. Thus Rilke, forgoing the felicities of Valéry's language in order to render its "core," ends up with a pure code, and Merrill properly emphasizes the look of the German letters, with the spirit of the French drained away.

Of course, translation is also possible, and Merrill himself has translated Valéry's poem – rhyme scheme intact – with many felicitous phrases and wordplays. But the possibility of translation here attests not to a core immune to displacements but to a core imaginable in and as its displacements and losses. For this reason, Merrill immediately asks:

Lost, is it, buried? One more missing piece?

But nothing's lost. Or else: all is translation
And every bit of us is lost in it
(Or found – I wander through the ruin of S

Now and then, wondering at the peacefulness)
And in that loss a self-effacing tree,
Color of context, imperceptibly
Rustling with its angel, turns the waste
To shade and fiber, milk and memory.

Quite possibly, the truth "found" in the losses incurred by the "translations" in this poem is the real "occasion" of the poem – the peaceful
"ruin of S," again presented in a parenthetical aside, as a textual find.
But how do we read "the ruin of S"? The senses of "S" proliferate.
It may be the capital initial of a lover's name, a device Merrill often
uses, whose "failing" may have again re-turned the poet to his
"mother tongue!" (1969: 20). Or "S" may stand for Sandover, Merrill's childhood home, the past that is lost and found in the poem's
acoustical chamber. In *The Changing Light at Sandover,* S calls forth
Stevens and "Sergei." Appropriately, then, S is also the letter designating a plural, the proliferation of senses that is a ruin. The original
site of experience becomes a ruin when the initial capital source S
hopelessly forks and multiplies in plurals. Thus the letter S is Satan's
sign, introducing time and loss, translating the initial S of a single
Source or origin into the final S of the plural ending. Finally, S is
simply a letter, the origin and the loss of all "underlying sense," all
symbolic readings, all meaning. The letter subsumes even time and
loss. And the "changing light" that rules over all, juggling stars and
periods (1985: 8), is perhaps a natural fact and, perhaps, a literary var-
iation of Marvell's "various Light," in whose difference we can dream
of the Garden.

    In all of its senses, then, the "ruin of S" is both a loss and a find.
Just as home is found in the loss of substitutive plots and puzzles, just
as a prewar peace is an effect of its cataclysmic loss and the primal
garden an effect of changing lights, the poem's recoveries follow from
its losses. The diachronic losses of various "translations" – of metaphor
and memory, as well as of interpretation and translation – are of the
essence, for they project sources, origins, and primal unities. The past
– personal, historical, or textual – cannot be imagined as a "prior"
source prior to such loss; it is loss that figures the past as prior, as a

source. This dialectic applies to intratextual unity as well; as Merrill writes in "Acoustical Chambers," "The unities of home and world, and world and page, will be observed through the very act of transition from one to the other." Since home is always already broken, long before the "Weathermen" accidentally blow it up, Merrill's echoing stanzas can sound a personal past partly in the inflections of "surrogate parents," as he calls his literary influences (1986: 7). The "translation" of interpretation retraces these transitions or substitutions, at once going back and forth, to recover textual sources and unities. But what is found differs from what was lost; what is found is always only textual, always "found" in a library, and cannot vouch for primal experience.

In Merrill's figuration of the temporal relation between the past and the present, the present poem is neither bound by the past and history – whether personal, public, or literary – nor free of them. The present is "parenthetical" to the past that is represented or recalled in the poem; in other words, it has only a textual relation to the past, a source that is a function of the present discourse. There is no existential loss prior to the textual loss, and no primary text prior to its translation or reappropriation by allusion, quotation, or any of the various figures that constitute tradition. Again, Merrill's poem appeals to the questionable "authority" of Rilke's appropriation; what he "ransacks" Athens to locate is not Valéry's original "gold" but Rilke's translation, the ruin of which belies the "truth" of the original "Palme," that "sunlit paradigm whereby the tree / Taps a sweet wellspring of authority."

Valéry figures his "authority" as a physical, natural, even physiological source; his palm can raise its erect, fibrous form to such heights because its "avid roots" delve deep to reach a "profound / Water," a spring buried in the desert waste of the present but readying "so much gold, / So much authority."[7] Yet in Valéry, too, the "gold" or "authority" is accumulated through temporal loss and accessed via the departure or deviation of metaphor, for the "sunlit paradigm" of a text as a tree posits such a natural source and offers the model of "one who, thinking, spends / His inmost dividends / To grow at any cost." A primal source, like a primal or proper meaning, is an effect of metaphor's deviation; the source does not exist before such a departure.[8]

In this deviation, the poem gives rise to its sources, the son begets the parents who can beget him, and metaphor figures the sources that would prefigure it. For just as a punning "spirits" alludes to, yet parodies, metaphysical spirits, the "changing light" of losing substitutions alludes to, while parodying, "sunlit paradigms" of authoritative, rooted languages.

If, for Pound, universal truths are found in translation, for Merrill any illusion of such grounds gets lost in translation, for what origins his translations recover are abysmally textual. The "truth" of the impossibility of transmitting truths across languages and time teaches a lesson different from Pound's: truths are historically, linguistically, and culturally contingent. In Pound, when we can accommodate more than one linguistic, cultural, or historical perspective, we prove truths that are not merely epistemological; in Merrill, when we shift perspectives, we change truths. Since we necessarily shift perspectives in translation, all translation entails persuasion. Merrill's postmodern international trade is not backed by bullion; rather, it operates as a network of credits and debits – of unstable political alliances and conflicts, violent assimilations and ransackings.

Thus Merrill's self-reflexive textuality in fact shows that no "transmission" – whether translation, representation, metaphor, interpretation, or tradition – is innocent of a will to power. For if truths are not metaphysical, they can only be political – rhetorical and consensual. Neither an authoritative past nor the immediacy of some unmediated present authorizes his texts, and his formal and rhetorical mediation robs both past and present of the privileged status of a stable reference point. Merrill's "abysmal" textuality alludes to and parodies the ideal value that would stabilize his transactions, which can thus be viewed as both losses and gains. Without a metaphysical "gold standard," the world is "opaque *and* transparent" – "cheerful *and* awful," as Merrill concurs (1986: 80) with Bishop – and poems, like lives, are constantly shifting puzzles of losses and finds, mixed blessings like "Sour windfalls of the orchard back of us" (1976: 4).

Notes

1. Readings of "contemporary" poetry typically privilege technical experiment and follow a modern or progressive model of history. For example, James Breslin writes, "In retrospect . . . we can see that in the fifties the only way to renovate literature was by annihilating it – the prototypical avant-garde gesture." Thus, "when [Frank] O'Hara strolled out of the Museum of Modern Art that noon [to pen "The Day Lady Died"], he had also, it seemed, stepped outside of Literature," and at that instant "poetry once again became disruptive – critical of its culture, of its immediate past, of itself"; by "repudiating orthodox modernism, American poetry once again became modern, 'of the present'" (1984: xiii, xv). Similarly, even in Perkins's balanced account, postmodern poetry is seen as a rebellion against the New Critical rationalization of the modernist legacy. The new poetry "did not repudiate the high Modernism of the 1920s, but in fact returned to it," remaining "open in form and antagonistic to the idea of form" (1987: 334, 339). Perloff's reading of postmodern poetry as an anarchic antiformalist repudiation of formalist-symbolist verse in closed forms repeats this model (1985). And Antin (1972) spells out the connection between poetic innovation and cultural criticism. His notion of a "metrical-moral" tradition remains firmly within a modernist framework.

   Paul Breslin's *The Psycho-Political Muse* (1987) is one exception in questioning this model of poetic history. His interest is in the psychopolitical rhetoric of liberation rather than the rhetoric of forms and techniques. I agree with Breslin that, "viewed as the liberation of creative energy from the death grip of outworn conventions, the recent history of American poetry is a boring melodrama. It is only credible as literary history if it is viewed as the displacement of one set of conventions by another. Even poetry that seems to come from 'experience,' or from the unconscious, or from Olsonian 'process' has conventions." By "conventions" he has in mind larger stylistic matters of voice rather than technical and formal conventions, and he dislikes the "alternation between genteel and neoprimitive forms of narrowness" (xv).

However, in arguing that the "several prominent group styles" of the 1960s "share a conception of poetry as engaged in the liberation of human consciousness from a false consciousness imposed by society" (1987: xiii), Breslin only shifts the liberational scenario to the poets' explicit, psychopolitical rhetoric and suggests that the perceptive critic (unlike one who buys the poets' rhetoric) will be able to see through it and show that such "liberation" simply adheres to different stylistic conventions.

In the end, then, Breslin stays within the dominant framework: he argues that sixties poetry claimed to be a liberation from outworn conventions, but it was not. The central "agon" holds – conventions versus "liberation," for which we are still waiting. For what disappoints Breslin is that this poetry makes false claims – it fails to liberate. While his study provides a good critique of liberational rhetoric, he provides no alternatives to the evaluative criterion of "liberation." I would suggest that the best poets very much question this rhetoric of liberation itself.

Nelson, reading modernism against contemporaneous poetic production, argues that the canonization of modernist poetry proceeded by opposing "genteel" and "sentimental" poetry in traditional forms to "innovative" or "modern" poetry (1981: 21–22). He suggests that the process of canonization cast literary history as a dramatic narrative of a contest between progressive and traditional poetries. Perloff's essay "Pound/Stevens: Whose Era?" (1982) argues that a similar drama of experiment versus tradition plays out within canonized modernism itself. These critical traditions shape the readings of postmodern poetry in terms of an antagonism between experimental and formalist poetics. What is at stake in all of these dramas is the big contest between Romanticism and modernism; the bid to decide which is the aberration and which the true development of poetry in English is a bid to control the terrain Eliot's criticism once ruled over. If we were to see a substantive continuity between Romanticism and experimental modernism, such dramas would lose much of their urgency.

2. In addition to Perloff and Antin, see Frank and Sayre (1988) and Easthope (1983). For a conservative perspective, see Turner and Pöppel (1983).
3. Most recently, Perloff's *Radical Artifice* (1991) and Conte's *Unending Design* (1991) show that this argument persists into the nineties; for a critique of such assumptions, see Steele's *Missing Measures* (1990).

4. In my reading of Pound I will focus on the features of his work that have been played up so that he can perform this literary-historical function. The Pound that has been critically appropriated for this purpose is itself open to question. See, e.g., Riddel's (1979) and Rabaté's (1986) deconstructionist readings of Pound against Kenner's (1971) organicist Pound. Cushman (1993) provides another kind of corrective – this time, to Perloff's avant-garde Pound – by arguing that his form achieves its effects by its dialogue with English and other metrical traditions.

5. See, e.g., Kenner (1971), Schneidau (1969), Géfin (1982), and Bell (1981).

6. The opposition of rhetoric and poetry may have even deeper roots. Kermode (1957), for example, has argued that this is a Romantic impulse. From this perspective, modernists would appear to be only technically revamping the Romantic-humanist concept of the imagination as a perceptive-creative shaping faculty, since "direct" presentation, as opposed to rhetoric and representation, is an ideal that marks the transcendent impulse of the Romantic image as well.

  Bender and Wellbery also locate this tendency in Romanticism: "What the Enlightenment accomplished in the domains of theoretical and practical discourse, Romanticism achieved in the aesthetic domain. Only with Romanticism was rhetoric finally and thoroughly evacuated from the realm of imaginative expression" (1990: 15). Their informative history of the fortunes of rhetoric concludes with the argument that modernism marks a return to rhetoric. I would argue that the modernism of Pound, the most influential on twentieth-century American poetry, is as implicated in the values of modernization as Romanticism is.

7. According to Steele (1990), modernists confused Victorian diction and rhetoric with metrical verse, and in reacting against the former, they also rejected the latter.

8. Hulme and Bergson would seem to be Pound's precedents here. For Bergson, a juxtaposition of "diverse images" makes for "intuitive," or preanalytic, perception (Coffman 1951: 55); for Hulme, thought consists in a "simultaneous presentation to the mind of two different images" (1962: 84). For a discussion of Hulme's debt to Bergson, see Coffman (1951: 54–56).

9. For example, in "Romanticism and Classicism," Hulme speaks of "a bad metaphysic of art" as characteristic of the Romantic attitude. The Romantic "is not content with saying that he prefers this kind of verse. He wants to deduce his opinion . . . from some fixed principle which can be found by metaphysic" (1948: 262). He also denounces the Romantic "confusion" of human and religious spheres, which renders Romanticism "spilt religion" (259). For Hulme, the realm of religious and ethical values is absolutely separate from the inorganic and organic natural spheres

(1924: 5–11). By contrast, Pound admires Greek humanism, for example, because the Greek concept of beauty is an "interpretation" of the "vital universe" – of "the tree and the living rock," the "universe of fluid force" – "by its signs of gods and godly attendants and oreads" (1968b: 92–93). Here aesthetic, natural, and divine spheres coincide.

10. This book complements and expands the synchronic rhetorical typology of my *American Poetry* (1987) by factoring in historical change. Focusing on the modern–postmodern divide, I want to examine the rhetorical negotiations of forms and extraformal values.

11. For this purpose I find their statements about their poetic programs most useful. For an evenhanded and perceptive extended discussion of both movements, including discriminating readings of specific poems, see Shetley (1993).

12. The term is the title of Scott's collection of essays (1990) on modernist writers of both sexes, which aims to show the important role of women writers in the modern period.

FRANK O'HARA: "HOW AM I TO BECOME A LEGEND?"

1. One index of O'Hara's trivialization in much critical commentary is how little care is taken in reading his poems. For example, arguing for O'Hara's nonsymbolist poetic, Perloff remarks that his trees do not have to be "plane" trees; "another tree would do just as well" (1979: 208). And Meyer concurs: "Exactly. This is a very disturbing and unnerving *modus operandi*. Especially for those in Pound's camp, those for whom each word, much less each image, is charged with selectivity to the point of being psychologically overdetermined" (1990: 90). But, of course, any other kind of tree would *not* do, for the "argument" of the poem is carried by such "puns." The poem may rely on an accidental resource, but within the poem's economy the kind of tree is not an interchangeable detail. In other words, the detail may be interchangeable from a metaphysical perspective, but not within this poem's economy. Here, again, value is exchange value and plane trees have "value" in this system. It is a unique detail, but no symbolic import is invested in its uniqueness. "How can we trust a poem that doesn't care if a tree is an elm, not a lime?" Meyer asks (91); how can we trust a reading that doesn't care if a tree is a plane tree, not an elm or a lime?

2. Gooch's biography shows how the war also weaned O'Hara from his parents and helped him achieve, for the first time, "a measure of adult independence" (1994: 91).

3. In this discussion of O'Hara's relation to Williams and the avant-garde

tradition, Lowney shows how O'Hara's vanguardism is also "an interrogation of the subtexts relating modernism and modernity" (1991: 248).

4. Longenbach's discussion of abstraction in Stevens's "Notes Toward a Supreme Fiction" provides interesting commentary on the politics of Abstract Expressionism through the forties and fifties. In the forties, when the pressure for politically engaged art came from the political Right, abstraction offered an alternative: "Scorned throughout the 1930s for being disengaged from historical reality, abstract art now seemed like a viable political alternative as the right appropriated the left's commitment to social realism" (1991: 254). Thus abstraction was "not a retreat from the political content of the social realism of the 1930s; it was a rebellion against the coercive demand for ideological explicitness, and it was an assertion of internationalist values" (253). During the Cold War, the political function of abstraction changed again: "By 1950 the Senate was calling for a worldwide 'Marshall Plan of Ideas,' and throughout the decade, the State Department subsidized the exhibition of Abstract Expressionist canvases in Europe. Jackson Pollock's splattered canvases became the badge of American individualism" (285). Longenbach quotes one rationale for such art from a 1952 symposium held at the Metropolitan Museum of Art: "Artistic freedom, experimentalism and diversity are products of democracy, and fundamentally opposed to authoritarianism. . . . In the troubled world of today, the artist's absolute freedom of thought, his uncontrolled expression of ideas and emotions, and his disinterested pursuit of perfection, are more needed than ever in our history" (285–86). O'Hara's admiration for Abstract Expressionism, with his emphasis on the individual perception of experience and individual responsibility, belongs to this phase. His dismissal of the notion of an avant-garde as "romantic nonsense" suggests his awareness of the complicity Guilbaud describes: "Avant-garde art succeeded because the work and the ideology that supported it, articulated in the painters' writings as well as conveyed in images, coincided fairly closely with the ideology that came to dominate American political life after the 1948 presidential elections." The ideology of "new liberalism," "unlike the ideologies of the conservative right and Communist left, not only made room for avant-garde dissidence but accorded to such dissidence a position of paramount importance" (1983: 3).

5. By contrast, Williams's aestheticizing working-class lives, neighborhoods, and so on is so troubling because it appeals to his legitimate distance as a poet – an aesthetic, objective observer – outside the system, who can appreciate beauty found in unlikely places. The city becomes the "background" that puts the poet in relief, so that he can posture and flaunt his

a master of her words, who speaks for one and all, getting "it" and passing "it" on, wheeling and dealing in "power," "guns," "scenarios," histories; the big production of "Harpers Ferry" is my case in point (1989: 38–42).

8. Said writes that "the imagery of succession, of paternity, of hierarchy" underlies such "genealogical connections" as "author-text, beginning-middle-end, text-meaning, reader-interpretation, and so on" (1985: 162).

JOHN ASHBERY: "THE EPIDEMIC OF THE WAY WE LIVE NOW"

1. "As You Came from the Holy Land" begins, with the title leading into the poem: "of western New York state / were the graves all right in their bushings / was there a note of panic in the late August air / because the old man had peed in his pants again" (1975: 6). The poem that rewrites Raleigh's "Walsinghame" defines itself as "the history of someone who came too late," and the juxtaposition of Raleigh's syntax with "bushings" highlights this lateness, for it doubly displaces the poet. While the poem is haunted by Raleigh, the "bushings" render him irrelevant, and vice versa, since the "new" and technologically inflected term "bushings" is deployed to return to Raleigh's questions and the issues of old age, death, and immortality. Ashbery is "too late" to both traditional and experimental norms; while invoking both, he has faith in neither. He comes from the "holy land" of the past, when poets could bank on a future (Christian or poetic immortality or the very possibility of "novelty"), but he finds himself in a present dispossessed of both past and future. The infirmity of the "old man" who is the subject of our solicitude here marks him as too late for a new beginning like Emerson's: "Late in the world, – too late perchance for fame, / Just late enough to reap abundant blame, – / I choose a novel theme . . . an unlaurelled Muse." Ashbery's poem rides on the "laurelled Muse" and cannot turn his lateness into a new earliness; it can only prove that "Youth is . . . / The fault that boys and nations soonest mend" (Emerson 1990: 491). Ashbery dwells between Emerson's opposing paradigms – "Old mouldy men and books and names and lands" and the youth's "I spurn the Past."

2. " 'How Much Longer Will I Be Able to Inhabit the Divine Sepulcher . . . ' " (1962: 25–27) covers the range of meanings light holds in Ashbery. The poem may be read as an allegory of the history of light: it traces the historical trajectory of the metaphor of light and darkness – the central metaphor, Derrida has argued, that grounds Western philosophical thought. It begins by invoking the divine or transcendent light of the Age of Religion ("And if some day // Men with orange shovels come to break open the rock / Which encases me, what about the light that comes in

then?"), but moves on to natural, pastoral light ("In the garden the sunlight was still purple") and then to modern, electrical light ("Darkness interrupts my story. / Turn on the light"), ending with a rhetorical "light," as in a manner of speaking ("Am I wonder, / Strategically, and in the light / Of the long sepulcher that hid death and hides me?"). By now, light is neither spiritual nor natural; it seems to survive only in certain discursive habits.

JAMES MERRILL: "SOUR WINDFALLS OF THE ORCHARD BACK OF US"

1. I am indebted to Goux's discussion of symbolic economies and the homologies he draws between linguistic and economic substitutive transactions (1990).
2. Ducrot and Todorov spell out the range and implications of the "transgression" that textual productivity represents (1979: 357).
3. The pun's subversive nature – working against institutions of academic thought, Aristotelian logic, Saussurian linguistics, and referential models of language – is argued by a number of essays in *On Puns* (Culler 1988).
4. Pound appeals to synechdoche to authorize his language yet upholds a prescriptive moral system, which entails hierarchies and in effect works against synechdochic logic. See my *American Poetry* (1987) for a reading of Pound as an anagogic poet, who distrusts analogical metaphor and seeks a language "beyond metaphor" (Pound 1968b: 33, 158). "Image," "vortex," and "ideogram" are various names for a figure that is less or more than a figure, an anagogic language that reveals natural isomorphisms and homologies.
5. See Goux (1990) on picture writing and barter as homologous systems.
6. In his valuable study of Merrill, Yenser remarks on the elusive origins of "Lost in Translation": "Is the poem's real source the relationship with Mademoiselle? Or is it indeed Valéry's lyric? Life or literature? To whose soft, imperative 'Patience' is it finally traceable? Or is the source better represented by Rilke's translation?" (1987: 13).
7. All quotations from Valéry are from Merrill's translation of "Palme" (1985: 72–74).
8. Discussing the "source" in Valéry, Derrida describes such an arrival through metaphoric divagation: "The proper meaning or the primal meaning (of the word *source,* for example) is no longer simply the source, but the deported effect of a turn of speech, a return or detour. It is secondary in relation to that to which it seems to give birth, measuring a separation and a departure from it. The source itself is the effect of that (for) whose origin it passes." Thus "proper meaning derives from derivation" (1982: 280). The whole essay on Valéry is of interest for Merrill as well.

Works Cited

Abrams, M. H. 1971. *Natural Supernaturalism: Tradition and Revolution in Romantic Literature*. New York: Norton.

Allen, Donald M., ed. 1960. *The New American Poetry*. New York: Grove.

Allen, Donald M., and George F. Butterick, eds. 1982. *The Postmoderns: The New American Poetry Revisited*. New York: Grove.

Allen, Gay Wilson, and Charles T. Davis, eds. 1955. *Walt Whitman's Poems: Selections with Critical Aids*. New York: New York Univ. Press.

Antin, David. 1972. "Modernism and Postmodernism: Approaching the Present in American Poetry." *Boundary 2* 1: 98–133.

Ashbery, John. 1956. *Some Trees*. New Haven, Conn.: Yale Univ. Press.

1962. *The Tennis Court Oath*. Middletown, Conn.: Wesleyan Univ. Press.

1966. *Rivers and Mountains*. New York: Holt, Rinehart & Winston.

1970. *The Double Dream of Spring*. New York: Dutton.

1974. Craft Interview with John Ashbery. By Janet Bloom and Robert Losada. In *The Craft of Poetry: Interviews from the "New York Quarterly."* Ed. William Packard, 111–32. Garden City, N.Y.: Doubleday.

1975. *Self-Portrait in a Convex Mirror*. New York: Viking.

1977. *Houseboat Days*. New York: Penguin.

1979. *As We Know*. New York: Penguin.

1981. *Shadow Train*. New York: Viking.

1983. "The Art of Poetry XXXIII." Interview with John Ashbery. By Peter Stitt. *Paris Review* 90: 30–59.

1984. *A Wave*. New York: Viking.

1989. *Reported Sightings: Art Chronicles, 1957–1987*. Ed. David Bergman. New York: Knopf.

1991. *Flow Chart*. New York: Knopf.

Auden, W. H. 1979. *Selected Poems*. Ed. Edward Mendelson. New York: Vintage.

———. 1989. *The Dyer's Hand and Other Essays*. Ed. Edward Mendelson. New York: Random House, 1962. Reprint, New York: Vintage.

Baudrillard, Jean. 1988. *America*. Trans. Chris Turner. London: Verso.

Bell, Ian. 1981. *Critic as Scientist: The Modernist Poetics of Ezra Pound*. London: Methuen.

Bender, John, and David E. Wellbery. 1990. *The Ends of Rhetoric: History, Theory, Practice*. Stanford, Calif.: Stanford Univ. Press.

Benjamin, Walter. 1969. "The Work of Art in the Age of Mechanical Reproduction." In *Illuminations*. Ed. Hannah Arendt. Trans. Harry Zohn. New York: Schocken.

Bernstein, Charles. 1992. *A Poetics*. Cambridge, Mass.: Harvard Univ. Press.

Bishop, Elizabeth. Drafts, manuscripts, and typescripts. Elizabeth Bishop Collection. Vassar College, Poughkeepsie, N.Y.

———. 1966. Interview by Ashley Brown. *Shenandoah* 17.2: 3–19.

———. 1981. "The Art of Poetry XXVII." Interview with Elizabeth Bishop. By Elizabeth Spires. *Paris Review* 80: 56–83.

———. 1983. *The Complete Poems, 1927–1979*. New York: Farrar, Straus and Giroux.

———. 1984. *The Collected Prose*. Ed. Robert Giroux. New York: Farrar, Straus and Giroux.

Blasing, Mutlu Konuk. 1987. *American Poetry: The Rhetoric of Its Forms*. New Haven, Conn.: Yale Univ. Press.

Breslin, James E. B. 1984. *From Modern to Contemporary: American Poetry, 1945–1965*. Chicago: Univ. of Chicago Press.

Breslin, Paul. 1987. *The Psycho-Political Muse: American Poetry since the Fifties*. Chicago: Univ. of Chicago Press.

Bürger, Peter. 1984. *Theory of the Avant-Garde*. Trans. Michael Shaw. Minneapolis: Univ. of Minnesota Press.

Byers, Thomas B. 1992. "The Closing of the American Line: Expansive Poetry and Ideology." *Contemporary Literature* 33.2: 396–415.

Carr, Helen. 1989. "Poetic License." In *From My Guy to Sci-Fi: Genre and Women's Writing in the Postmodern World*. Ed. Helen Carr, 135–62. London: Pandora.

Coffman, Stanley K., Jr. 1951. *Imagism*. Norman: Univ. of Oklahoma Press.

Cohen, Keith. 1980. "Ashbery's Dismantling of Bourgeois Discourse." In *Beyond Amazement: New Essays on John Ashbery*. Ed. David Lehman, 128–49. Ithaca, N.Y.: Cornell Univ. Press.

Conte, Joseph M. 1991. *Unending Design: The Forms of Postmodern Poetry*. Ithaca, N.Y.: Cornell Univ. Press.

Costello, Bonnie. 1991. *Elizabeth Bishop: Questions of Mastery*. Cambridge, Mass.: Harvard Univ. Press.

Crane, Hart. 1966. *The Complete Poems and Selected Letters and Prose*. Ed. Brom Weber. Garden City, N.Y.: Doubleday.

Culler, Jonathan, ed. 1988. *On Puns: The Foundation of Letters*. London: Blackwell.

Cushman, Stephen. 1993. *Fictions of Form in American Poetry*. Princeton, N.J.: Princeton Univ. Press.

de Man, Paul. 1983. *Blindness and Insight: Essays in the Rhetoric of Contemporary Criticism*. Minneapolis: Univ. of Minnesota Press.

    1984. *The Rhetoric of Romanticism*. New York: Columbia Univ. Press.

    1986. *The Resistance to Theory*. Minneapolis: Univ. of Minnesota Press.

Derrida, Jacques. 1982. *Margins of Philosophy*. Trans. Alan Bass. Chicago: Univ. of Chicago Press.

Diehl, Joanne Feit. 1990. *Women Poets and the American Sublime*. Bloomington: Indiana Univ. Press.

Ducrot, Oswald, and Tzvetan Todorov. 1979. *Encyclopedic Dictionary of the Sciences of Language*. Trans. Catherine Porter. Baltimore: Johns Hopkins Univ. Press.

Easthope, Antony. 1983. *Poetry as Discourse*. London: Methuen.

Emerson, Ralph Waldo. 1990. *Ralph Waldo Emerson*. Ed. Richard Poirier. Oxford: Oxford Univ. Press.

Fenollosa, Ernest. 1936. *The Chinese Written Character as a Medium for Poetry*. Ed. Ezra Pound. London: Stanley Nott.

Frank, Robert, and Henry Sayre. 1988. *The Line in Postmodern Poetry*. Urbana: Univ. of Illinois Press.

Freud, Sigmund. 1963. *Jokes and Their Relation to the Unconscious*. Trans. James Strachey. New York: Norton.

Frost, Robert. 1979. *The Poetry of Robert Frost*. Ed. Edward Connery Lathem. New York: Holt, Rinehart & Winston.

Géfin, Laszlo. 1982. *Ideogram: History of a Poetic Method*. Austin: Univ. of Texas Press.

Gooch, Brad. 1994. *City Poet: The Life and Times of Frank O'Hara*. New York: Knopf, 1993. Reprint, New York: HarperCollins.

Goux, Jean-Joseph. 1990. *Symbolic Economies: After Marx and Freud*. Trans. Jennifer Curtiss Gage. Ithaca, N.Y.: Cornell Univ. Press.

Graves, Robert. 1980. *The White Goddess: A Historical Grammar of Poetic Myth*. New York: Creative Age Press, 1948. Reprint, New York: Farrar, Straus and Giroux.

Guilbaud, Serge. 1983. *How New York Stole the Idea of Modern Art: Abstract Expressionism, Freedom, and the Cold War*. Trans. Arthur Goldhammer. Chicago: Univ. of Chicago Press.

Harrison, Victoria. 1993. *Elizabeth Bishop's Poetics of Intimacy*. New York: Cambridge Univ. Press.

Harvey, David. 1989. *The Condition of Postmodernity*. Oxford: Blackwell.

Hatlen, Burton. 1989. "Kinesis and Meaning: Charles Olson's 'The Kingfishers' and the Critics." *Contemporary Literature* 30.4: 546–72.

Heaney, Seamus. 1990. *The Government of the Tongue: Selected Prose, 1978–1987*. London: Faber, 1988. Reprint, New York: Farrar, Straus and Giroux.

Hoover, Paul, ed. 1994. *Postmodern American Poetry*. New York: Norton.

Hulme, T. E. 1924. *Speculations: Essays on Humanism and the Philosophy of Art*. New York: Harcourt, Brace.

————. 1948. "Romanticism and Classicism." In *Criticism: The Foundations of Modern Literary Judgment*. Ed. Mark Schorer, Josephine Miles, and Gordon McKenzie, 257–65. New York: Harcourt, Brace.

————. 1962. *Further Speculations*. Ed. Sam Hynes. Minneapolis: Univ. of Minnesota Press, 1955. Reprint, Lincoln: Univ. of Nebraska Press.

Hutcheon, Linda. 1988. *A Poetics of Postmodernism: History, Theory, Fiction*. London: Routledge.

Huyssen, Andreas. 1986. *After the Great Divide: Modernism, Mass Culture, Postmodernism*. Bloomington: Indiana Univ. Press.

Jameson, Fredric. 1991. *Postmodernism, or, the Cultural Logic of Late Capitalism*. Durham, N.C.: Duke Univ. Press.

Kalstone, David. 1989. *Becoming a Poet: Elizabeth Bishop with Marianne Moore and Robert Lowell*. Ed. Robert Hemenway. Afterword by James Merrill. New York: Farrar, Straus and Giroux.

Keats, John. 1982. *John Keats: Complete Poems*. Ed. Jack Stillinger. Cambridge, Mass.: Harvard Univ. Press.

Keller, Lynn. 1987. *Re-making It New: Contemporary American Poetry and the Modernist Tradition*. New York: Cambridge Univ. Press.

Kenner, Hugh. 1971. *The Pound Era*. Berkeley: Univ. of California Press.

Kermode, Frank. 1957. *Romantic Image*. London: Routledge.

Kristeva, Julia. 1980. *Desire in Language: A Semiotic Approach to Literature and Art*. Ed. Leon S. Roudiez. Trans. Thomas Gora, Alice Jardine, and Leon S. Roudiez. New York: Columbia Univ. Press.

Leithauser, Brad. 1987. "The Confinement of Free Verse." *New Criterion* 5.9: 4–14.

Lentricchia, Frank. 1988. *Ariel and the Police: Michel Foucault, William James, Wallace Stevens*. Madison: Univ. of Wisconsin Press.

Longenbach, James. 1991. *Wallace Stevens: The Plain Sense of Things*. Oxford: Oxford Univ. Press.

Lowney, John. 1991. "The 'Post-anti-esthetic' Poetics of Frank O'Hara." *Contemporary Literature* 32: 244–64.

Manley, Lawrence. 1981. "Concepts of Convention and Models of Critical Discourse." *New Literary History* 13: 31–52.

Mendelson, Edward. 1981. *Early Auden.* London: Faber.

Merrill, James. 1962. *Water Street.* New York: Atheneum.

    1966. *Nights and Days.* New York: Atheneum.

    1969. *The Fire Screen.* New York: Atheneum.

    1972. *Braving the Elements.* New York: Atheneum.

    1976. *Divine Comedies.* New York: Atheneum.

    1982. *The Changing Light at Sandover.* New York: Atheneum.

    1984. *From the First Nine: Poems, 1946–1976.* New York: Atheneum.

    1985. *Late Settings.* New York: Atheneum.

    1986. *Recitative.* Ed. J. D. McClatchy. San Francisco: North Point.

Messerli, Douglas. 1987. *"Language" Poetries.* New York: New Directions.

Meyer, Thomas. 1990. "Glistening Torsos, Sandwiches, and Coca-Cola." In *Frank O'Hara: To Be True to a City.* Ed. Jim Elledge, 85–102. Ann Arbor: Univ. of Michigan Press.

Milton, John. 1993. *Paradise Lost.* Ed. Scott Elledge. New York: Norton.

Moi, Toril. 1988. *Sexual/Textual Politics: Feminist Literary Theory.* London: Methuen, 1985. Reprint, London: Routledge.

Moore, Marianne. 1982. *The Complete Poems.* New York: Penguin.

    1987. *The Complete Prose.* New York: Penguin.

Nelson, Cary. 1989. *Repression and Recovery: Modern American Poetry and the Politics of Cultural Memory, 1910–1945.* Madison: Univ. of Wisconsin Press.

Norris, Christopher. 1990. *What's Wrong with Postmodernism: Critical Theory and the Ends of Philosophy.* Baltimore: Johns Hopkins Univ. Press.

O'Hara, Frank. 1971. *The Collected Poems of Frank O'Hara.* Ed. Donald Allen. New York: Knopf.

    1975a. *Art Chronicles, 1954–1966.* New York: Braziller.

    1975b. *Standing Still and Walking in New York.* Ed. Donald Allen. Bolinas, Calif.: Grey Fox.

    1977. *Early Writing.* Ed. Donald Allen. Bolinas, Calif.: Grey Fox.

Olson, Charles. 1966. *Selected Writings.* Ed. Robert Creeley. New York: New Directions.

Ostriker, Alicia Suskin. 1986. *Stealing the Language: The Emergence of Women's Poetry in America.* Boston: Beacon.

Palmer, Michael. 1989. Interview with Michael Palmer. By Keith Tuma. *Contemporary Literature* 30.1: 1–12.

Perkins, David. 1987. *Modernism and After.* Vol. 2 of *A History of Modern Poetry.* 2 vols. Cambridge, Mass.: Harvard Univ. Press.

Perloff, Marjorie. 1979. *Frank O'Hara: Poet Among Painters.* New York: Braziller, 1977. Reprint, Austin: Univ. of Texas Press.

1982. "Pound/Stevens: Whose Era?" *New Literary History* 13.3: 485–514.

1985. *The Dance of the Intellect: Studies in the Poetry of the Pound Tradition.* Cambridge: Cambridge Univ. Press.

1990. "Frank O'Hara and the Aesthetics of Attention." In *Frank O'Hara: To Be True to a City.* Ed. Jim Elledge, 156–88. Ann Arbor: Univ. of Michigan Press.

1991. *Radical Artifice: Writing Poetry in the Age of Media.* Chicago: Univ. of Chicago Press.

Plath, Sylvia. 1981. *The Collected Poems.* Ed. Ted Hughes. New York: Harper & Row.

Pound, Ezra. 1960. *ABC of Reading.* New York: New Directions.

1968a. *Literary Essays.* Ed. T. S. Eliot. New York: New Directions.

1968b. *The Spirit of Romance.* New York: New Directions.

1970a. *Gaudier-Brzeska.* New York: New Directions.

1970b. *Guide to Kulchur.* New York: New Directions.

1975. *Selected Prose, 1909–1965.* Ed. William Cookson. New York: New Directions.

1976. *Collected Early Poems.* Ed. Michael John King. New York: New Directions.

1981. *The Cantos.* New York: New Directions.

1990. *Personae.* Ed. Lea Baechler and A. Walton Litz. New York: New Directions.

Proust, Marcel. 1982. *Swann's Way, Within a Budding Grove.* Trans. C. K. Scott Moncrieff and Terence Kilmartin. Vol. 1 of *Remembrance of Things Past.* 3 vols. New York: Vintage.

Rabaté, Jean-Michel. 1986. *Language, Sexuality, and Ideology in Ezra Pound's "Cantos."* Albany: State Univ. of New York Press.

Rich, Adrienne. 1986. "The Eye of the Outsider: Elizabeth Bishop's *Complete Poems, 1927–1979.*" *Boston Review* April 1983: 15–17. Reprinted in *Blood, Bread, and Poetry: Selected Prose, 1979–1985,* 124–35. New York: Norton.

1989. *Time's Power.* New York: Norton.

Riddel, Joseph N. 1979. "Decentering the Image: The 'Project' of 'American' Poetics?" In *Textual Strategies: Perspectives in Post-Structuralist Criticism.* Ed. Josué V. Harari, 322–58. Ithaca, N.Y.: Cornell Univ. Press.

Ross, Andrew. 1990. "The Death of Lady Day." In *Frank O'Hara: To Be True to a City.* Ed. Jim Elledge, 380–91. Ann Arbor: Univ. of Michigan Press.

Said, Edward W. 1985. *Beginnings: Intention and Method.* New York: Basic Books, 1975. Reprint, New York: Columbia Univ. Press.

Schneidau, Herbert N. 1969. *Ezra Pound: The Image and the Real.* Baton Rouge: Louisiana State Univ. Press.

Scott, Bonnie Kime, ed. 1990. *The Gender of Modernism: A Critical Anthology*. Bloomington: Indiana Univ. Press.

Shelley, Percy Bysshe. 1960. *The Complete Poetical Works*. Ed. Thomas Hutchinson. 1943. Reprint, London: Oxford Univ. Press.

    1967. "A Defence of Poetry." In *English Romantic Writers*. Ed. David Perkins, 1072–87. New York: Harcourt, Brace & World.

Shetley, Vernon. 1993. *After the Death of Poetry: Poet and Audience in Contemporary America*. Durham, N.C.: Duke Univ. Press.

Steele, Timothy. 1990. *Missing Measures: Modern Poetry and the Revolt Against Meter*. Fayetteville: Univ. of Arkansas Press.

Stevens, Wallace. 1951. *The Necessary Angel*. New York: Vintage.

    1954. *The Collected Poems*. New York: Knopf.

Turner, Frederick, and Ernst Pöppel. 1983. "The Neural Lyre: Poetic Meter, the Brain, and Time." *Poetry* 142.5: 277–309.

Vattimo, Gianni. 1988. *The End of Modernity*. Trans. Jon R. Snyder. Baltimore: Johns Hopkins Univ. Press.

Vaughan, Henry. 1981. *The Complete Poems*. Ed. Alan Rudrum. London: Penguin, 1976. Reprint, New Haven, Conn.: Yale Univ. Press.

Vendler, Helen. 1990. "Frank O'Hara: The Virtue of the Alterable." In *Frank O'Hara: To Be True to a City*. Ed. Jim Elledge, 234–52. Ann Arbor: Univ. of Michigan Press.

von Hallberg, Robert. 1985. *American Poetry and Culture, 1945–1980*. Cambridge, Mass.: Harvard Univ. Press.

Whitman, Walt. 1964. "Death of Abraham Lincoln." *Prose Works, 1892*. Vol. 2. Ed. Floyd Stovall. New York: New York Univ. Press.

    1965. *Leaves of Grass*. Ed. Harold W. Blodgett and Sculley Bradley. New York: Norton.

Williams, William Carlos. 1954. *Selected Essays*. New York: New Directions.

    1986, 1988. *The Collected Poems*. 2 vols. Ed. A. Walton Litz and Christopher MacGowan. New York: New Directions.

Wordsworth, William. 1979. *The Prelude: 1799, 1805, 1850*. Ed. Jonathan Wordsworth, M. H. Abrams, and Stephen Gill. New York: Norton.

    1981. *The Poems*. 2 vols. Ed. John O. Hayden. New Haven, Conn.: Yale Univ. Press.

Yeats, William Butler. 1961. *Essays and Introductions*. New York: Macmillan.

    1989. *The Poems*. Ed. Richard J. Finneran. Vol. 1 of *The Collected Works of W. B. Yeats*. New York: Macmillan.

Yenser, Stephen. 1987. *The Consuming Myth: The Work of James Merrill*. Cambridge, Mass.: Harvard Univ. Press.

Index

Abrams, M. H., 84, 86, 97, 106
Abstract Expressionism, 42, 159, 203n4
aesthetic ideology, 2, 9, 18, 19, 21; *see also*
  Ashbery, John
aesthetics and politics, 9, 20–22, 24; *see also*
  Ashbery, John
Allen, Donald M., 3
Allen, Gay Wilson, 98
Andrews, Bruce, 27
Antin, David, 33, 199n1, 200n2
Arnold, Matthew, 140
Ashbery, John: and aesthetic ideology, 118,
  126, 128, 145, 155; aesthetics and
  politics in, 20, 142, 145–46, 155; and
  alienation, 117, 128, 138, 146;
  allusiveness of, 134–35, 150;
  anachronisms of, 132–35, 147; and
  Auden, 119–20, 121; and
  autobiography, 148–50, 154–55; and
  avant-gardism, 111–13; and Baudelaire,
  126–28; and blank verse, 136; and
  bourgeois art, 127, 142–46; and
  business, 117–19, 121; on communism,
  123; and consumer economy, 121, 144,
  150–55; and critical distance, 113–14,
  123; darkness in, 116–17, 154; and
  Eliot, 132, 134, 137, 145, 151; and
  form, 12, 122–23; and history, 113–16,
  123–24, 136, 138, 139, 140–41; and
  humanism, 127, 135–37, 140–41, 149,
  153; and the individual, 112, 115, 118,
  119, 129–31, 135, 138–41, 152, 154–55;

and Keats, 133; and light, 206–7n2; on
nature and the imagination, 113–15,
117, 122, 124–28, 133–34, 143; on
O'Hara, 33–34; and Olson, 122, 147,
151; and the poet's function, 114–15,
118–19, 121, 126, 128, 130–33, 144–46,
148–55; and politics, 119, 120–23, 141,
142–46, 147; as postmodern, 3, 10, 11,
12, 13, 124, 141; and postmodernity,
112–15, 117, 128, 135–36, 138, 141,
145, 206n1; and Pound, 119, 122, 126,
135, 147; and private life, 130–31, 140–
41, 144; relation of literature and culture
in, 111, 116, 118, 131, 140–41, 144–46;
and rhetoric, 120, 123, 129, 130; and
the Romantics, 113–14, 124, 126–29,
130–31, 135, 136–37, 141, 147, 153; on
Surrealism, 122, 123; and technology,
123, 124, 126, 129, 140–41, 145; towers
in, 118–19, 121, 123, 125–27, 132; and
tradition, 11, 111, 133–41, 150, 206n1;
and Wordsworth, 113, 137, 148–51,
153–54. Works: *As We Know*, 123; "As
You Came from the Holy Land," 115,
206n1; "Business Personals," 117, 133;
"The Cathedral Is," 123; "Daffy Duck
in Hollywood," 134–35; "Decoy,"
120–21, 136; "Definition of Blue," 130;
The Double Dream of Spring, 137; *Flow
Chart*, 146–55; "Friends," 116;
"Houseboat Days," 139–40; " 'How
Much Longer Will I Be Able to Inhabit

215